I was lying on my back with my weapon across my chest when shots rang out, and green tracers (glowing bullets from enemy ammunition; ours were red) flew over my body and hit Hines. He fell over Limey, and all hell broke loose. I grabbed Hines, rolled him onto his back, and checked to see if he was breathing and had a pulse. He was stone dead. I yelled at Danny Williams that Hines was gone. Hines had been on radio watch and had been sitting up when the incoming fire swept through our area. Bacak yelled for a "mad minute" (all the team members fire their weapons on full automatic, covering their preassigned areas of responsibility from the defensive wheel), and everyone on the heavy team complied. Limey couldn't find his weapon because I had rolled over onto it. Williams decided to throw grenades through the thick vegetation. The first one got through, but the second one bounced off a bush and landed really close to us. Fortunately, my rucksack took most of the shrapnel. Bacak yelled that we were not to throw any more grenades, then started calling in 81 mm mortars, which were set up on the firebase.

The first round was white phosphorous and landed about fifty meters from us. Too close for comfort, I thought. Then he started working the area around us with HE (high explosives). Saturating the sides of our position with mortar rounds, he moved the fire like an artist with a paintbrush. During all this time, we could hear and smell the enemy around us.

Books published by The Ballantine Publishing Group
are available at quantity discounts on bulk purchases
for premium, educational, fund-raising, and special
sales use. For details, please call 1-800-733-3000.

GONE NATIVE

An NCO's Story

Alan G. Cornett

BALLANTINE BOOKS • NEW YORK

A Ballantine Book
Published by The Ballantine Publishing Group
Copyright © 2000 by Alan G. Cornett

www.randomhouse.com/BB/

Library of Congress Catalog Card Number: 00-190522

ISBN 0-8041-1637-7

Manufactured in the United States of America

First Edition: June 2000

10   9   8   7   6   5   4   3   2   1

"For he today who sheds his blood
with me shall be my brother."
—Shakespeare, *Henry the Fifth*

This book is dedicated to my father, who stood by me when times were bad and taught me to survive in situations where another person would have failed. He is my mentor and my idol and the greatest person alive. I also dedicate this book to Rey Martinez. It would not have been completed without his pressure to write, his editing, and his advice. I cannot be remiss and forget my brothers: Doug Scherk, Teddy Bear Gaskell, Jaybird McGill, Limey Walker, Marty Dostal, John Chadwick, George Murphy, Walter Bacak, Gunther Bengston, Sully, Hines, Terry Swanke, and all the other old Foul Dudes I served with.

Special thanks to Teresa Oxendale, who guided me through the writing of this book, and to Connie Hills, who has patiently waited for its release. Extra-special thanks to my wife, Lori, who pushed me to complete it. To my children, Alan III, Shannon, Erich, I love you and am thankful you are my children.

☆
FOREWORD

My editor wanted me to title the foreword "Kids—Don't Try This at Home!" As with most human endeavors, my history in the military cannot easily be lumped into a single moral category. My experiences encompassed the good and the evil, the cherished and the regretted, the honorable and the dishonorable. I've pride in much of my career choices and military performance. The positive portion of my time in the service earned me a Master Parachutist Badge, Pathfinder Badge, Ranger Tab, Canadian, Cambodian, and Vietnamese jump wings, Combat Medical Badge, two Bronze Stars for valor, the experience of serving with some of the finest people alive, and, most important, friendships that mean more to me than even my own life.

Unfortunately, my military career has also been blemished by several unsavory acts, deeds that have earned me humiliation, guilt, and regret. The worst of them, my attempt to kill an American officer, earned me a general court-martial and time in Long Binh Jail (LBJ), Leavenworth Disciplinary Barracks (DB), and the Army Retraining Brigade (USARB) at Fort Riley, Kansas.

My maturing has given me a clear understanding of how drugs and recklessness can cause irreparable harm and why they have no place in the military, among young men with strong passions and available weapons. But I did the best with what I had and knew at the time, and only hope God and my victims can find a way to forgive my offenses.

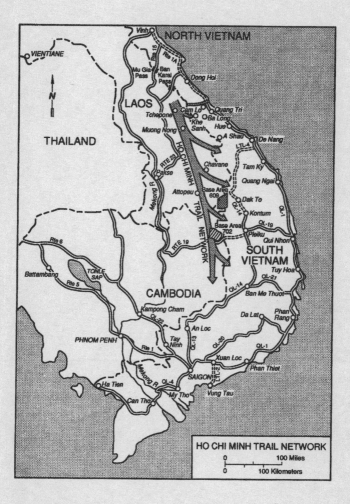

VIENTIANE

NORTH VIETNAM

Vinh

Rte 15

Rte 1A

Mu Gia Pass

Ban Karai Pass

Dong Hoi

LAOS

Cam Lo
Quang Tri

Tchepone
Ba Long
Khe Sanh

THAILAND

Muong Nong
Hue
A Shau
De Nang

LTL-4

RTE 23

Chavane
Tam Ky

Mekong R.
Quang Ngai

Pakse

HO CHI MINH TRAIL NETWORK

Attopeu
Base Area 609
Dak To
QL-1

QL-14
Kontum

QL-19

Base Area 702
Pleiku
Qui Nhon

RTE 19

SOUTH VIETNAM

Tuy Hoa

Rte 6

QL-21

Battambang

TONLE SAP

CAMBODIA

QL-14
Ban Me Thuot

Rte 5

Da Lat
Phan Rang

Kampong Cham

QL-2

An Loc

PHNOM PENH

Tay Ninh

QL-13
QL-20
QL-1

Rte 1

Mekong R.

Xuan Loc

QL-4
SAIGON
Phan Thiet

Ha Tien

My Tho
Vung Tau

Can Tho

HO CHI MINH TRAIL NETWORK

0   100 Miles

0   100 Kilometers

☆

PROLOGUE

It was first light, and the rains were a downpour. From where we were hiding, visibility was impossible. We couldn't see or hear anything that might be hostile. The huge leaves that provided cover doubled as spouts for the rainwater, funneling it down on us. The foliage and my rag of a boony hat gushed rivulets that streamed down my body. I was soaked to the core.

A new member of the 302d Vietnamese Reconnaissance Company, I had been lying in triple canopy, waiting and watching for any sign of the enemy. Our group consisted of myself, the only American, and five members of the AK squad, South Vietnamese soldiers dressed in black Viet Cong garb. Our commander, Captain Phong, had picked the area because he knew it to be well traveled by the enemy.

I had positioned myself by a large tree for cover and some relief from the torrential rain. The rain was making every noise I heard sound like the enemy, giving me the impression they were closing in from all directions. My nerves were frayed, and my unfamiliarity with my new team just added to my unease. But as suddenly as the rain had started, it stopped, and the jungle came alive with the sounds of many creatures. So, too, returned the large mosquitoes, which immediately exercised their ability to find their way into every exposed area of the body. Their cohorts in bloodletting, green slimy worms that transformed into bulging red leeches as they extracted

1

blood from the body, were back as well. As miserable as conditions were, we couldn't move. We had to lie there, immobile, drained of our lifeblood by hundreds of the greedy little vampires.

I watched as an ant moved across a large green leaf, only to be snatched midjourney by a lizard with a tongue that would give any man bragging rights in a cathouse. The lizard speared its target with pinpoint accuracy, then lazily consumed the insect. My attention was wandering, but I tried to focus on the trail the team was watching, all the while restraining the urge to swat the areas of my body that were under attack. I was learning to coexist with the rain. When it poured, the stinging vampires disappeared, and I could go to sleep to the sounds of the raindrops dripping from the trees and vines and to the occasional cooing of a spider monkey. But when the rain stopped and the terrain became inundated with these pesky blood-drinking creatures and the false alarm of the fuck-you lizard, I went back to an agonizing state of alert stillness. But without the security I felt with the old team, the agonizing alertness persisted, rain or no rain.

The sight of a dark figure moving through the trail of wet leaves and vines brought me to full awareness. Fear and excitement rose inside me, blending into an anxiety high. Everyone on the team had seen the figures moving through the jungle slowly but with purpose and at the ready.

What am I doing here? I thought to myself. I could be in the rear area, teaching medical classes in the comfort and security of a whole division of American boys.

The figures moved from the trail toward where we lay in wait. As I watched, the thought that there were only six of us and at least thirty of them went through my mind. I wanted to close my eyes and believe they couldn't see me, something I had done when I was three years old. But my eyes wouldn't close. I had to watch and be ready to kill or be killed. My finger moved to the trigger of my AK-47. I prayed it would respond if I needed it. Unlike the M-16 I carried when I worked with an American unit, this weapon had never failed me.

The dark figures stopped, kneeled, and took up defensive positions. They must have heard or found something. I feared that "something" was us. All of them were now hidden from our view. My anticipation of combat heightened.

One of the ominous figures stood and began moving again. In my direction. I prayed again for invisibility. The dark figure stopped about two feet from where I was lying. My finger tightened on the trigger. The figure looked around and then stood his weapon against the tree I was behind. I waited in absolute silence and stillness, wondering what the fucker was up to. My question was answered by the hot, putrid steam of his urine. I lay there counting the toes I could see through his black rubber sandals while clenching the trigger of my AK-47 as his urine saturated my uniform and the stench filled my nostrils.

I just knew the guy was going to hear my heart beating. I had stopped breathing and began to pray that it would be just a quick golden shower. I became one with the ground and vegetation around me, but I was starting to struggle for air and felt I would have to kill this enemy "pisser" just so I could breathe. But as I began to pull the trigger of my weapon, the figure finished his business, shook the last few drops on me, then picked up his AK and moved back toward his companions, oblivious of the fact that his mortal enemy had just had an up-close-and-personal with his John Thomas.

I wished I could have blown the guy's balls off, but knew that would have been a short-lived satisfaction. Then the rains began again, with great intensity, washing the enemy's urine from my body. The dark figure who had relieved himself on me reached the other members of his unit, and they moved back to the trail. They took up the path once again, slowly and deliberately, keeping an eye out for the enemy.

My lungs were desperate for air, and my heart was pounding

about two hundred beats a minute. But I couldn't just gasp for air; they were still too close; I had to exhale and inhale slowly. The process was excruciating and did little to alleviate my desperate need for oxygen. It wasn't until all of the dark figures were out of sight that I was finally able to take a desperately needed deep breath.

As we watched the last dark figure move into the cover of the rain and vegetation and out of sight and earshot, a feeling of calm came over me, followed by an adrenaline rush. I had been pissed on by the enemy, and I couldn't do a thing. Later, I was willing to bet that if I had jumped up that dark figure would have done more than piss. I would have thoroughly enjoyed making that man shit in his pants as he was presented with a bullet from a weapon of his own army, courtesy of his unappreciative urinal.

We lay there another hour before the AK-squad team leader, through hand signals, motioned us to move out. One at a time, we got up, moved a few feet, and waited for the next guy to get up, until we all were ready to patrol to a safer place.

Slowly, we moved to our extraction point. Our trip took most of the day, and the sun was going down when we reached our destination. My size and my unfamiliarity with the environment compared to the rest of my team had made the excursion miserable. I was relieved when I found out we would be picked up by trucks rather than have to walk out of the hostile countryside the way the team usually did.

As we drove back to our base camp in Da Lat, I reflected on how the hell I got to that place. It was my first mission with the unit, and Captain Phong and I weren't sure what to expect if and when we came under fire. I really missed the old Foul Dudes from my last American team and the security they had provided. Those were men I could trust and relate to. If I had a problem, there was always one of the Foul Dudes I could talk to like a brother.

☆

CHAPTER 1

There's no doubt that the army goes a long way in turning a civilian into a soldier. It teaches him skills, supplies him with the latest combat equipment, then gives him the time and place to become familiar with the two. The army even goes as far as attempting to instill strength, discipline, and an ability to think quickly under harrowing conditions. But, through my experience, I've learned that the qualities that will save your ass when faced with the hell of war are qualities developed long before Uncle Sam comes knocking at the door.

Those qualities *can* make the difference between whether you fly home in your uniform or are shipped back in an aluminum box. And if you make it home, those qualities can make the difference between whether you live again or simply exist. Those qualities find their origin in your upbringing and your heritage. For me, I see the seeds of my personality being sown as far back as the 1800s with the birth of my paternal grandparents.

Robert Alan Cornett was born in 1878. Robert was a salesman with a gift of gab and was loved by everyone, including Helen Talent, the nurse he was to marry. Though he was known as a nice guy, a "lifelong drunkard" may have been a more fitting career title. Because of my grandfather Robert's alcoholism, Grandmother Helen basically functioned as a single parent to my father and his sister from their birth on. She was officially left a single parent when Grandfather

Robert abandoned her completely, leaving her to deal with their children and the Great Depression on her own. His drinking would eventually land him on the streets and out of my father's life. Before the age of ten, my father had to rely on his own wits, skill, and instincts for survival, a habit that deepened when Grandmother remarried to a man who was mentally abusive to her and to her children as well.

His dysfunctional upbringing and the absence of a strong fatherly presence led the empty boy in my father searching. He landed in a military summer camp, CMTC (city military training camp). It was offered for thirty days each summer and gave my father a much-needed sense of belonging. His positive experience in CMTC resulted in my father's joining the Boy Scouts. There he was able to find the structure, morals, and the father figure every boy needs. There, too, he found his mentor, retired Lieutenant Colonel Scott. Between the colonel's guidance and the Scouts' standards, my father flourished. He eventually achieved the highest honor in scouting, that of Eagle Scout. My father had discovered his niche, an outside source of direction and belonging, and a pattern was established, one that would be transmitted down through the next two generations.

The lack of a healthy atmosphere at home combined with my father's great success within the structured and disciplined world of the Scouts made the military an obvious and enticing place for him to seek his future. As millions of other men did in the forties, my father joined the army to fight the Germans, Italians, and Japanese. With that act, he gave birth to a tradition of military service for the males in the Cornett family that followed him. My father qualified for officer training and graduated from the officer basic training course at Fort Benning, Georgia, in 1942. From there, he was assigned to an infantry unit in Oregon, but he eventually made it to France and to his first taste of combat as a platoon leader of the 90th Infantry Division.

For several years, my father utilized the instincts and self-reliance cultivated during his youth to avoid death, capture, or injury. But time and circumstance caught up with him; in 1945, an injury had him on his way to England with a wounded hand. By the time he had recovered from the wound, the war was over, and he was discharged with the permanent rank of master sergeant* and assigned to the 2d Philippine Scouts. Soon, in the Philippine Mountains, he was hunting and killing the Communist-rebel Huks. Eventually, an encounter with a regimental commander who had known him from the Big War resulted in an offer of commission to second lieutenant. But the job at hand was essentially unchanged: for another six months, he ran the hills and jungles, digging out the Huks.

That successful stint of combat was ended when my father was sent to Japan for more surgery on his wounded hand. Though my father had chosen a rough and hard career path, it seemed to be working for him. The strengths he'd cultivated throughout his youth had served him well while he was still wet behind the ears. And now, the instincts and skills acquired from combat experience were in place. Those skills, combined with fate, would help my father to survive the challenging missions yet to come.

When the Korean War broke out, my father, by then recovered from the second surgery to his hand, was assigned as platoon leader to Company K, 34th Infantry, 24th Infantry Division on 15 August 1950. K Company was one of three companies that occupied several important hills close to the Naktong River, which ran through Pusan, South Korea. My father was responsible for seventy-nine men, few of whom had actual combat experience, and a company commander who refused to leave his tent. The only contact my father had

---

*A common practice since World War II; when officers with commissions in the reserves elected to remain in the downsized army, they frequently reverted to permanent senior enlisted positions.

with his commander was a handshake through a tent flap. My father reported to his platoon and immediately realized he was taking command of a poorly led unit. Recognizing the disarray of their position, he started making things right. Adding and rearranging defensive fighting positions, he beefed them up by adding sandbags, placing them in fields of fire for his machine guns and BAR men. He met all the men in his platoon, and made sure they knew who he was and what he expected of them. He did what all good infantry platoon leaders do: he led the men. Feeling good about the job he had done, he went to the commander and asked him to inspect his defensive positions. The commander said he was too busy checking out the other positions but would inspect my father's area the first chance he got. The positions were never inspected, and the company commander left his tent only once, to return to the rear and out of the army.

My father was made company commander. The hill his company occupied overlooked the river and was strategically important because of its commanding view. From that huge mound of earth, the enemy could be seen moving miles away. The hill had few trees and little brush. As time went on, scheduled resupplies stopped coming in. My father noticed an apparent increase in enemy movement on the opposite side of the river from his position. His company watched the enemy building an underwater bridge out of sandbags filled with rice. It was an unconventional technique, but the bridge was strong enough to hold tanks. Food was down to raw peanuts and overripe watermelons. Communications were out because the batteries were old and had lost their charge. He didn't hear from his command element for over two weeks, and then friendly artillery suddenly started sporadically impacting around his position. My father, quite alarmed, got one of his sergeants with a half-track and went looking for his battalion commander. The first unit he ran into happened to be the regimental headquarters commanded by Col. Fireball Mc-

Calister. My father told him about the underwater bridge they had been observing and his troops' being out of food and communication for several weeks. At the same time my father was talking to the regimental commander, jets were overflying his position, preparing to bomb the hill. Overhearing the regimental staff in communication with the jets, my father managed to convince the regimental commander to call off the bombing mission. The regimental command post also got in touch with the artillery to stop them from killing my father's troops. Colonel McCalister then got my father transportation back to the hill with food, ammunition, and fresh batteries.

By that time, the enemy was making a strong push toward my father's hill, causing other American units to retreat. Again my father's company was left on the hill. As the enemy pushed across the river, retreating troops ended up on the hilltop with my father, and my father's command went from 79 to 388 people in a matter of hours. To complicate things, the battalion commander told my father to pull back, but the regimental commander ordered my father to stay and hold the hill.

The enemy tried to take the hill but couldn't because of the positions my father and his men had built. Throughout the fighting, my father continued to receive conflicting orders from his regimental commander and his battalion commander. For a month, my father's unit of stragglers defended that hill against the North Koreans without further rations or communications. The men relied on locally grown rice and watermelons for food, sheer will for endurance, and ammunition for existence. They were down to only a few rounds of ammunition when relief, in the form of an infantry battalion, finally arrived. To this day, my father can't stand to eat rice or watermelon. When word finally arrived to move out, only four trucks were sent to move the 388 men. Every available space on those trucks was covered by a soldier. When my father returned to the rear area, he was told the battalion commander wanted to see him. My father couldn't wait to have a few choice words with him also, and it was a good thing my father left his weapon outside the commander's quarters, because he wanted to end the man's life and the problems he had caused.

My father wasn't just angry; he was also sick from malnutrition and malaria. He soon collapsed and was sent to a field hospital, where he awoke to the friendly face of a doctor who was an old acquaintance. My father told him about the problems with his battalion commander. The doctor put an evacuation ticket on my father's toe, sending him to Japan for treatment.

During the wars, my father received two Bronze Stars for valor and two Purple Hearts for wounds. But more important, he'd found an organization that would acknowledge and reward his strengths. He eventually had a twenty-two-year career of respect and honor.

My father's childhood, career choice, and combat experience gave birth to his no-nonsense, no-excuses, and no-second-chances attitude. That in turn bred in me a familiarity with fear and an inner strength that would serve me well later in my own military career. My father also cultivated in me a sense of competition, a love of physical challenge, and a desire to come out on top. But strength and determination alone won't have you surviving a war, at least not intact. To successfully survive the madness of war, a soldier's strength needs to be tempered with perspective, humor, and compassion. Those qualities I took from my mother's family tree.

My mother was born to a small Irish woman just sixteen years old. My mother's father abandoned her when she was still very young, and she had no recollection of him at all. Just as my paternal grandmother had been, my maternal grandmother was a single parent during hard times. She survived by finding employment in an automobile factory, earning a salary that enabled her to support the family. Both my parents were born of women who knew from firsthand experience the meaning of and requirements for survival.

As my mother grew, she absorbed the messages of her time and the lessons of her mother as well. She was raised with old-fashioned standards during a time when women were supposed to stay home, cook, clean, and raise the children. My mother was a beautiful woman who not only mastered those skills (I can still smell the wonderful home-baked goods) but broke the stereotype by not being afraid to show she was very smart and by possessing a great sense of humor that could make even the worst situation seem not so bad. Her own mother's precarious situation and resulting resourcefulness instilled in my mother a sensitivity to the needs of others and an innate sense of timing when delivering help to those in desperate straits. When soldiers in my father's unit were killed, my mother was always at the widows' sides, taking care of the women's children and making sure the loss was not forgotten by the military. She was always there to help others in their time of need, with grace and compassion guiding her every move.

She showered us children with patience and selflessness. No matter how many bonehead stunts I pulled, how many new school outfits I destroyed, or how many times my antics got me in trouble, my mother's love never wavered. She somehow accepted my need to play hard, and early on resigned herself to the fact that domesticating a rattlesnake would have been an easier job than curbing my zest for living life to the fullest. As I watched my mother work endlessly to counter the damage I did, I was unwittingly acquiring the very patience and good nature that would allow me to successfully treat and teach the thousands of scared, reckless, and always rowdy soldiers I would later encounter as a medic. I was also learning what it meant to be a true friend: to accept people, warts and all, and be there when they need you.

Fate, in the form of my parents' experiences and personalities, had me on my way to becoming a successful soldier. I can see now that my father's encouragement of my childhood athleticism provided me with the endurance that long field excursions would demand. It's clear that his strict discipline and Spartan expectations prepared me for the military lifestyle. I can also acknowledge how dealing with my fear of that man's temper and punishments toughened me to what the world's darker side has to offer. And I've seen more of that, including my spells as a "guest" at Long Binh prison and Fort Leavenworth, than most successful career soldiers.

As well, I see how my mother's sense of humor guided me in infusing humor into the classes I taught in Nam, classes that would save soldiers' lives if the information was properly absorbed. I reaped the benefits of friendships that would see me through the worst of times. These friendships were based on selflessness and acceptance, qualities that my mother had instilled in me. I can also see how my mother's ability to make the best of a bad situation influenced me, resulting in my seeking out beauty in the people and culture of the land I was defending. But my own childhood and my own experiences and circumstances also affected my development, leading to other resources I would need to survive in Vietnam.

Being the son of a career military man means moving, all the time and all over. My first memories are of my father's parents' home in Royal Oak, Michigan. It was there that my mother, older sister, and I lived until my father's return from his World War II and Korean War excursions.

I remember waking up early in the morning to the smell of fresh hot bread and the sound of Grandfather working in his basement. Grandfather repaired and recovered antique furniture, and he wouldn't let us sleep beyond 7:00 A.M. My sister and I were put to work stripping furniture for Grandfather to repair. When done as well as Grandfather expected, stripping furniture was a hard job: we removed the old varnish or paint; we hand-sanded the wood until it was clean. We started our work after breakfast, and one piece of furniture took us a day to complete. The reward for our effort was for our grandfather to take us fishing. Even as a young child, I was able to tell that the act was more for him than for us kids.

By the time my father returned from Korea and moved the family to his next military assignment, in Japan, I knew the meaning of a hard day's work. As much as I'd disliked the grueling labor of stripping furniture, I would gladly have chosen it over what life had in store for me next.

My father had been placed in charge of a military resort hotel. As well as adjusting to the duties and responsibilities of his new job, he was making the transition from warrior to father, husband, and businessman. The difficulty involved in making those changes was something I wouldn't understand for another couple of decades, when I had to go through the same transitions. But as an eight-year-old, all I knew was that it seemed he was taking out on my butt some of those anxieties and pressures. I'll never forget my first taste of my father's wrath. I had called my mother a skunk because I was upset over not getting something I wanted. My mother made me sit in my room until my father got home. I sat in that room watching the clock tick until I heard my father enter the house and my mother telling him of the day's events. I sat there gulping and waiting for the door to open. Then it did, and there stood my father, six feet four inches of anger and disappointment, making the room look small and me feel puny. Belt in hand and the look of hell on his face, he calmly asked if I knew what I had done wrong. I didn't speak because my throat was paralyzed. I managed to nod. Then, with one step and a swing of his arm, the belt hit my butt. My father proceeded to apply corporal punishment on my body and mind. The more he struck me, the more enraged he became. When it seemed he wasn't able to stop of his own accord, my mother interceded and put an end to the onslaught. Though I learned not to call my mother names, the lesson that was really beaten into me was not to piss off my father. From that day on, when I knew I was going to get a spanking, I just ran away until I got hungry or got caught. That ritual succeeded only in delaying my punishments, but the thought of my father and his belt kept me repeating it.

During the first two years we spent in Japan, I not only learned a healthy wariness for those with the upper hand but experienced my first exposure to the people and customs of the Orient. The exposure and familiarity would later enable me to learn Oriental languages easier than most Americans. I had no idea how important that would end up being to me.

In 1953, we returned to the States. We landed in Fort Carson, Colorado, where my father bought our first home, in the city of Colorado Springs.

At Fort Carson, I had my first experience in the field with soldiers. When my father evaluated an exercise, he would take me with him. I got to patrol with some of the elements and to set up ambushes. To this day, I don't know if my father really wanted me to go with him or if my mother just wanted me out of her hair, but during each of the next three summers I got to tag along with the soldiers on three-week field exercises.

During one of these exercises, the units were divided into the Red and Blue Armies. My father dropped me off at the base of the Blue Army to wait for his return after evaluating an exercise. I spent about thirty minutes watching the cooks prepare for the upcoming meal. While surveying the area around the camp, I noticed some soldiers getting ready to go on patrol. I wandered over to them and watched as they put on their rucksacks. One of the soldiers asked if I would like to come along. I said yes, and he handed me an M-1 carbine. As I walked with them, I felt like John Wayne and probably looked ridiculous. We were on patrol for about half an hour when I noticed some guys hiding in the bushes. I told my soldier friend, and he reacted by firing (blanks) at them and causing a surprise ambush to be a failure. The soldiers I was with praised me for reacting so well, and I was adopted by the patrol. Once back at the base camp, I was given my first cigar, unknown to my dad.

During our time in Colorado, my family grew to six, with the addition of a younger brother and sister. From that time on, I was the first at the dinner table.

I had been exposed to combat and the customs of the Orient, two of the three main components of the lifestyle I would be experiencing in Vietnam. It was now time for fate to complete my pre–boot camp training and expose me to the third component, the art of drinking. That art I quickly mastered at my family's next destination, Schweinfurt, Germany, to which we went in 1956. By then, I was twelve years old, tall enough to reach a *gasthaus* counter, and in the possession of enough money. So I had all that was required to purchase and consume beer in Germany. Drinking sure as hell beat stripping furniture for my grandfather and being the object of my father's wrath. Germany is the source of many fond memories.

Having been an Eagle Scout as a boy, and as an adult a scoutmaster, my father encouraged me to join the Scouts. I made it as far as a Life Scout, then gave up scouting to spend more time chasing girls and drinking. Unlike my father's, my childhood wasn't devoid of a sense of belonging or a strong male presence; where there were girls and beer to be had, the Boy Scouts just didn't have enough to offer a secure young man.

Germany was also where I started my athletic career. The military had excellent programs for dependents: football, basketball, wrestling, baseball, and even bowling. I didn't bowl a lot but frequently got the chance to improve my reaction time by setting pins for the base bowling alley. I could set four alleys and never get hit by a bowling pin or bowling ball. For that sterling accomplishment, I earned eleven cents a line, just enough to keep me in beer.

Our years in Germany were, for the most part, great fun for

the family. But while we were in Germany our family endured one of its most tragic times as well. When my little brother was just five he was hit by a motorcycle while chasing a foul ball during a Little League baseball game. We all waited, prayed, and hoped for him to regain consciousness. After a month, he finally came out of the coma, but he needed extensive physical rehabilitation. The family rallied, and aided by the determination and strength of my brother, we helped him in his struggle to learn to walk, talk, and function normally again. The experience taught me what effort and determination can accomplish.

With that tragedy behind us, in 1959, we headed back to the States once again. That time it was in Park Forest, Illinois, that the family settled. My father had been appointed the Fifth Army inspector general and traveled all over a five-state area inspecting Reserve and National Guard units. That was to be his last active-duty assignment before retiring from the army as a lieutenant colonel after twenty-two years of service. For me, that meant spending four years at Rich TWP (township) High School, Park Forest, Illinois.

Our family was experiencing good times, and I was to become really spoiled with all that America has to offer. At school, I played football, wrestled, and ran track. My academics suffered, but because of my athletic ability and having been a state champion in wrestling, I received a scholarship to Midland Lutheran College, Fremont, Nebraska. Considering that I hadn't studied a day in my life, I thought that was particularly funny. I would pay for my poor study habits for the rest of my life.

In the fall of 1963, with the scholarship, a good family, and the freedom of the sixties, I had no use for the lessons I'd learned during my youth. Rather, I was learning to play, a habit that's much harder to break than to form. I spent *all* my time partying and no time studying. I had met a beautiful girl named Lana Ludwig, blond, blue-eyed, and tall, with a body like a goddess. I spent too much time chasing her and playing sports trying to win her favor. I first met Lana at Midland's student union. I was a freshman and, as I was later to discover, she was a junior majoring in education. She was also the homecoming queen. I tried acting cool, and I found the courage to ask the beauty on a date. My acting paid off, and she accepted.

From that moment on, all I could think about was Lana. Money I received from home, I spent trying to impress her—flowers and simple little gifts, anything to make her like me. After three months, she told me that she had fallen in love with me. I immediately went out and bought an engagement ring, on credit, and couldn't think of anything but Lana.

In the spring of 1964, because of my poor scholastic performance, I became ineligible for sports. Lana demanded I do better in school, and I managed to bring my grades up enough to be returned to eligibility for football and to be taken off probation. Time went fast, and it was the end of the school year. Everybody went home except me; I got a job shoveling horse manure at a local ranch for room and board. During the weekends, I worked as a lifeguard at a local pool. After a day on the ranch, I was too tired to do anything but sleep. Consequently, I didn't write or call Lana the whole summer.

After only one month at the pool, the manager realized I was more interested in the girls sunbathing than in watching the pool for drowning people, and I was fired after a concerned mother told the manager that I hadn't noticed that her son was in danger of drowning. Without a lot of money to spend, I passed the remainder of the summer hanging around the ranch doing odd jobs. It wasn't until the middle of August that football-practice reporting time finally arrived. Needless to say, I was back well before the other students.

Of course, when Lana returned to school, she wasn't happy with me. Two months passed before I could get on her good side, and even then she didn't trust me. But finally she decided she wanted me back in her life and asked me to go with her to her home for Thanksgiving, 1964. I thought that would be my redemption and the path to her heart, but the trip to her parents', who lived in Denver, Colorado, was the worst I ever took. The weather was snowy and extremely cold, as was the reception I received from Lana's family. I could sense her parents' dislike for me the moment we met. With the loving instincts of good folks everywhere, they could see how immature I was.

The Thanksgiving dinner was excellent but became unbearable when Lana's parents asked me what I wanted to do with my life and I told them I didn't know. The conversation then veered from me to the other people in the family, all of whom seemed to know what they wanted to do and where they were going. For the rest of the time I spent there, I stayed out of everybody's way. I couldn't wait to get back to school, and that was not a common feeling with me.

That was the last time I saw her parents. When we got back to school, I started spending less time with Lana, and when she asked why, I told her it was because I had to study. That wasn't a lie, but I never spent the time studying.

After Lana graduated, she taught high school in Longmont, Colorado. I was eligible for the first semester of my sophomore year but became ineligible for the remainder of the year. My coach, Max Kitzelman, a former Giants football player, even took to checking in on me at the dorm, at one point assigning someone to watch over me to make sure I was studying. All his efforts failed. In February 1965, I received a welcome letter from our government. I was being drafted into the service of its choice. I'd been enjoying the good life that freedom made possible. I was about to learn firsthand the price for that freedom.

I called my father from school and told him of the letter. Of course, he told me I would have to go. He added that if I wanted my choice of service, I would have to join voluntarily.

So, tail between my legs, I went home to sign up for the army. Somehow I had to make amends for my disastrous college career. I signed up "Airborne Unassigned"—I was guaranteed Airborne training, but my assignment would be determined later—and three years of service. I called Lana and told her what I was going to do. I promised to see her before I was to leave, but, like all the promises I made to her, I didn't keep it.

☆
CHAPTER 2

The induction center in Harvey, Illinois, is where Uncle Sam and I got married. I arrived for our union in an air-conditioned car. Had I known that it would be my last experience with creature comforts for some time, I'd have savored every Freon-chilled moment of it; as with the rest of my charmed life, I'd taken it for granted.

I stepped out into the sweltering July afternoon and headed toward the huge, prison-gray building. The place was packed with young men just like me, all wondering what was going to happen next. Air seemed in low supply. The heat, the hundreds of competing lungs, and the heaviness of the fate that was surely to befall us made what air was available quite unpalatable.

I don't know whether it was a mix of denial and a love of adventure, or if it was just that I was about to be fully absolved of all responsibility for decision-making for the near future, but for whatever reason, I found myself actually excited about my predicament. All my life, I had vowed to steer clear of a military career, and suddenly there I was, feeling pleasant anticipation about just such a fate. Though I had always been mentally opposed to a foray into the military, on some level inside me, the move felt unbelievably right. I've heard it said that the soul speaks to us through hunches, intuition, and feelings. If that is true, I suspect that though my mind was saying no, my soul knew differently.

As we waited, I perused the flock around me. Most of them were asking questions to anyone who would answer. Others, however, quietly kept to themselves. They were all too aware of what would happen next, of what to expect. For those men, all the nervous talk and questioning in the world couldn't block that truth; they were men who were going back into the service. Conversations continued until we were all herded into one huge room to be sworn in. All two hundred and fifty of us were greeted by an officer in a starched uniform and spit-shined boots. From that moment on, there would be no more talking, only the following of instructions.

After the swearing-in, we were herded once again into a locker room and told to strip down to our underwear. The first stop was to have our blood pressure and vital signs taken, and a vision check, including a test for color blindness. That was followed by lab work, a blood test, and a urinalysis. It was funny to see huge, well-muscled guys pass out just because their blood was being sampled. After numerous shots and in-oculations, we entered a room and were told to drop our drawers and bend over while a medical technician with huge hands stuck his finger up our butts to check our prostate glands. After the finger wave, we finally got to talk to a doctor, who asked us about past medical problems, then pronounced us fit for duty. At that point, we were officially in the army. We were then loaded onto buses and on our way to learn how to soldier. On the bus, sleep won out over nervous exhaustion. The ride's quiet seemed ominous to me.

We arrived at Fort Knox, Kentucky, early in the morning, greeted by a six-foot black man wearing a Smokey-the-Bear hat and using language I had heard only in bars. He barked commands with a strange cadence and intonation that seemed to hypnotize everyone around him. His voice and demeanor left no doubt as to his place in our chain of command. His eyes glowed with an intelligence and power that instantly won our respect. Not only did we fear that man, but we came to idolize him. His name was Sergeant First Class (E-7) Grimes, a veteran of twelve years of military service. He was Airborne, i.e., a trained parachutist, and wore a Combat Infantryman Badge, signifying that he had seen combat. The CIB is the most coveted badge of an infantryman. What he was saying could be translated into "Get the fuck off the bus and stand in a straight line."

Sergeant Grimes's uniform was impeccable, and I saw my face in his highly shined boots as I did push-ups at his personal request. That man made the uniform beautiful, and I wanted to look like him. Over the time I was in basic training, I tried to get my boots to shine like his but never was able to accomplish that mission. At any time throughout my military career, if I didn't feel that I looked the part of a professional soldier, I had guilt feelings about what Sergeant First Class Grimes would say if he'd seen me not groomed to his standards. Consequently, when in garrison, I always made a special effort to look my best. I had that feeling not only about my appearance but when learning job skills. To this day, I still try to emulate Sergeant First Class Grimes.

There wasn't anyone in my platoon who'd had formal military experience, so Sergeant Grimes selected me to be platoon guide because I came from a military family. The platoon guide was the person the drill sergeant yelled at if things weren't up to his standards. That meant I had to make sure all details (minor military tasks) were properly performed and that everybody was where they were supposed to be at the time they were supposed to be there. At first I thought it was an honor to be selected as platoon guide, but I quickly learned that the position wasn't at all easy. Not only did I have to deal with every soldier's thinking I was a kiss-ass, but I got my ass chewed every day by the drill sergeant. The only benefit I received for being the platoon guide was to share a two-man room with the assistant platoon guide and to get out of details such as kitchen police and fire watch.

At first I tried to be the nice guy and be everyone's friend, but that made people think they could get away with sloppy performance and that I would take care of them. People took advantage of every situation. Even the simplest chore took them longer to accomplish than necessary, and most of the time, the job had to be done over because it wasn't up to the drill sergeant's standards. So after a couple of weeks' frustration, I asked the drill sergeant to assign someone else to the job. The first words out of Sergeant First Class Grimes's mouth were: "Quitters never win, and winners never quit." He told me that anytime I felt like quitting I should just repeat those words to myself. He then explained that people in leadership positions had to take a hard stand to make sure the job or mission got done. My priority was to my mission first, only then to my troops. He also said I didn't have to be a "total asshole" but that some people would respond properly only to my being tough. Sergeant First Class Grimes said that with time I would come to know when to be very tough and when just to be persuasive.

The whole purpose of boot camp was to develop men who could function properly as part of a team while having necessary discipline and the basic infantry skills. If there was an individual in our platoon who didn't develop with the rest of the platoon, he was either discharged from the service or retrained. People with bad hygiene habits weren't tolerated. We had a trainee who didn't like to take showers. After several days of putting up with his smell, I told him that he was to take a shower every day or someone would help him. I then put the biggest man in the platoon in the bunk next to his and told the big guy he was responsible for ensuring that the reluctant bather took a shower after daily training. We never had another problem with the man's body odor. There were stories about how other platoons with the same problem had handled it by giving the smelly recruit a "GI shower" (i.e., a group of men threw the man into the shower) with harsh GI soap and a scrub brush. Other platoons would give the individual a "blanket party" (throw a blanket over his head during the night and pummel him), telling him to correct his behavior. Different techniques, but effective.

Our platoon was the Airborne platoon of the basic training company; everybody in it was going to try to be Airborne. But because of the extra physical requirements levied on us as potential paratroopers, some ended up being transferred to another platoon because they didn't have the ability or the desire to try to succeed. When other platoons ran two miles, we ran five. If the drill sergeant said "Hit it!" we had better immediately spring into a "tight" body position (feet and knees together, knees slightly bent, head down with our hands to our front—the position a paratrooper had to take when exiting an aircraft) or be able to do fifty push-ups at a stretch. Before I was to leave basic, I could do several sets of fifty push-ups and enough pull-ups to spell Airborne. We also had to answer our drill sergeant's commands with the word "Airborne" instead of "Drill Sergeant." At graduation time, our platoon was the honor platoon, and I was selected honor graduate because I had the highest physical training test score of the company. My father was able to attend my graduation, but I had forgotten to mention to our company commander that he was an officer, so I got my ass chewed as I was informed that it was proper protocol to let a commander know if a higher-ranking officer was going to attend graduation.

Because of my being honor graduate, I was sent to leadership school before beginning advanced individual training. Leadership school took place during the post–boot camp leave. So while everyone else got to go home for a few weeks, I was learning to be a leader. The course was two weeks long and basically taught us the leadership traits and methods of motivating soldiers to get the job done or a mission accomplished. It was optional, but I wanted to learn all I could about my new career field. Of course, as my career progressed, I learned that really good leaders are born. A person can learn the attributes of a leader and the well-known techniques of leadership, but the ability to motivate and make sound decisions (particularly in combat) doesn't always come out of a book. Only a few people on earth are blessed with the ability to be a natural leader, and some of the best leaders I met in the army never attended any kind of leadership school. I never had the desire to be an officer because I wanted to be the person who got to do the hands-on job, not the planning. As it turned out, when I became an NCO, I found out I would have to plan as well as lead.

My advanced individual training was at Fort Gordon, Georgia. Somehow the army had decided that I was best suited to be a military policeman (MP). All that was required of that military operational specialty (MOS) was average intelligence and a height of at least six feet. The whole course was built around the structure of the military police. As a platoon guide once again, I had essentially the same privileges as before: a two-man room and freedom from details.

During my time off at leadership school, which was also at Fort Gordon, I went to the gym and worked out with weights or played basketball. On one occasion, I noticed some people wrestling in a corner, preparing for a tournament to be held at the gym the following week. One man was larger than everybody else and looked to be a heavyweight. Everyone he wrestled, he dominated, mostly because of his weight. It got so I couldn't watch without participating, so I challenged the big guy to a match. To his surprise, it took me only a few seconds to put him on his back. After a couple more matches, and in need of a shower, I quit and headed back to my barracks. As I was leaving, the big guy stopped me and introduced himself as the post chaplain and a major (O-4). He was hosting a wrestling tournament and wanted me to take part. I told him that I was about to graduate from leadership school and start military police school, so I didn't know if I would be able to participate. From that day until I was to leave Fort Gordon, the chaplain picked me up from my billets and took me to the gym to work out.

After he spoke with my commander, he had me representing my company in the wrestling tournament. I wrestled three matches and won all of them, winning the post championship. But no good deed goes unpunished: because the chaplain assisted me in getting away from the company, he insisted that I attend his church services every Sunday. I also had to serve as an usher. To my surprise, I met more women during those Sundays than I had in all my civilian years combined. The chaplain also spoiled me by letting me use one of his two cars anytime I wanted to go to town or go out on a date. It was cool to drive through the post gates and have everybody salute me as I did because the sticker on the chaplain's car identified it as belonging to an officer.

A week before graduation from military police school, we students received orders for our next duty station. My orders said 1st Cavalry Division, Vietnam. I couldn't believe it: I had been looking forward to being Airborne, and to do that I'd have to attend jump school at Fort Benning. Even so, I had almost accepted the orders and was going to blow off jump school. But when I called my dad to let him know where I was being sent, he told me to tell my drill sergeant that I wanted to talk to personnel about jump school. Dad said that in the meantime, he would make some calls to find out what had happened. I didn't realize I was making waves until I was told to report to the command sergeant major of the personnel office. The sergeant major chewed my ass about going over his head to complain to my dad, but I explained that I'd just been telling my father where I was being sent and hadn't been crying about going to Nam. At that point, the sergeant major offered to let me decline jump school so that I could join my buddies going to Vietnam, but I refused because I really wanted to attend jump school.

I was a little embarrassed about my dad's doing the dirty work, but the results were great. The next day, the drill sergeant told me that my orders had changed and I was going to Fort Benning, Georgia, to jump school.

From my military police class, only ten people were going to jump school; the rest were going to be "permanent party," assigned somewhere on Fort Benning. On the way to jump school, we again traveled by bus a short eight hours or so. We had left Fort Gordon after graduation, about 1600 hours. I really don't remember the trip because I slept all the way. I do remember coming to my senses as someone was yelling in my face to wake up and get off the bus. I had heard stories about jump school and how mean the cadre there were. All I wanted to do was get through the school without getting injured or killed.

After off-loading the bus and lining up for a quick roll call, we were ushered to a quick breakfast, then to supply to draw a footlocker and bedding. I couldn't wait to hit my bunk and get some more sleep. Our cadre escorted us, at double time, to the barracks. We ran with the footlockers on our shoulders. Once inside, we each grabbed a bunk, and the cadre informed us that we would have physical training (PT) at 0400 hours, followed by an in-ranks inspection. It was already 0300 hours, so we had one hour to make sure our boots were shined and our uniforms perfect. By the time I finished my boots and uniform, a cadre member was screaming up and down the barracks floor that everyone was to line up outside for PT in T-shirt, fatigue pants, and boots. After a quick roll call, we double-timed to the PT field and did our daily dozen, followed by a five-mile run in formation. I expected that to be more difficult than it was. Despite the slow pace, people fell out. But I could have run another five miles without any problems. The conditioning we'd endured during basic training and the chaplain's getting me into the wrestling program had paid off.

Jump school was broken down into three phases. The first

week was ground week, during which we learned to do the parachute landing fall (PLF) and to assume the proper body position when exiting an aircraft. At the end of the week, we were tested by exiting from the top of a thirty-foot tower while strapped into a harness attached to a skate that rode on a cable. We had to successfully demonstrate the correct body position by exiting properly from the tower three times. When exiting the tower, we assumed a tight body position and counted to four, then looked up to check the (imaginary) canopy; all while we slid wildly down the cable to end up slamming into a dirt berm fifty yards away. After our wild ride, each of us would have to act as the "rope man," attaching a length of rope to the harness and running it back up to the tower. While the rope man, we were subjected to numerous calls for push-ups from the "black hats," our instructors.

The second week was tower week, during which we spent a lot of time suspended in a harness that squeezed the testicles until many of us felt we'd become eunuchs. The week was devoted to learning how to control the—real, this time—parachute canopy. At the end of week two, we were tested by being hauled up 250 feet and dropped while in harness and beneath a parachute canopy, weather permitting. If the winds were too high, we couldn't jump from the tower. During the 250-foot-tower jump, if we didn't slam into the tower and landed without injury, we moved to the final week.

The third week was jump week, when we found out if we really had what it took to be Airborne by making five jumps and living through the experience. Everybody was herded into a huge building to be briefed about the jumps to be made each day. This was called a MACO briefing (military airborne command operation), and at it, we learned what aircraft we were jumping from and which drop zone we would use. After the briefing, we went to the staging area, where we put on our parachutes and related equipment. Then a jumpmaster checked to make sure our parachutes were in good working order, after which we were moved to the Green Ramp, where we waited to load onto the aircraft. It was hot sitting in the sun as we waited to climb on board the aircraft, and everybody was sweating. We were to jump from a C-130 aircraft at twelve hundred feet. From the time we had entered jump school, we had been addressed by numbers rather than our names, and we were herded like animals everywhere we went. Now we were on our own. The ultimate test of courage would be the jump.

The wait to load the aircraft seemed to last forever, and all I could think about was whether I had what it took to jump. Would I be a coward? When the order finally came to load the aircraft, all my senses seemed to become sharper. And so did my unease; my stomach was queasy. We boarded the aircraft via the tailgate. We were seated so close to each other that I could smell the breath of the men sitting on both sides of me. With the exception of the jump cadre and the flight crew, everybody had wide eyes, and sweat was running down their faces. I could smell the fear. I tried not to look scared, but I don't think I was any more successful than the people around me.

It was very hot on the aircraft, and when the crew chief closed the rear ramp for takeoff, it became even warmer. When the aircraft took off, everybody lurched forward, pressing us even closer together. I closed my eyes and tried to simulate an air of relaxation; I didn't want anyone to see the real fear I was feeling. All I could think was, What the fuck am I doing here?

For what seemed like hours, we flew low level, and the aircraft bounced us up and down, left to right, causing stomachs to revolt and the vomiting to start. Finally the jumpmaster gave the six-minute warning. We prepared to stand up on the command of the jumpmaster, who was hanging out the jump door looking for our drop zone. Once the jumpmaster was satisfied we were at the right location, he turned and faced the jumpers and shouted, "Stand up!" to my side of the aircraft. I had wanted to be the last person out, but we were to jump first. By that time, though, I was glad to get out of that hot, smelly plane: the man next to me had thrown up, and the smell was overpowering and caused a chain reaction of vomiting people. The jumpmaster told everyone who had puked into a barf bag to take it with them. Just one more incentive not to heave.

Finally, the jumpmaster shouted, "Hook up!" and we all snapped our static lines to the cable running through the aircraft. The static line pulls the parachute open when the jumper leaves the aircraft, so everybody was careful to hook up right.

Next the jumpmaster said, "Check static line!" The assistant jumpmaster then checked everyone's static line, and all of us then rechecked ours.

On the command to "Check equipment!" using the buddy system, we each checked the person in front of us to make sure all straps and gear were securely attached.

The jumpmaster then shouted, "Sound off for equipment check!" From the last man to jump up to the man in the door, with a slap on the ass of the man in front of us, we shouted "Okay" all the way up to the jumpmaster. When the last man in each of the two sticks (lines of jumpers in each doorway of the aircraft) looked at the jumpmaster and said, "All okay," the jumpmaster pointed at both doors and gave the command, "Stand in the door!" The first man in the stick "airborne shuffled" (with the foot next to the side of aircraft leading, we advanced toward the doorway of the aircraft; shuffling that way prevents stumbling). Once in position in the doorway, my hands, outside the aircraft, slapped the side of the plane. The jumpmaster then leaned out the jump door for the final drop-zone check. Seeing that the aircraft was nearing the right DZ, the jumpmaster shouted, "One minute," signaling that the first jumper had one minute before he was to exit the aircraft. At that point, everybody would jump whether they wanted to or not. One minute out, the two lights by the jump door become very important: red means don't jump; green means go. When the jumpmaster turns and says, "Stand by!" the first jumper prepares to exit the aircraft. Once the green light comes on, the jumpmaster yells, "Go!" On my first jump, everybody exited the aircraft without hesitation. Of course, I'm not sure anyone could have refused to jump because of the momentum of all the people pushing toward the door. Normally, the two biggest meatheads are put at the rear of each stick. Their job is to shove forward and get the stick out of the aircraft as quickly as possible. Any chickenhearted jumper will literally be carried out of the aircraft. But the real reason for getting everyone to exit the aircraft as quickly as possible is to ensure that the jumpers all have a shot at landing in the designated drop zone.

My first jump was a night jump, because when I exited the aircraft I had my eyes closed. Just as I opened my eyes my parachute opened and jerked me like a puppet on a string. I had multiple line twists in my canopy, probably because of bad body position when I exited the aircraft. I was immediately afraid I'd land on top of someone else's parachute or just run into someone because I'd have no control over my parachute until I got the twists out. Kicking my legs as if I were riding a bike (the school solution for untwisting shroud lines) caused me to gyrate, which undid the twists. Once I was able to control my canopy, I shouted, "Airborne!" at the top of my lungs. It was a great ride down until I hit the ground. I had forgotten to watch the horizon and prepare for impact, so I ended up hitting with my heels first, then my ass, followed by my head slamming into the ground and almost knocking me out. It was amazing that I didn't sustain any injuries.

I quickly gathered the parachute, stuffed it into the bag carried for that purpose, and double-timed to the transportation area to be taken back to the airfield for another jump. We had one week to make five jumps, but because of the unpredictability of the weather, the cadre tried to get as many jumps out of the way as possible while conditions were good. That day we did three jumps. For the rest of my jumps, I remembered to maintain proper body position when I exited the aircraft, and I remembered to prepare for a proper parachute landing. It was amazing how easy it was to jump if we only did what we were taught. Since bad weather was approaching, the following day we made two more jumps to finish up the requirement.

Our graduation was still scheduled for Friday, and because of rain, the ceremony was held inside.

Graduation took forever, as we had several guest speakers, but finally we received our jump wings. Airborne has a tradition of "blooding" wings when they are pinned on the chest for the first time. In the army at the time, that meant we could choose whomever we wanted to put the wings on our chest and punch them, pushing the pointed pins into the chest hard enough to cause some blood to flow and touch them. I didn't have anyone with me, so the first sergeant blooded mine.

Finally, fully qualified parachutists, we were ready to kill Communists.

I really didn't want to be a military policeman, so while we had free time, I talked to the Special Forces recruiter and volunteered to try out for the coveted green beret. I figured chances were excellent that I would end up in Vietnam, so I wanted to learn as much as possible to survive. I went through the battery of tests and physical examinations and was selected for Special Forces training. Of the over eight hundred Airborne students in my group, twenty people tried out for Special Forces. Ten of them made the selection. Before I graduated on Friday, I had received my orders to Fort Bragg, North Carolina, home of Special Forces. I was glad that I was to be trained by the best, and knowing how popular the Green Berets were with young women gave me something to look forward to as well. The biggest motivation for my volunteering, however, was wanting to be part of the best. The danger of what I would be exposed to never entered my mind.

With the demobilization of Gen. William J. "Wild Bill" Donovan's Office of Strategic Services (OSS) after World War II, the United States lost whatever ability it had had to conduct unconventional warfare. The Communist involvement in the so-called national wars of liberation in the emerging third-world countries highlighted the necessity for a national defense policy to counter the threat of aggressive Communist expansion. The start of the Korean War exposed how inadequate our military was to counter that kind of threat without the use of massive conventional troop deployments or atomic weapons.

On 20 June 1952, the first volunteers were organized at Fort Bragg, North Carolina, into the 10th Special Forces Group under the authority of the army chief of psychological warfare. The men were trained to infiltrate deep into enemy territory by air, land, or sea to conduct unconventional and guerrilla warfare; sabotage operations; organize, train, and equip guerrilla forces; support resistance movements; and escape and evade enemy forces. Special Forces operators were highly trained and skilled in operations, intelligence, demolitions, communications, medicine, and light and heavy weapons. They were capable of operating as small teams for extended periods in enemy territory with minimal support. They adopted the insignia of the Trojan horse as their symbol, and *De Oppresso Liber* (To liberate from oppression) as their motto.

After a year of training, the 10th Special Forces Group was deployed to Bad Tolz, Germany, in November 1953. The 77th Special Forces Group was activated at Fort Bragg that same year. In 1957, the 1st Special Forces Group was activated on Okinawa to support unconventional warfare missions in the Far East. By 1961, Special Forces teams were operating in

Thailand, Laos, Vietnam, Philippines, Korea, Taiwan, and other nations, primarily as training teams.

During the Kennedy administration, the role of Special Forces was to teach the techniques of guerrilla warfare to indigenous personnel. The idea was to form a twelve-man team, two officers and ten enlisted of different job skills—i.e., light weapons, heavy weapons, engineering-demolitions, communications, operations and intelligence, and medical—and drop them into enemy-held territory to train the host country's forces to fight against insurgency. In Vietnam, Special Forces carried out counterinsurgency operations, most of them covert, along with training the South Vietnamese and montagnard peoples in counterinsurgency and counterguerrilla warfare.

I was on my way to Fort Bragg, North Carolina, once again by bus, late in the day. On the bus with those of us selected for Special Forces training, there were paratroopers who were assigned to the 82d Airborne Division, which was also located at Fort Bragg.

Of course we arrived early in the morning, when the usual big, badass-looking black sergeant got onto the bus and yelled that all of the people assigned to the 82d were to get off the bus. As the bus pulled away, I watched out of the window of the bus as that big, mean-sounding sergeant continued to yell. Before I lost sight of them, those new paratroopers were doing push-ups. At every school I had attended in the army, someone ended up screaming at us to get off the bus. Later in life, when I traveled on civilian buses, I kept expecting some big black guy to lunge aboard and order me to get off. After watching what happened to those people assigned to the 82d, I wondered what was in store for us. After all, from what I understood, we were going to be trained by the baddest, toughest guys in the land. All of us on our bus looked at each other and shook our heads in unhappy anticipation.

Our bus pulled up to a modern brick building surrounded

by World War II–era barracks (two-story wooden buildings with open bays and toilets), each of which could accommodate fifty people. All of us were nervous about the torture we were about to endure. Outside the modern structure, a short, thin man wearing a green beret stood like a statue at the position of parade rest, waiting for the bus doors to open. Every one of us took a deep breath without moving, waiting to scramble off the bus at the first command of the man boarding our bus. The doors opened and the Green Beret stepped up into the bus and with a big grin welcomed us to Fort Bragg. I was thinking that he was smiling because he was about to lower the boom on us poor soldiers. He was small in stature but looked like he was chiseled from stone. He introduced himself as Staff Sergeant Norton. He asked how many of us were hungry and wanted to eat. There were only ten of us, but all of us were hungry. We all raised our hands. The sergeant told us to get off the bus and get into a formation. I thought, Here it comes: time for push-ups and loud yelling about how stupid we are. Instead, we formed up in a squad formation, and he asked for copies of our orders. After collecting them, he marched us to the "dining facility" (mess hall); we filed in and were offered fresh eggs, bacon, and SOS (shit on a shingle, or creamed chipped beef on toast). That was quite a surprise; we were used to eating whatever was being served as fast as we could eat it before some sergeant yelled that we were to get out of his mess hall.

After we ate at our leisure, Sergeant Norton took us to get bedding and then led us to our billets. The only thing the 82d had over the Special Forces were their new billets; we slept in World War II billets, and we had to pull fire watch for an hour each at night because the billets were heated with coal, and someone had to stoke the furnaces a couple of times each night. I kept thinking that the next day we would be treated like scum again because the nice-guy image we were getting of Special Forces had to be too good to be true.

The next morning a different sergeant came into the billets.

We had a formation, and he marched us to in-processing. To decide what job specialty we would be trained in, we had to go before a board of Special Forces noncommissioned officers headed by an officer. I reported to the officer in charge, and he asked what I thought my job skill should be. I had heard that Special Forces medical training was the best and the most fun because the training was at Fort Sam Houston, Texas, and the area was said to be well stocked with friendly women. I was also eager to get away from the rigid Airborne standards of Fort Bragg. So I said, "Medic." The board NCOs asked several questions while looking over my record. They noted that I had some college education and agreed that medic training would be for me. I was glad they didn't have my grades in front of them.

The other Special Forces job skills were communication, light weapons, heavy weapons, engineer, or demolitions. Medical training was the longest of the schools available and the most difficult. Before we could start training, we had to wait for a class date. Since the medical classes had the longest waiting period, that meant I had many days and nights of kitchen police (KP) and fire watch to look forward to, not to mention twenty-four-hour duty as runner for the charge of quarters. Those became our everyday chores. I couldn't wait to start training to get away from the details.

Special Forces training was broken down into three phases. In those days, the first phase was the job-skill training. At Fort Sam, the first eight weeks of basic medical training were very basic: we learned the lifesaving steps and the techniques used in applying them, and for those eight weeks we were treated like basic-training students. I thought that by that point in our military careers we would be finished with petty details and be concentrating on medical studies, but KP was once more a part of our lives. And it quickly became obvious that the Special Forces students were getting more of the kitchen duty than the other soldiers, and some of us were upset about it.

One morning, a couple of our trainees were peeling potatoes, and, while doing so, cut the potatoes open and put soap in them. Later, when the cooks started to boil them, the pots and pans started to foam. We had a formation the next day, and the two men who'd been on KP were sent back to Fort Bragg. We pulled more duty while at our basic medical training than we had at Fort Bragg, and we weren't allowed to leave our area of training except to visit a local enlisted club that served only weak "near" beer.

After the basic medical training, we were to spend twelve weeks at advanced medical training, still at Fort Sam but under much better circumstances and across from the women's billets. And we all ate at the same dining facility. That was the best assignment I'd yet had in the military: we could live off post and weren't assigned details like kitchen police or fire watch. Although we had more time to ourselves, the circumstances and curriculum required more studying. The hands-on portion was more detailed, and there was a book of terminology we had to learn. Any of the hands-on procedures I could master without a problem, but come time for the written tests, and I struggled.

A couple of other students and I rented an apartment and, of course, partied way too much, almost to the point of failing. The first weekend in our new digs, we bought a keg of beer and invited as many women as we could. After having been locked up in the basic medical course for eight weeks, we were all horny as hell. Even so, we couldn't have accommodated all the willing females who showed up at the apartment. Our classes were located next to the women's barracks, so every time I saw a good-looking girl there, I invited her to the party. So did the other guys. I got into trouble because every girl I invited thought she was with me. At one point, three girls were ready to fight over who was going to get me. Having women fighting over me was a different experience. Problem was, there just wasn't any privacy—we had fifty guests and just a two-bedroom apartment, so most people ended up drunk by the pool. I don't know why the police never came, because we were loud, drunk, and obnoxious.

The next day we had a visit from the landlord, who ordered us to clean up the mess and not to repeat that kind of party again or we would be out on the street and she would make sure we wouldn't be able to rent an apartment anywhere in town. It took me three days to recover from my hangover, and I still hadn't gotten laid. I thought a lot about Lana but never wrote to her. She would not have approved of my behavior if she could have seen me. Not communicating was just one of the many mistakes I had made with that woman.

On one occasion, several of the women challenged three of us to make a panty raid on the female barracks. They promised us all sexual favors if we succeeded. Being the macho young bulls we were, the next night we borrowed some ropes from a mountain-climbing buddy, went to the roof of the female barracks, tied the ropes so we could retrieve them, then rappelled into a bay window that had been left open by one of the women who'd offered the bet. We swung through the window, pulled the rope down, and ran through the barracks, grabbing underwear from footlockers. We were out the fire escape before the person on duty knew what the women were screaming about.

The next morning we had a mandatory formation, and the whole Special Forces class was accused of carrying out the raid, but no one admitted to anything, and nothing could be proved. That weekend we all partied and collected on the bet without any protests from the women. But out of fear of flunking or getting caught for our shenanigans, I decided to study more and party less. On occasion, though, we did journey with a few of the friendly females and a blanket to the polo field for extracurricular activities. Occasionally, a passing horseback rider out for an evening's ride would be surprised by the sight of a couple of naked people on the field.

Luckily, we all finished our training successfully and moved to the next phase, twelve weeks of on-the-job training. I was to report to Fort Jackson, South Carolina.

I flew into Columbia, South Carolina, where a shuttle bus ran to Fort Jackson. After in-processing through personnel, we were taken to our medical training company and received a brief welcome by the first sergeant and the company commander. I was introduced to my liaison, who provided me with a schedule of rotation through all of the services offered by Moncleaf Hospital, where we would receive training. My first rotation was the emergency room. I was scheduled for the night shift, and on the third night, a patient came in complaining of rectal pain. He was admitted and taken to an examination room, where a corpsman prepped him prior to meeting the doctor. The corpsman came out of the examination room a minute later, laughing hysterically. A couple of trainees and myself went in to see what was so funny. The patient was straddling the exam table, chest down, with his buttocks exposed so the doctor could examine him. Upon closer examination, I could see a beacon of light emanating from his anus like a lighthouse on a lake. The individual ended up having a flashlight surgically removed from his anus!

When I arrived at Fort Jackson, two Special Forces medical students were finishing rotation through that period of training. They warned me about the hazards of partying too much and said that the women going through training there were off-limits. On the other hand, the women in town didn't like the military at all, probably because so many of them had had bad experiences with soldiers. Anyhow, our time was taken up with work and learning as much as we could. The next training would be the dog lab. Training at Fort Jackson was excellent because we got to work every service in the hospital from emergency room to surgery. It was a great experience, and we didn't have much time for the kind of fun we'd had at Fort Sam.

The last phase of medical training was the Advanced Medical Lab at Fort Bragg, North Carolina. It was also the most intense training. After a couple weeks of lectures and some lab procedures, another student and I were given an animal with a gunshot wound. In advanced training at Fort Sam, we did get to work on goats, but that was a combined effort. Now we were solely responsible for the well-being of our dog.

The wound the animal received was made by machine. In lectures and demonstrations, we had covered veterinary medicine, including anatomy and physiology. My partner and I administered local and general anesthesia, after which our animal was given a wound simulating a war wound. It was our job to ensure that the animal didn't suffer and to provide adequate treatment so that the animal would live. After the treatment, the animal would be put to sleep.

Some of the animals had problems that had been present when we received them. If so, we had to identify and treat those problems, too. There was never time enough to establish any warm feeling for the animal; it was used to ensure that we medics could identify and treat combat injuries and environmental diseases to save the lives of our soldiers. I had heard that animal-rights groups were formally protesting our use of the animals but never personally encountered any of them. I can say from personal combat experience that if we hadn't used those animals, many of our wounded soldiers would have died.

Upon successful completion of dog lab training, we went into Phase II of Special Forces training, in which we studied the history of special-operations forces and Special Forces, dating back to Roger's Rangers, through World War I, II, Korea, and finally when Special Forces was recognized by President Kennedy and became the first American unit formally authorized to wear a distinctive item of uniform (the green beret) by presidential proclamation. Phase II concentrated on teaching us efficient methods of instruction so that we could teach others how to defend and protect themselves, which was Special Forces' primary mission. We learned patrolling, communications, camouflage, ambush techniques, and a wide variety of weapons—domestic and foreign. The most important class taught was the history and practice of guerrilla warfare.

Phase III was a field exercise treated like a real war situation. We were assembled into a standard Army Special Forces A-detachment team of twelve men. Each man had the necessary job skills called for in the TOE (Table of Organization & Equipment) makeup of an A-team: detachment commander (officer); detachment executive officer (officer); operations sergeant (team sergeant); heavy weapons leader (heavy weapons NCO); light weapons leader (light weapons NCO); intelligence sergeant (intel sergeant); medical specialist (team medic); radio operator supervisor (senior radio operator); assistant medical specialist (junior medic); demolitions sergeant (engineer NCO); combat demolitions specialist (demo NCO); chief radio operator (junior radio operator). We were issued a warning order to prepare for the field and given a detailed operation order and mission objective describing exactly what we were to accomplish while we were in the field.

Under the cover of darkness, we were to jump into a designated area and link up with our "indigenous" force (soldiers portraying freedom fighters being supported by our government). At the same time, we were to gather intelligence that would be utilized by conventional troops. We would provide the indigenous force with classes in our fields of expertise, as we later did in the jungles of Vietnam. Occasionally, in the middle of a class, we would be attacked by the aggressors (enemy force) and have to move to another secure location in order to continue instruction. That part of the exercise was followed by a mission to attack a known enemy village, after which we had to escape and evade the reaction force of the enemy. Men from an element of the 82d Airborne were the aggressors, and the word was not to get caught or captured. Those folks thought of themselves as the army's elite and felt as if Special Forces had taken some of the "shine" away from them. If we got caught, the boys of the 82d would treat us like prisoners of war under conditions not much different from those accorded real prisoners of war in Vietnam.

Our team made a successful raid on a mock enemy village, then broke into two six-man teams and quietly and quickly moved toward the designated safe area. Along the way, we ran across an old still that had jars of moonshine. One of the men on our team was from Tennessee and could tell good liquor from poisonous. Our find was good stuff, so we filled our nearly empty rucksacks with as many jars as we could fit into them. With our rucks packed and hoping not to get caught with the goods, we patrolled to the extraction area. We each promised not to tell anyone of our find and not to drink any until we completed the mission. We reached the extraction area without being captured. The other half of our team arrived about the same time we did, and we shared our fortune with them on the trip back to Fort Bragg. The mission wasn't complete until we were debriefed and all of our equipment was accounted for, so none of us was able to indulge until the cadre told us we were done. We kept our mouths shut about our find of white lightning so we wouldn't have to share it.

Finally, after all was said and done, and with a sense of accomplishment, we broke out the jars of shine and became totally intoxicated. We were fully qualified Green Berets and proud of it.

Our graduation was on a Friday, but we all had already received orders to our next duty stations. Mine read Headquarters, 5th Special Forces Group, Republic of Vietnam.

I called my parents after I learned my assignment. My parents, especially my mother, didn't like the idea of my going to Vietnam. My dad was concerned but understood that I had to go, just as he had. I told them on the phone rather than wait until I got home so that I wouldn't have to deal in person with their reaction to my going.

I had mixed emotions about going to Vietnam. While in training, I never heard much about Special Forces men dying, and I couldn't picture myself getting killed. Our instructors did make references to death in Nam in the context of "You fuck up, you die, and get all of your team killed in the process."

Before I could take leave en route to Nam, I had to attend a course in the Vietnamese language for eight weeks. Language school was boring, probably because I didn't study hard enough to understand. While being monitored by an instructor, we sat and listened to a tape recorder, then repeated what the tape said. If we didn't pronounce the words right, the instructor would interrupt and correct us. I passed all of the quizzes and the final exam but still couldn't speak the language as well as I could have had I tried harder. The eight weeks went fast, and I couldn't wait to get out of North Carolina. I hoped to see Lana before I went to Nam.

I flew to Denver, Colorado, then caught a Greyhound bus to Longmont, Colorado, to see Lana. I had tried to call her, but it seemed she was never home. After arriving in Longmont, I called her home and was lucky enough to catch her. She agreed to pick me up, but I could sense a chill through the phone line. She arrived at the station exuding the same coldness she'd delivered over the phone. The first words out of her mouth were, "What are you doing here?" I explained that I was going to Vietnam and wanted to see her before I left, and then said that I still loved her. She laughed at me and reminded me I hadn't written or called her in months. Playing on her naivete about the military, I told her I hadn't been able to call because of the special training I'd been undergoing. She must have believed me because she insisted that I stay, but not with her. She took me to a hotel, dropped me off, and said she would pick me up after work.

Dressed in my green uniform and beret, I went into the hotel to get a room. The place became silent. I didn't impress Lana, but I did impress the hotel owner. She asked where I was going, and I told her I was en route to Vietnam. She gave me a room, then invited me to the hotel bar for a drink on the house. I sat in the bar and drank beer all afternoon while talking to the owner, a very nice woman about the age of my father. She appreciated soldiers. When I checked out the next day, she told me to forget about the bill; it was her way of showing her appreciation for a man fighting for his country.

Still looking angry, Lana picked me up for dinner. She told me that I was no longer her boyfriend, but I pulled out every line I could think of to get back into her confidence. I even told her again that I loved her. While at dinner I kept telling her how much I wanted her and that she was the only woman I would ever love. I told her I was on my way to Vietnam and wanted her there for me when I returned. After a couple of cocktails, she started warming up and even admitted that she still loved me in spite of the fact that my actions had taught her not to trust me. She was one smart woman! She told me there would be no real intimacy until I proved myself by writing her while I was in Vietnam. She would wait for me unless I didn't write; then it would be good-bye. We spent the night sitting on her porch, kissing and holding one another. I left the next day on the Greyhound bus to Denver as she watched with tears in her eyes. I had every intention of doing what Lana wanted, but after arriving in Vietnam, I wrote one letter to her before I got caught up in the war without regard to any of the ones I loved. As I boarded the plane in Denver to visit my parents, I was thinking about Lana and couldn't get her out of my mind the whole trip to South Bend, Indiana.

My father was at the airport when I arrived. I was hungry and just about broke, so my father and I found a quiet place to eat and drink before going home. I had only a week's leave left before I was to report to Oakland Army Terminal for the flight to Vietnam. During my stay at home, my mother cooked every meal I wanted as if it were to be my last supper, and I must have gained twenty pounds. That leave was the closest I had ever been to my family. It was as if they felt they would never see me again. But the week flew by, and soon I had to say good-bye to my mother, who was in tears out of fear for me. My father managed to rein in his emotions until it was time for me to board the aircraft, when he grabbed me and told me to keep my eyes open, my mouth shut, and to listen to the old NCOs. Most important, he told me he loved me, something he had never done before. We hugged, and again I left someone in tears.

☆
CHAPTER 3

August 1966

As far as I know, I was the only person to receive orders directly to Vietnam from my graduating class. My point of embarkation was Oakland, California. I checked in at the airline terminal, then proceeded toward my boarding area, keeping my eyes open for a bar in which to quench my thirst like a professional soldier while attracting the attention of any young woman who might be interested in an adventure with a Green Beret.

I found the boarding area, received my boarding pass, and was told that it would be a couple of hours before my flight would be available. The flight attendant pointed me to the closest pub.

I sashayed up to the bar, catching the attention of a group of older gentlemen. One of the men, heavyset with gray hair and a lot of experience showing on his face, was staring at me with a look of curiosity and admiration. Once our eyes met, he lifted his glass and toasted me, then told the bartender to give me whatever I wanted to drink. He said something to the men he was with and walked toward me. He must already have had a few, because he was having a hard time maneuvering around the other people in the bar. As he got closer, his lips spread into a grin, and he asked me where I was going. I told him Vietnam. His face lost its smile momentarily, and for an instant he looked the way my father had when told I was going to Vietnam.

Several drinks and long but interesting conversation made the time fly. The old man related to me his experiences during World War II. We must have drunk gallons of beer; I would finish one, and before I could set my glass down, another would appear in front of me. I was feeling no pain, and the kind old man refused to let me buy. It seemed like only minutes, but in reality about two hours passed before I heard my boarding call. I got an adrenaline rush with the thought that my time in that bar could be the last time I would be able to enjoy a cold beer in a nonhostile environment. I finished my beer and told my drinking companion that I had to go. He suddenly became sober, took out one of his cards, handed it to me, and told me to keep in touch. He then gave me a hearty hug and told me to keep my head down. As I boarded the plane, I glanced back, and the old man threw me a salute that I returned. I entered the plane, and the old man disappeared from my view. That incident stands out in my mind because my next visit to the U.S. would be marked by a different reception and farewell.

FUI (Flying under the Influence)

The first leg of the flight passed relatively quickly because I had consumed so much alcohol in a short period of time that I passed out as soon as the aircraft took off. I awoke as the flight attendant told me to put my seat into the upright position for landing; we were landing at Clark Air Base in the Philippines. There we had to get off the aircraft while the crew refueled and took on more supplies.

Again I went looking for a bar or somewhere to find a drink to ease my hangover, but all that was available was a small, air-conditioned snack bar. The humidity was high, and the cool interior of the snack bar was a relief. As I walked inside, I saw an empty seat by a couple of men who were on my flight. I sat down and struck up a conversation and found out they, too, were suffering from dehydration due to overconsumption of alcohol.

One of the guys sitting at the table was a paratrooper going to the 101st Airborne. He had smuggled a bottle of vodka aboard and was sharing it with the rest of us. After we swapped a few Airborne lies, it was time to board the aircraft again. I was still suffering from an alcohol buzz, but I spent the rest of the trip talking with my seatmates about what we expected to encounter in Vietnam. Male ego definitely dominated part of that conversation; there was never any talk of our dying, only of our killing the enemy. Of course, we were all cherries and had no idea what was in store for us. The general consensus was that we were going to rid the world of communism through the means of firepower.

A Saigon Welcome

We landed early in the morning at Tan Son Nhut Air Base in Saigon. When the aircraft shut down, the air-conditioning also stopped, and it seemed like hours before we could get off the aircraft. The longer we sat, the hotter it became and the more difficult to breathe.

The flight attendant finally opened the aircraft doors, and we were allowed to get off the aircraft. As I stepped onto the stairs leading from the aircraft, the *really* hot air outside hit me like a blast furnace. At the bottom of the steps, an OD green bus with metal screens across its windows waited for us. By the time we reached the terminal, I was soaked with sweat from head to toe.

We were led to a huge open hangar where hundreds of large fans buzzed in a futile effort to cool the impossibly hot and humid air. The fans provided minimal relief if you stood directly underneath them.

The terminal building was lined with makeshift offices representing every unit in Vietnam. At each one, clerks were typing orders, and sergeants were telling people where to go. The center of the terminal was taken up by benches filled with baggage and the sleeping forms of military people waiting for flights out or transportation to their new units.

I didn't see a Special Forces representative, so I went to the booth marked REPLACEMENT CENTER. It was there I saw a Green Beret talking to a group of Vietnamese. The airport was deafening because of all the aircraft coming and going and the noise of the big fans, so I couldn't make out what the sergeant was saying or even whether he was speaking English or Vietnamese.

Finally, he concluded his conversation and spotted me. With a wave of his hand, he motioned me over to him. He asked for a copy of my orders and introduced himself as Staff Sergeant Horton. He wanted to know how my trip was and if I was hungry. I told him I would rather be drinking than eating. He smiled, picked up one of my bags, and told me to follow him.

Horton had a jeep parked outside. He threw my bag in the back of the jeep and told me to get in. Outside, the heat and humidity were still stifling, and the roads were crowded with hundreds of bicycles and small vehicles called Lambrettas. Horton's driving abilities amazed me. He must have been going fifty miles an hour, and he never slowed down for anything; everybody and everything got out of his way. How we ever made it through the maze of people, bicycles, and vehicles without hitting anything was a miracle. After a couple of miles, we arrived at a Special Forces hideaway called Camp Goodman. A little jungle in the middle of the city of Saigon, it was surrounded by every kind of vegetation known to man or animal. From the outside, the compound looked like a small park.

As we passed the Vietnamese guards and entered the compound, I distinctly smelled insect repellent, but the fragrance of the magnolia trees quickly made me forget the more distasteful odor. After several days, I became completely unaware of the insect repellent. The compound was small but had everything a soldier could desire in a war zone. The men of Special Forces were given the worst missions but had no wants when they were in the rear; they knew how to make the best of a bad situation.

The compound housed an A-team (smallest unit in Special Forces) and a small transient area for people coming into the country. It also had a small club, and boats were available for the use of those off duty. The interior of the compound was very colorful and exotic because of the great number of flowering shrubs with blooms of every color and fragrance imaginable. Still, to a newcomer, all that beauty was at first overshadowed by the smell of the insect repellent and the noise from the streets outside the compound. Besides the plants and flowers, there were many colorful species of birds. I would learn to sit and enjoy watching these beauties for hours.

I was taken to the guest room, shown where to drop my bags, and then immediately escorted by Horton to the local bar to satisfy my thirst. He said he, too, would rather drink than eat. The whole evening, Horton never talked about himself, and when I asked him a question he would respond with, "You'll find out." After quenching my thirst, I told Horton I was exhausted and would like to retire for the night. He said he would be at my billet in the morning to finish my in-processing. I thanked him and staggered back to my waiting bunk.

The first night there was my most difficult. I had two choices: be eaten alive by the thousands of miniature vampires, called mosquitoes, that mercilessly buzzed my ears all night, or use the mosquito net to cover my bed and sweat to death because I wouldn't get any air circulation to cool me down. I resolved to sweat because I was worn out and intoxicated. I soon passed out and didn't rouse until Horton woke me the next morning.

To my surprise, someone had polished my boots and picked up after me, a service of the facilities, I learned. Horton took me to the dining hall, where I could actually order whatever I wanted to eat. No lines or waiting. It made me feel like an officer. On the table in front of me were a couple of bottles of antimalaria tablets that, as long as I would be in country, I would have to take. One was a huge orange tablet called chloroprimaquine and the other a small white tablet called dapsone. After a couple of years of making all GIs take dapsone, the military found out that the medicine had an adverse affect on blacks with sickle-cell anemia. It took government specialists a couple of deaths before they figured out why the men died.

It was explained to me that I would be at Camp Goodman waiting for orders assigning me to a unit and allowing myself to acclimate to the hot, humid weather. While at Camp Goodman, I wandered into the city of Saigon, taking in all the sights and sounds. Saigon was a crowded city where the slums were mixed in with the homes of the wealthy. To this day, the ever-present noise of the motorcycles and Lambrettas is etched into my mind, and once in a while, when I hear a rice-burning motorcycle, I have flashbacks reminding me of Saigon. In Saigon there was always heavy pollution and the smell of oil. Despite the curfew, hundreds of food stands stayed open twenty-four hours a day, serving everything from soup to dog. There were as many Indian shops selling gold and jewelry as there were Chinese restaurants. And all the merchants and salespeople were trying to get as much out of passersby as they could. Some shops sold weapons and equipment that our soldiers couldn't get through normal supply channels. That was the black market. The vendors treated customers nicely until receiving their money; then they would quickly move on to the next prospect.

Taxis were plentiful, but the best way to see the city was by man-powered rickshaw carriages. It was cheap transportation, and those guys could go where taxis couldn't. In Saigon, anything a person could possibly want—well, those guys knew where to get it. Most of the rickshaw men could speak and understand English, but unless it benefited them, they pretended they didn't understand anything a GI said. At that time, my grasp of the Vietnamese language was limited to exchanging pleasantries and being able to order food and drink.

During my excursions, I stopped into a couple of bars that were loaded with young women who wanted me to buy them drinks or whatever else they were selling, but I quickly learned that it cost more for the drink than it would to spend an hour alone with them. The drinks GIs ordered for the girls were called "Saigon tea," and most of the time tea was all that was in them; the girls usually weren't allowed to have alcoholic drinks while working. They got a very small percentage of the house take for the Saigon teas they talked GIs into buying for them.

The "working girls" had several universal sayings, "I love you long time," "No money, no honey," and "Hey, GI, you want boom-boom?" being three of the most common. Being a clean-cut American boy and broke, I didn't get laid. A class I remembered most distinctly from medical school was the one on veneral disease (VD). In the Korean War, the Americans had more VD cases than war wounds. It wouldn't have looked good for a new medic in country to be asking for medication to cure VD. It was smarter and cheaper just to eat and drink in Camp Goodman. On the weekends, the club on Camp Goodman had enough entertainment to satisfy most of my needs until I reached my final duty station.

After two weeks at Camp Goodman, I was finally notified that I was being sent to Nha Trang, to the 5th Special Forces

Operational Base (SFOB). Horton took me to the airfield, right up to the waiting aircraft, a C-130 with four huge turbojet engines pushing its props. We loaded onto the aircraft using the tailgate. With the props blasting hot air and the sound of the engines rising to a deafening roar, the crew chief told me to find a spot somewhere in the fully loaded cargo hold. Then the ramp closed, and we took off. That would be the last I would see of Saigon for a while. At that moment, my thoughts were on the location of the front and of the war. The city had a carnival atmosphere, and the Vietnamese were barkers trying to get every penny we had. Had I stayed one more day, my impression would have been different; the city and airport were attacked by rockets, killing a lot of soldiers and civilians.

Nha Trang

The trip didn't take long, but after we landed in Nha Trang, I could tell the difference in climate as soon as the ramp lowered to permit off-loading. Nha Trang is a small coastal city lined with white beaches along the crystal-clear South China Sea. The French colonial influence was reflected there in the huge mansions that sat along the coast. Compared to Saigon, the air was cool, and the smell of the sea prevailed over the smell of insect repellent.

After I got off the aircraft, personnel inside the terminal told me where to catch a shuttle bus to the Special Forces Operational Base. The SFOB compound was close to the shore, a couple of miles from the airport. It was a small compound located within a larger conventional army compound. The SFOB had only a few buildings and a sandbagged concrete bunker, the command post, that was nestled between wooden buildings. Surrounding the SFOB were elements of the Nha Trang Mike Force, a battalion-size group of montagnards (the generic name for the non-Vietnamese ethnic-minority peoples of the highlands who were considered savages by the Viet-namese) and their Special Forces advisers. The Mike Forces were countrywide Special Forces reaction units whose mission was reinforcement of camps under attack or construction, conducting small-scale conventional combat operations, and performing raids and patrols. There were also conventional American units that supported the SFOB. Except for all the military equipment, weapons, and men in uniform, it was hard to tell there was a war going on; the area looked like a tropical paradise.

The bus let me off in front of personnel, where I once again processed in. After filling out what little paperwork there was, I was sent to supply to be issued a weapon number, flak jacket, web gear, and gas mask. I was in a war zone, but I couldn't even keep my weapon with me. By the time I finished collecting everything I was to be issued, I looked like a pack mule. Then one of the supply clerks led me to the first sergeant's office, and I received a brief orientation and indoc-trination about what was expected of me while serving with his unit. That was the last time I saw the first sergeant. Then I was turned over to the company clerk, who assigned me a place to stay. I was shown my bunk and where to stow my gear. I had only a few minutes to get settled before I was to report to the aid station, where I would be working.

The company clerk introduced me to the noncommis-sioned officer in charge, (NCOIC) Master Sergeant Guess, and the next man in charge, Staff Sergeant Arnold. I never associated with the master sergeant or even saw him much; everything was run by Arnold.

The company clerk then brought me to the dispensary. It was small for the amount of troops who used it: just two examination rooms, a minor-surgery room, and a laboratory. The NCOIC and the doctor each had his own office. After I met everyone, Staff Sergeant Arnold had Dave, one of the medics, show me the rest of the compound and take me to process into the Mess Association. Eventually Dave became a friend, even though I can no longer recall his last name. Sorry, Dave, I've always been terrible with names! When Dave took me to in-process at the Mess Association, I met the most obnoxious person I've ever met in my entire life, the NCOIC, Master Sergeant Childers, who stood about six feet nine inches tall and used every bit of it to intimidate people. He was as massive as he was tall and had a mouth that was proper issue for his body. If you didn't have a rank equal to or higher than his, he clearly considered you to be shit. And Childers was a very senior man at pay grade E-8. His function was to handle the money for the association and the running of the enlisted club. To me, even the worth of his job was questionable: the Mess Association was used to provide the soldiers with some of the comforts of home. A club with stateside entertainment and steaks on Friday nights! And it wasn't free. Every month, every SF soldier in Nha Trang had to pay dues. After signing up, I couldn't wait to get out of the asshole's presence. In retrospect, I often wonder if I would have had a different opinion of Childers had I been of higher rank.

Playboy Club

Since by then it was chow time, Dave wanted to take me to the Playboy Club because the mess hall had terrible food. I was broke, but Dave insisted on treating me, so I swallowed my pride and vowed to pay him back the next time I had money. It wasn't long before the rest of the dispensary, with the exception of the doctor, arrived. We ate, drank, and had one of the best times I'd experienced since arriving in country. At that time, I felt I had found some good friends, but I learned later in my tours in Vietnam that my lifelong friends would be the ones I spent the most time in combat with.

The night went fast and, after consuming more beer than a human should, so did I. I was told the next day that it took two men to help me to my bunk. The next morning, Dave woke me to a hangover I would remember for a long time. He escorted me to the showers and then to the dispensary. We were at work before 0600 hours and found Staff Sergeant Arnold already checking medical records. When I first worked at the dispensary, I made it my goal to beat Staff Sergeant Arnold to work, but after a couple of weeks, my goal became just to show up on time.

The first day at work, I was put in triage, taking temperatures and blood pressures, writing up patients' complaints and their brief medical histories, then passing them on either to the doctor or to Staff Sergeant Arnold. Dave worked in the lab and spent the day doing blood counts, smears, cultures, and whatever else the doctor ordered.

I had the opportunity to observe Staff Sergeant Arnold working up a patient, and quickly decided he should have been a physician. Even the doctor asked him questions. For the rest of my time in the dispensary, whenever I had the opportunity I followed Sergeant Arnold around, trying to absorb as much of his knowledge as possible. I learned more in the short time I watched him than in all the time I spent in training. Arnold explained every procedure and diagnosis in detail so that I could understand. The next day he would question me to see if I remembered what he had taught me. After a couple of weeks observing the various minor surgical procedures, I was given the opportunity to do most of the simple things, like cyst removals and removing foreign bodies from cuts and wounds, then suturing the patient. Since Dave didn't like being confined in the lab all the time, I asked to work there to refresh my lab procedures. That way he could do more screening and procedures.

I had been at SFOB about three weeks when Staff Sergeant Arnold asked me to go to the medical warehouse to prepare pallets of medical supplies that were needed fast. I finished early, and Arnold gave me the rest of the day off. One of the clerks had earlier given me a joint of marijuana. I told him that I had never even smoked a cigarette, let alone a joint. He advised me to smoke it after work, assuring me that the grass would "relax me." I had to take a dump, so I thought the latrine would be the perfect place. I could lock myself in, and the smell of the diesel fuel used to submerge the excrement, and of the excrement itself, would cover the smell of marijuana.

First Date with Mary Jane

I sat down, pulled out the tightly rolled joint, and lit up. The clerk had told me to get the most out of the joint by inhaling as much as I could without coughing, then holding my breath as long as I could without passing out. So I slowly drew the smoke into my waiting lungs, filling them to the point of explosion. I was light-headed but figured that was because I was holding my breath. I thought something was wrong with the grass because the light-headed feeling passed quickly, and I felt normal. Soon the joint was down to nothing, and I discarded it into the fifty-five-gallon drum-half that was under the shitter.

I sat, waiting for something to happen. After I thought I'd given the marijuana enough time to work, I said to myself, "Man, that wasn't anything." Thinking it was really stupid for people to smoke that stuff and believe they were going to get something out of it, I pulled up my pants, got up to leave, reached for the latch that locked the door from the inside, and couldn't get it open. Then the smell of diesel fuel and human waste started to make me feel sick. After several attempts to open the door, and what seemed like an eternity, paranoia hit me: sooner or later, I thought, someone is going to have to take a dump, and he'll find me locked in the latrine. Either that or I'll have to spend the night in it. Of course, by then I realized that if anyone saw me, they would know that I was high. I continued to work the lock until I'd had enough: I kicked the door open and stumbled into the blinding sunlight, trying to find my way to my hootch. I was praying that I wouldn't run into anyone on the way, because anyone who saw me would have thought I was drunk or retarded. I couldn't get my feet to work right, and I couldn't remember where my bunk was. I was getting even more paranoid until, finally, I recognized a prominent terrain feature and concentrated on moving to that point, eventually making it to my hootch. I lay down and thought to myself, "Man, that was good shit!"

After that experience, the rest of my time with SF, I drank. I felt it was safer for me.

It Can't Last Forever

After I'd been in country for three weeks and still not been into town, mostly because of monetary reasons, Dave decided to take me to a restaurant that had great seafood. For three weeks, I had seen and treated numerous GIs with venereal disease, so sex was not a priority. Before we ate, Dave took me to several of the bars that lined the beach of Nha Trang, beach houses with very little food but a lot of beer and women. We consumed a lot of *Bier* 33 and *Bier Larue* and finally landed in a restaurant called the Nautique. Not realizing how big the creatures were there, we both ordered lobster. We sat at the table munching on French bread, waiting for our orders. Then the waiter came out of the kitchen with lobsters in each hand. He put them on a huge tray and displayed them to us. They had to weigh at least five pounds each. He took them back to the kitchen, returning about fifteen minutes later with both lobsters red and steaming. I tried to eat all of mine, but I could barely finish the claws. We probably sat for three hours trying to finish that meal. I'd been hungry, but not hungry enough to eat all of the food that was presented to us.

Filled to the brim, we left the restaurant and hit Kim's, another bar that SF people frequented in the middle of town. We had just one drink, and even that was difficult to get down because we were so full, so we decided to watch a Chinese movie that was playing at the theater next to Kim's. After the movie, I was ready for the sack.

Of course, I knew it would be too good to be true for me to spend my entire tour in a tropical paradise. At the end of my second month in country, Staff Sergeant Arnold told me that a unit needed a medic as soon as possible. Dave was senior in rank to me, but he was not given the option to go. He was upset, but took my assignment graciously and wished me well. I knew he was a better medic than I, and to this day I feel that the dispensary didn't want to lose him. I was expendable. I received orders assigning me to B-52, Project Delta.

☆
CHAPTER 4

October 1966

Project Delta

On 15 May 1964, a select number of Vietnamese and
Civilian Irregular Defense Group (CIDG) under the leadership of Special Forces personnel began classified long-range
patrolling within the borders of South Vietnam. This program
was referred to by the code name Leaping Lena. Reorganized
in October 1964 as Detachment B-52 Project Delta, it was
assigned the mission of conducting secret long-range reconnaissance into enemy-held sanctuaries within South Vietnam.
Project Delta recon teams incorporated two Americans and
four indigenous personnel tasked with collecting intelligence
for strategic or tactical exploitation, capturing of NVA and
VC personnel for interrogation, planning and directing air
strikes on enemy targets, performing bomb-damage assess-
ments (BDA) in enemy-controlled areas, employing wiretap
methods on enemy communications, recovering allied prisoners, assassinating specific enemy personnel, and conducting photo reconnaissance of targeted areas.

Another branch of Project Delta employed Road Runner
teams within enemy-held territory. Utilizing the equipment,
dress, and documentation of the NVA/VC within the specific
area, the Road Runner teams openly traveled the same trails

and base areas that the enemy used. Made up primarily of Vietnamese personnel, the Road Runner teams could infiltrate enemy-held areas and conduct reconnaissance and gather valuable information on the enemy. Backed by the South Vietnamese 91st Airborne Ranger Battalion as a reaction force, Project Delta was a formidable force that the enemy had to deal with. Another mission Project Delta undertook was establishing the MACV Recondo School at Nha Trang to train select allied personnel in long-range reconnaissance patrol techniques.

Project Delta's compound was about five hundred meters outside the gate of the SFOB. Bag and baggage in hand, I walked to the Delta compound, which was guarded by Chinese mercenaries called Nungs. I had heard that Project Delta had suffered numerous casualties and needed medics as soon as possible. I was nervous about going and yet had heightened anticipation of what I was getting into. Project Delta shared the compound with a Vietnamese 91st Airborne Ranger battalion, a Korean (ROK) unit, and the MACV Recondo School.

The Chinese guards claimed not to speak a word of English, and they wouldn't let me onto the compound. But one of them called someone on the landline, and an SF soldier escorted me to my new home. In the command section, I was introduced to the project's top enlisted man, Sergeant Major Garfolio, a short, older man with graying hair. He was stocky and, by his handshake, very strong. He greeted me like a long-lost friend. For the first time since arriving in Vietnam, I was made to feel welcome by my unit; I had been at the SFOB for two months and had never met the group sergeant major. I never met or even saw the group commander. At Project Delta, in just fifteen minutes I had met the sergeant major and was on my way to be introduced to the project's commander, Lieutenant Colonel Hayes, who greeted me in the same fashion as had the sergeant major. They proceeded to tell me about the project and all the good people involved. They made me feel important to their mission. Their enthusiasm set off such an adrenaline rush in me that I couldn't wait to get into action and prove my worth.

After filling them in on my background, I was taken to meet my team sergeant and some of the people I would be working with. Since the team sergeant was teaching a class, I was next taken to be assigned a place to sleep and to store my duffel bag. After stowing everything, I was given a tour of the area. The most important facility was located next to my quarters. It was called the Conrad Hilton, the guest house that was home to Project Delta's own club and restaurant. It had the cheapest drinks and food in Nha Trang. Whatever you could find in town, you could get at the Hilton, with the exception of women; soldiers had to go into town for sex.

When we returned from the tour, my team sergeant was still teaching a class to some Recondo students, so I went to watch. The students came from units serving in Vietnam—Americans, Australians, Koreans, Thais, and Filipinos. Recondo School was established 15 September 1966 by order of General Westmoreland to train allied personnel for long-range reconnaissance patrol (LRRP) units. At Recondo School, the students learned land navigation, patrolling techniques, hiding, observation and reporting methods, and insertion and extraction methods. There were also emergency medical classes that, I eventually would have the opportunity to teach. The students were taught how to pack their rucksacks most efficiently and how to assemble, disassemble, and use enemy weapons such as AK-47s, SKSs, RPDs, etc. They were also taught how to control and utilize gunship and fixed-wing aircraft support. Rappelling, ladder extraction, and the use of the McGuire rig in a helicopter were practiced extensively.

Built of nothing but muscle and bone, my team sergeant stood about six feet five inches tall. He wore his hair short and had the face of a well-conditioned athlete. He was the epitome of a well-trained professional soldier. It was very interesting, and the way he got the students' attention using humor had a big influence on how I would later teach my classes. He finished his class, and my escort introduced me to the huge man, who reached out with both hands to shake mine. The strength of his grip proved my first impression of him was right. He was M.Sgt. Ernest Stamper.

Master Sergeant Stamper welcomed me to the project and asked if I had been taken care of as far as a room was concerned. I told him that I had had the tour and was getting hungry. He said he was through for the day and he was thirsty for a beer, so we departed the training area and walked to the Hilton for liquid refreshment.

By the time Stamper and I arrived at the Hilton, several other guys were already drinking. I told Stamper I was broke, and he said he had more than enough chits to get us drunk. (Chits were tickets we bought from the club system to purchase drinks; we weren't allowed to give currency to the indigenous people working for the club system.) I followed him up to the bar, and he took out a couple of books of chits, threw them on the bar, and told the bartender to give me whatever I wanted for however long I wanted it. We both got a beer and joined our teammates, who were already enjoying themselves.

When we sat down, Stamper introduced me to the men. They were in heavy conversation, so I just sat there and kept my mouth closed. I was feeling inferior because of the wealth of knowledge that was sitting at the table. I remember being afraid that one of them would ask me a question and that whatever answer I gave would sound stupid. Luck was with me, though, and their conversation stayed on women or weapons. Eventually people started leaving. Finally, only Stamper and myself were left, and I told him that I thought I was way out of my league with those guys. But Stamper said that every one of them had to start somewhere. As time went on, I met other men who were with B-52: S.Sgt. Russell Bott, SFC Willie Stark, and Sgt. Irby Dyer III, who was the other medic on the team. The remaining men I can't recall. Staff Sergeant Bott and Sergeant First Class Stark had reputations as quiet professionals who never bragged about their abilities, where they had been, or what they had accomplished. Very silent guys, but very deadly. Dyer was the only guy with a rank as low as mine, so we developed a rapport from that day forward.

Irby Dyer was from Midland, Texas, and twenty-three years old. He was tall, lanky, and had a pleasant, easygoing demeanor. Irby was the type of person who was always first to step up and do whatever needed to be done. He never asked anyone for help with tasks that he was assigned. This is what a Special Forces soldier is supposed to do. I didn't realize how important that trait was at the time, and was probably disliked for it. I was out of my league with the real professional soldiers I was assigned to work with, and it would come to pass that my lack of professionalism would surface. I was young and dumb! Dyer left for Khe Sanh shortly after I got to Project Delta.

After I'd been in the project for a couple of days, Stamper gave me a warning order to give a medical class to the Recondo School students. He handed me a lesson plan, and I worked on giving the best class I was ever to teach. It took a couple of hours to go over my presentation and to gather the things I needed, but the next day I told Stamper I thought I was ready. He said that I could teach his class the same day but only after he listened to my pitch. So I gave it to him, and he approved my presentation and said he would be there in case I needed him. But the class went well, and from that day forward I got to teach the medical part of the curriculum.

After I'd spent only two weeks at Delta, I was to join the rest of my team, which was already pulling missions in Khe Sanh, in the northwestern corner of South Vietnam. That was hot lurping* country, and we had to watch every step carefully because we were hunting khaki-uniformed NVA regulars.

Khe Sanh

We flew out of Nha Trang on C-130s early in the morning along with some of the Vietnamese Rangers. After a couple of hours' flying, we landed in Da Nang and hit the NCO club. We had just enough time in Da Nang to down a hasty lunch and take a tour of the club. A lot of money had been spent on building the facilities; the club had indoor toilets and huge glass windows overlooking the most scenic area of Da Nang. From inside, it was difficult to tell there was a war going on.

While we were eating and scoping out the scenery, our higher element was preparing for our mission. I found out later that Project Delta had suffered several casualties at Khe Sanh, and our team was to replace them. With rucks and weapons in hand, we loaded back on the refueled C-130, taking off and flying the nap of the earth (NOE). My stomach would never be the same. Too much lunch to take aboard an aircraft bouncing up and down for a couple of hours. At so low an altitude, the air in the aircraft was hot and humid, and after only a couple of hours of fighting nausea, we were told the landing strip was in sight. The crew chief told us that the landing strip became a hot LZ whenever aircraft landed, so we had to be ready to get off the C-130 even if it was moving. The best time to get off was when the aircraft was turning around to take back off. This later became known as the "Khe Sanh shuffle." He also mentioned that there were bunkers on both sides of the airstrip and that should we come under mortar or rocket fire, to head for one of the bunkers. Then the aircraft

---

*Patrolling, from long-range reconnaissance patrol—abbreviated LRRP and pronounced "lurp."

started to gain altitude instead of landing. Puzzled, I looked out one of the small windows and could see the PSP (perforated steel plate) landing strip below. I could see another aircraft landing, and it had to use every bit of the strip to land. After the aircraft taxied around and took off, our crew chief lowered the ramp in the rear of the C-130, and we started a "tactical" descent that sent my stomach hurtling toward my head: it was like falling out of the sky with the aircraft as our parachute. My heart was pounding as we hit the landing strip with a very loud *thud*. Everything and everybody was thrown forward as the aircraft reversed thrust to slow down enough to be able to turn around. The crew chief signaled us to be ready to get off.

Everybody on board looked scared except Stamper. The Rangers were pushing toward the ramp as though they were going to jump before the aircraft turned around. I got behind the mass of people and equipment and waited for the exodus off the back of the aircraft. The aircraft came to a momentary halt as it turned around, and everybody left the aircraft. The whole process took only a minute.

The First Dance—The Khe Sanh Shuffle

It felt good to touch the ground running; I'd really felt vulnerable in the aircraft. But just as I was getting over the nausea from the jarring ride and the adrenaline rush, the ground around us started to explode. I saw Stamper heading for one of the bunkers, so I followed suit. So did about fifty other people. Fortunately, I was faster, and I hit the bunker in a dive that wouldn't have gotten high marks for style. It was my first taste of war and of having that uncomfortable feeling that I was a big target. I'd never before tried so hard to get small. I didn't look heroic, but I wasn't alone; everybody was covering themselves up as best as they could. If that bunker had received a direct hit, there would have been a lot of casualties. I wanted to look out of the bunker to see what was going on, but the shells kept coming in, and no one else was trying to see outside. I expected at any time to look up and find an NVA soldier either trying to take me prisoner or shooting me. I could hear American voices and the sound of outgoing artillery fire. The Marines were shooting back at the hidden enemy.

As soon as the incoming shelling stopped, someone shouted, "All clear." I carefully peered over one of the sandbags that were protecting me to see what was going on. It seemed like a lot of people running around without purpose. I was waiting for my training to kick in and make me do the right thing, but all I could think about was being hit by flying metal. I cannot put into words the gut feeling I had during my first encounter with the reality of war. There was nothing I could do; we were like cattle going through a slaughterhouse, confined to a small space, waiting for that big hammer to fall. What seemed like hours actually took only a couple of minutes.

☆

CHAPTER 5

Stamper got up and out of the bunker, and I followed, not sure where to go or what to do; Stamper knew right where to go and took me to my new home, a tent surrounded by sandbags, some of which were torn and leaking sand. A composed Irby Dyer was walking from one of the bunkers, and he welcomed us to Khe Sanh. I was to share the refuge with Dyer and our ARVN Ranger counterpart. After getting settled in, I took it upon myself to replace the bad sandbags with new ones. After I finished that, Dyer told me we had to construct a latrine with a cover for the officers.

Dyer and I had just finished the latrine when it started raining enemy mortars and rockets, and I ran to the nearest bunker. How anyone could endure these incident attacks and live was beyond me. I felt the odds would eventually run against me, and one of those rockets or a mortar round would hit my bunker. Then I became afraid that the officers would ask us to build them their own bunker. Fortunately they didn't. It was not a bad day otherwise; my first two experiences with enemy mortars and still no casualties.

Dyer and I decided to take a tour of the underground hospital that was manned by two SF medics. A navy doctor posted on a ship on the South China Sea gave assistance by radio or by flying in when needed. The hospital complex was on the other side of the airstrip, and on the trip to the hospital, Dyer and I had the opportunity to observe the defenses manned by the Marines, who were experiencing the worst conditions a human should have to endure. In trenches that had been turned into bunkers, the Marines had placed wooden crates on the ground because the water level was high. In addition to the mud and the water, they had to coexist with all the creatures of the land, especially rats. I talked to several Marines who said that it was not unusual to wake up with rats chewing on their feet. Also providing security at Khe Sanh was a Mike Force (montagnards advised by SF and LLDB Vietnamese Special Forces) company.

Made out of concrete, steel, and sandbags, the hospital was the best-constructed facility in the area. Inside that fortress was enough equipment to accommodate doctors and nurses. The SF medics there had the facilities for minor and major surgery, but more serious procedures would be performed with the aid of the doctor on the ship. Of course, that would happen only if the wounded couldn't be evacuated.

When Dyer and I returned to our hootch, Stamper was waiting for us. He told me I would have to accompany Master Sergeant (E-8) Campbell and the Vietnamese Rangers on a search-and-destroy mission. Master Sergeant Campbell was a big man with a square jaw that gave him the appearance of John Wayne. He was a veteran of Korea and had been in Vietnam a long time. He was a no-nonsense guy who hated unprofessionalism; he would come to dislike me very soon. Early the next morning, under the cover of fog and light rain, we walked away from the security of our Marines to look for signs of NVA activity or buildup. Several Road Runner teams were out, and they all reported large movements of NVA troops in our general area. Our mission was to engage and kill as many of the enemy as we could.

The Field of Reams

It was my first exposure to the field and the most memorable. It was also the beginning of my downfall in SF. Due to my inexperience, I didn't pack enough food for the extended patrol, and that created more problems than I could have imagined at the time. After moving through the hills covered with vines and triple-canopy forest all day, we finally stopped for the night. I set up my hammock, ate my last can of food, and watched as the Vietnamese Rangers built fires to cook their food. Too tired to sleep, I watched and wondered how we could ever surprise anyone with the amount of noise and light we were giving off. Seeing that light discipline was very lax, I decided to read myself to sleep, and I took out a penlight. I had just started to read when, looking like he wanted to kill someone, Campbell walked over. He ordered me to put out the light or *someone* would get killed.

That was the first major strike in my demise with Project Delta. I was such a cherry at the time, and way over my head. Master Sergeant Campbell was so obviously pissed that I wasn't about to tell him I was already out of food. I made a concerted effort to stay out of his way and wandered over to where the Vietnamese Rangers had a small bonfire going and were cooking something in a pot hanging over the fire. My intentions were to try out my limited Vietnamese vocabulary. About ten Vietnamese Rangers were huddled around the fire, poking it with long sticks, making sparks fly into the darkness like tiny fireflies. As I watched them, I thought about Campbell's anger over my little penlight. I prayed he wouldn't show up; he'd probably blame me for the sparks going into the air. Later in my years in Vietnam, I learned to appreciate what Campbell was teaching me. At that moment, though, I thought everybody hated me and was picking on me.

The Vietnamese Rangers greeted me with grins on their hardened faces. I didn't know if the grins were from the way I spoke Vietnamese or about the food I was ready to ingest. The Vietnamese who was doing the cooking handed me a bowl while the rest watched in anticipation of my reaction to what they had given me. I was hungry and didn't want to insult anyone. I ate everything on my plate, including the fish heads with huge slimy eyes. After I'd taken a couple of big bites, the Vietnamese started to eat, shoveling rice into their mouths as if they were worried there wouldn't be any food left tomorrow. From that day, whenever I saw one of those Rangers, he would greet me with a smile and a handshake. I might have made an enemy with my American counterpart, but I crossed a valuable threshold in relationships with the Vietnamese. That would pay dividends for me in the years to come.

We must have walked a hundred miles in our two weeks in the bush, and we never made contact. There were trails, and signs that a large force recently had been through the area, but the enemy chose to stay out of our way. The light and noise we made probably had a lot to do with our not finding an enemy to fight. Finally, command decided that we were accomplishing nothing by staying in the field, and we walked back into base camp.

I knew that Campbell had told Stamper about my using the penlight and that I'd been mooching food off the Rangers, but Stamper never said anything to me. Even so, I was feeling alienated.

From Bad to Worse

Because of the poor diet, I soon developed diarrhea and severe stomach cramps. I usually couldn't eat, and even when I did, it came back up or out the other end. Then a succession of powerful stomach cramps would follow.

At the same time, the weather decided it was monsoon season, and the rain fell in bucketfuls. At one point, the wind was so strong that it blew the top off the officers' latrine. Of course, it was the medics' job to fix it. Dyer knew how sick I felt and never asked for any help, but Campbell came into my tent and told me to get up off my lazy ass and help Dyer, so I did. The winds were really howling, and it took several tries to get the top back on and secured so that it would not fly off again. At that time, I was at my lowest point, feeling sorry for myself. Everybody thought I was a hazard in the field and lazy in the rear. Nothing seemed to be going right. Except for my Ranger counterpart, Dyer was the only person who sympathized with me and knew how I felt.

I returned to my dry bunk thinking I was going to die. My Ranger counterpart gave me some opium-based medication that made me feel good and offered a brief relief from the pain of the cramps. I still couldn't keep anything down, though.

I know now that because I was a Special Forces soldier I should have ignored my illness and continued with the mission, but I was immature and couldn't fully conceptualize the reality of war; I failed miserably even though I knew I was hanging out with a bunch of high-speed bad boys who were older and years more mature than I was. That was one of the low points in my career in the army.

It was taking time, but with the opium and the soup my Ranger buddy was giving me, I slowly recovered. That guy was wise beyond his years. As I think back, I'm embarrassed that I didn't have greater mental and physical fortitude. Finally, feeling physically better but still thinking of myself as pretty worthless, I tried to thank the old Ranger by giving him my only possession of worth, my watch. He smiled and politely refused. I couldn't help but feel a closeness and kinship to that man who selflessly helped a foreigner and did it with kindness and understanding. I was beginning to feel a warmth for the people whose country I thought I was defending.

Strike Two

The next day, Stamper came to my tent and wanted to know if I was well enough to go out with the Rangers again. He told me to be sure I had enough food to last a couple of weeks. He didn't say what we would be doing, but I wasn't going to make the same mistake twice; I carried enough food and supplies to last me a month. My ruck must have weighed a ton.

We left the perimeter under the cover of fog and light showers. I made an effort to be sure I was quiet in movement and always at the ready. I never touched my penlight unless it was to look down someone's throat. When we stopped for the night, I either kept to myself or wandered over to the Rangers' fire to listen to their stories and learn about the years that they had endured war. I couldn't understand everything they were saying, but I picked up enough to keep interested. Those fireside nights helped me learn the language and learn to love the people.

For three weeks, we walked up and down hills and crossed large and deep streams. But we never made contact. In my heart, I knew that the Rangers were making noise so the enemy could hear us coming. Finally, we headed back to our base camp, only to be greeted by NVA mortars and rockets slamming into our perimeter. I quickly concluded that it was safer in the field, and from that period on, I stayed in the field as much as possible.

During that engagement when sappers tried to get into the perimeter, Campbell asked me if I knew how to fire the M-79 grenade launcher, and I unwittingly said yes. I was familiar with the weapon but had never fired one. During the heat of battle, he told me to put a round about two hundred meters in the direction of the incoming fire. I locked and loaded and fired the round, but on a flat trajectory. Horror of horrors, it landed in the middle of our Vietnamese Ranger battalion. In disgust,

Campbell grabbed the weapon from me and called me a few well-deserved choice words. Fortunately, no one was hurt.

After the all-clear was given, I crawled out of my bunker and found a small Vietnamese boy on the ground behind our bunker. He had taken some shrapnel in his legs and back. I gathered him up and took him to our underground hospital and watched as the Special Forces medic removed the metal from the boy's riddled body. The boy was conscious, but not making a sound. After the medic finished working on the boy's wounds, I took him back to the area he was staying in. I then returned to my tent to resupply my ruck and aid bag in case I had to go out again. While I was repacking, Campbell came into our tent and told me that the next time a civilian was wounded the Vietnamese were to handle it. I had threatened the security of the hospital by taking that child there. Another strike. The night came fast and sleep did, too.

Team Viper, "We're Hit Bad!"

The next evening, Wednesday, 29 November 1966, I watched as Sgt. Russ Bott and Sgt. Willie Stark and four Vietnamese loaded onto a waiting UH-1H helicopter. Their call sign was Team Viper, and their AO (area of operation) was tucked up close to Laos and North Vietnam. Everybody was camouflaged and dressed to kill.

The weather was "dogshit," with rain showers, gusting winds, and a very low cloud ceiling. When the team left to be inserted, the flying weather was marginal, and I thought the mission should have been aborted, but knowing how many people respected my opinion, I wasn't going to say a thing. I learned later that as the insertion helicopter got closer to the operational area, the higher elevation put the team right into the cloud ceiling. That forced the helicopter to weave around the mountains as the pilot tried to maintain a course to the designated LZ in the growing darkness. The pilots could have aborted the mission, but they were under intense command pressure to insert the team. From so low an altitude, the pilots made a very critical navigational error, mistaking a swollen stream for a river checkpoint. When the helicopter pilots returned to base, the consensus was that they had missed the LZ and had inserted the team somewhere in Laos. At Khe Sanh, the winds howled that night as sheets of rain blasted my tent.

Command was in the shit because of the potentially embarrassing political fallout of having had a United States Army helicopter land operating ground forces outside the borders of South Vietnam. An honest mistake made in the midst of high-risk combat operations was being aggravated by distorted politics.

The next morning, Thursday, an army radio-relay plane from Da Nang arrived on station and reported that the entire operational area was socked in. Team Viper made contact with the relay and wanted to know its exact position. They had realized they were in the wrong area and wanted a forward air controller (FAC) to pinpoint the team's location. During the early morning, the team reported a brief contact and firefight with the enemy, but broke the contact and reported that it was moving east and north.

By midmorning at Khe Sanh, the winds had died down to about twenty knots. I could see about two hundred yards, and the clouds were at two hundred feet. A FAC plane, piloted by John Flanagan and carrying a Delta recon sergeant in the backseat, left at midday to try to locate Team Viper. After some exceptional flying by the FAC, the team was pinpointed in Laos but close to the DMZ (demilitarized zone)—and in the center of a suspected North Vietnamese regiment. On arriving back at Khe Sanh, the pilot pointed out on the operations map that Team Viper was four or five klicks northwest of where we'd thought they were. Flanagan also informed command that he had sighted numerous armed NVA around Team Viper.

But the team's mistaken position on the operations map was not changed to reflect the FAC's information. The winds that night were so strong that I had to go out and secure the tent to keep it from blowing away.

Friday dawned to horrendous weather. A thirty-knot wind was blowing clouds across the Khe Sanh plateau. It was raining intermittently, but the rain was coming in horizontally due to the wind. It was extremely bad weather, and my thoughts were with Team Viper and another recon team led by Staff Sergeant St. Laurent that was also out in the storm. The radio-relay plane from Da Nang had picked up a garbled radio transmission from Team Viper and understood they had again made contact with the enemy and, in the ensuing firefight, several members of the team had been wounded. Just prior to my learning of Team Viper's new problem, one of the Vietnamese Rangers had come over to me and asked if I would remove a cyst from his leg. I removed the cyst, and while I was suturing him up, Master Sergeant Stamper came into the tent and told me to get my aid bag and be ready to go at a moment's notice. At that same moment, Sgt. Irby Dyer walked into the tent and Stamper told him he would have to go, not me. That hurt.

The commander had decided to launch a rescue extraction. Involved were a pickup ship, a spare pickup, a command-and-control (C & C) helicopter, and two gunships. Stamper went back to the TOC to monitor the radios, and Dyer went to the helicopter pad. He was to be the belly man on the extraction helicopter. More important, he would be able to help with the wounded. I quickly finished up with the Ranger, then hurried over to listen with Stamper to the radio transmissions between the rescue ships and Russ Bott. We could hear only the C & C's portion of the radio transmission as it repeated what was being transmitted by Team Viper. The team was asking if the choppers had launched and reported that one American (Willie Stark) was badly wounded and that the team was unable to move. A short time later, we heard another one-sided conversation. Team Viper was receiving sporadic fire. By then, they had one seriously wounded and two others with lesser wounds. That news was fueling our anxieties. Adding to Team Viper's problems was the fact that the rescue ship couldn't locate the team. Occasionally, the team could hear the sound of the choppers, but they couldn't figure out which of the five helicopters they were hearing. Finally, a radio transmission was relayed back to Khe Sanh asking if the FAC (John Flanagan) could fly out in his aircraft and pinpoint the team.

Some incredibly brave flying was done that day by Flanagan. With Delta recon sergeant Tommy Tucker outfitted in ass-kicking gear in the backseat, they took off into a vicious shearing wind. The winds at Khe Sanh were gusting to fifty knots. When Flanagan arrived in the operational area, the helicopters had only twenty minutes of fuel left. Talking to Team Viper, Flanagan recognized Russ Bott's voice immediately, and he heard the background chatter of automatic weapons and grenades exploding as a vicious firefight was in progress. Bott told Flanagan that Stark was hit bad, that the Americans had become separated from the three Vietnamese on the team and were completely surrounded. Flanagan told Bott to key the handset on his radio so that the FAC could home in on the signal. Guided by the signal, Flanagan overflew Team Viper's position, and Russ Bott gave him the code word "payoff." Flanagan then told Bott to pop smoke so that he could direct the rescue ship in. Purple smoke was observed and confirmed, and Flanagan saw that the team was located in elephant grass on the crest of a small knoll. When Flanagan overflew the team's position, he drew no ground fire, so he cleared the pickup helicopter in. When the rescue helicopter came to a hover ten feet above the team, the whole world exploded. The elephant grass parted, and from dozens of camouflaged spider holes and gun emplacements, vicious automatic weapons fire was brought to bear on the helicopter. It had been a trap, and Team Viper had been the bait.

The FAC launched a marking rocket so the gunships could pour fire into the enemy positions to protect the pickup helicopter. But the pickup helicopter rose, banked to the left into the air for about two hundred feet, then continued banking to the left, finally rolling over and plunging straight down, augering nose first into the ground. It burst into a ball of flame as it rolled down the small knoll, killing the two pilots, the two door gunners, and Sgt. Irby Dyer in the process. On the second pass, the lead gunship had its fire control system shot out. That was a bad day for our Project Delta.

Back at Khe Sanh, we were catching bits and pieces of the horrible drama as it unfolded. We heard the commander order Team Viper to break up and escape and evade. Then the helicopters transmitted that they were at critical fuel levels and returning to base. The team was being abandoned, and not by choice. It was a gut-wrenching moment, and I could see the gears churning in Master Sergeant Stamper's head. He looked at me and voiced something like, "We've got to help them." I knew then I was soon going to be part of it.

Meanwhile, above Team Viper's position, Flanagan was witness to a heartbreaking moment. The last radio transmission from Russ Bott was, "FAC, please help us; we're hit bad." It was from a brave soldier who wouldn't abandon his best friend even though he had been told to do so. Alone, armed only with marking rockets and smoke grenades, Flanagan tried what he already knew was futile, but try he did. He expended his marking rockets on the active gun emplacements and then flew a wide turnaround, flying back over the team's position. All he saw was trampled grass. He found no sign of the team. When he flew over the downed helicopter, all that he saw was a wisp of smoke rising from the charred hulk of the helicopter wreckage. There was no movement and no sign of life. Flanagan flew back to Khe Sanh. I witnessed the hair-raising landing he performed in a vicious fifty-knot cross-wind. So many brave men.

Political Fix

That evening and into the night, radio traffic between commands in Nha Trang and Saigon was intense. Because the helicopter was downed outside South Vietnam, political football was being played all the way to Washington. Denial was a priority, and Bott and Stark were being written off. Cover-up coordinates had already been submitted for the downed helicopter. The FAC pilot, Flanagan, was instructed by the project commander that under no circumstances was he to search for Team Viper along preplanned E & E routes, which would take them farther into Laos. He was to stay within the team's assigned area of responsibility. Those orders came directly from Saigon. Flanagan countered that although he was op-con (operationally controlled) to Delta, he was an air force pilot, and his rules of engagement did allow him to overfly Laos. The commander hastily brought in another officer to bear witness that Flanagan had stated that he had authority to fly into Laos. The commander further stated that if Flanagan was brought down in Laos, Project Delta had no responsibility to assist in his recovery. Flanagan had been set up, and the commander's action was pure chickenshit.

A politically motivated recovery plan had been formulated. A "sterile-deniable" Hatchet Team would be inserted to search for survivors or recover bodies from the downed helicopter. Master Sergeant Stamper would lead the team, and I would go with him. Two Vietnamese Rangers would accompany us for added firepower. Because of improving weather in the AO, we would rappel onto the crash site in coordination with planned air strikes around the surrounding areas.

Fear was knotting my stomach, and I thought that my turn to die had arrived. I had no idea what to do; I had been trained to treat wounded, but no one had taught me how to control my emotions or feelings. I thought I was a coward. As that thought of being a coward crossed my mind, I decided to show everyone that I wasn't.

I went to my tent and grabbed my weapon and aid bag. Stamper was waiting for me at the helicopter pad. He had already prepared the ropes for rappelling. We loaded into the helicopter and took off on what I thought would be my last day alive. The weather was clearing so at least we could see below us. We were going to rappel into a hot area, and every NVA and VC in the place would have a chance to take a shot at us.

As I moved onto the helicopter skid, preparing to rappel down, I saw the bottom of the downed helicopter. Burnt debris was scattered everywhere. Stamper and one of the Vietnamese Rangers were on the starboard skid; the other Ranger and I were on the port skid. I was scared to death. It was the longest fifty feet I would ever rappel. I must have made it down in record time because my gloves were smoking when I hit the ground! I had beaten everybody down. Meanwhile, adding to the excitement of the moment, jet aircraft were making bombing runs all around us. Every time a bomb exploded, I thought we were receiving incoming; then the ground shook.

I watched as Stamper got off his rope, made sure everyone was ready to move out, then, with the instincts of a cat on the hunt, moved toward the downed aircraft. I learned a lot from watching him move. His weapon at the ready, he was moving slowly but with purpose, his eyes constantly moving over the terrain to his front and flanks. Nothing escaped his vision. For the rest of my six years in Vietnam, I would mimic the way Stamper had prowled that day.

As we closed in on the downed helicopter, I could smell death. That salty, coppery smell of dried blood and decaying flesh was another thing I would never forget. When we got close to the wreckage, Stamper held me back, pointing to a trip wire that was connected to one of the three bodies lined up in a perfect row in front of the helicopter. Demolition wasn't my forte, so Stamper had to clear the area of booby traps. If I had touched one of those bodies, I wouldn't be writing about that mission. This was my first experience with the sight and smell of death in combat. The bodies had been so mutilated by the enemy that I couldn't distinguish which of the hunks of meat laid out in front of the helicopter was Dyer. The pilot and copilot were already stiff and difficult to get out of the wreckage, so we decided to concentrate on getting the more accessible bodies out of there.

Stamper called in a Marine CH-46 with a hoist cable and basket to retrieve the bodies, but just as the helicopter could be seen and heard, we started receiving heavy incoming fire, and it had to leave, taking with it my hopes of surviving the mission. We were forced to leave the wreckage site to save our own skins, and we had to leave all of the bodies. With the aid of gunships and Stamper's survival skills, we fought our way out and made an escape and evasion (E & E) to a more favorable extraction site. A McGuire rig (a rope that looked like a huge rope swing, which enabled small units to be lifted out of areas where helicopters couldn't land) was dropped on us, and Stamper, myself, and the other two Rangers were being lifted out. We were up in the air about fifteen feet when the Ranger closest to Stamper was suddenly hit several times through the back, killing him instantly and knocking him out of the rig. The loss of the Ranger caused the McGuire rig to twist, and we had to compensate by doing a spread eagle, our arms and legs spread out. I feared I would be the next person to take an enemy round in the ass or the back, but Stamper was in control the whole time, telling me what to do. He even had a grin on his face; at least, I thought it was a grin. The three of us continued our ascent as rounds cracked all around us. While I clung to the rope, all I could think about was one of us getting hit or the helicopter being shot out of the sky. Base camp never looked so good. As soon as we touched down, Stamper ran to the radio to find out what might be going on with Bott and Stark.

Because of the bad weather, it was several days before a SOG Hatchet Team (the Studies and Observation Group subordinate to MACV, in Saigon, conducted secret long-range recon missions in Laos, Cambodia, and North Vietnam), Campbell, and half the Vietnamese Ranger battalion would be inserted. The SOG team, Campbell, and the Rangers recovered the bodies of the helicopter crew and the Special Forces dead, and found our dead Ranger on the way out. But the Americans on Team Viper were never seen or heard from again. Two days after that tragic loss, two of the indigenous personnel who had been with Team Viper and had managed to escape and evade the NVA walked into base camp with only minor scratches. They explained during their debriefing that Bott told them to leave and make it out any way they could. Bott and Stark are still listed as MIAs, and their names are carried on the Vietnam Veterans Memorial.

As I think back on the lives wasted for that tragic mission and how it was politically more important to cover it up rather than make amends for it, I grow angry. The team should never have been inserted. Given the poor weather forecast for that area, command should have realized that the timeliness of any intelligence gathered by Team Viper would have been nullified because the weather would have prevented anyone's acting on it while it was still usable. Common sense should have guided the commander's decision, but it didn't. Consequently, the team went from being an asset to being a very dangerous liability. Later, I listened as some of the officers and the enlisted men talked about how great Bott and Stark were. But nothing was said about Irby Dyer or the helicopter crew who had given their lives to try to save Bott and Stark. I might have come in too late to hear the whole story, but I had a bad feeling in the pit of my stomach about it all. I held my own memorial service to remember them for the heroes they were. I promised myself never to forget them, and through this book, their heroic effort will be remembered. I matured a lot during that mission, feeling a great loss of innocence and more vulnerability than I had ever felt in my life.

My First Hit

It hadn't been a week since the Team Viper debacle, and another team was in trouble. Stamper and I went out with a re-action force made up of half of the Vietnamese Ranger battalion. We were inserted into an area close to the Laotian border, northwest of Khe Sanh. A Mike Force element was also working in the area, and it had reported large numbers of enemy troops heading toward the team that had been compromised. We were cautiously moving toward the team's location, but night came upon us, and it became too dangerous to continue. At first light, we linked with the team and prepared to be extracted. As I heard the helicopters approaching, I had a feeling that something bad was going to happen. It was like a flashback: I kept seeing the Ranger falling from the McGuire rig and flash pictures of the dead at the helicopter crash site. The helicopters were on final approach to the landing zone (LZ) when the Rangers initiated an ambush on enemy troops that were closing in on the LZ, and ordnance was flying every which way. I felt helpless, and everything seemed to go into slow motion. I didn't like it; I wanted to move fast and get the hell out of there.

As we left the shelter of the tree line, moving toward our waiting helicopter, a B-40 rocket hit a tree I was passing and exploded. A piece of shrapnel took my legs out from under me. I didn't feel any pain, but my pants were wet from the blood I was losing. I got up as fast as I went down, but my left leg was numb. Adrenaline fueling my movement, I managed to move as though I wasn't wounded because I wasn't about to be left behind. Stamper was already on the helicopter and was yelling something at the pilot; then he turned toward me, making hand signals to hurry up. But the helicopter was taking a lot of enemy fire, and the pilot wouldn't wait. I had to jump with my good leg to reach the skid of the chopper. Stamper reached down and pulled me the rest of the way into the helicopter with hands that gripped like vises. Once inside the chopper, I put a bandage on my bleeding leg while trying to hide my fear from Stamper's view. As we approached our base camp, I saw that a C-130 had just landed and people were getting on board. We landed, and a jeep was waiting as we came down. The jeep took me to the waiting C-130, and that was the last I saw of Khe Sanh. I was being medevacked to the 6th Convalescent Hospital in Cam Ranh Bay.

It took several hours to reach Cam Ranh Bay. The pilot had radioed ahead, and an ambulance was waiting when we landed. The dose of morphine I had given myself was wearing off by then, and my leg was in great pain. The medics hurried on board the aircraft and carried me off, their every move causing pain to shoot through my leg.

My stay at Cam Ranh Bay was like an in-country rest and recuperation (R & R). After surgery and several weeks of healing, I was allowed to stretch out on the beach all day. By then, two months had passed since my arrival in Vietnam, and my thoughts turned to what I had left at home. I remembered what I had thought, then, were rough times, with my girlfriend leaving me and the poor grades in college. How trivial that all seemed compared to what I was involved in now. I recalled my friends and I complaining (whining) about our way of life and how hard we thought we had it. Now I had a better under-standing of some rights and privileges that Americans have and take for granted. I was grateful to be an American.

While at Cam Ranh Bay, we had movies at night and all the beer we could steal. I wasn't being paid, and was told that I would have to wait until I returned to my unit. But money really wasn't necessary because the hospital provided everything we needed. Once it was determined that my leg had healed, it was time to return to reality and to the war. My flight out of Cam Ranh Bay was scheduled for early the next morning, but not before one more good night of celebration. Turned out I departed just in time: after I left, a squad of sappers (Viet Cong soldiers who handled demolitions and specialized in blowing up ammo dumps and anything else they could to destroy morale and people) hit the 6th CC Hospital in Cam Ranh Bay, killing a couple of recovering Americans. The security was so bad, the whole squad got away without a shot being fired at them. And no weapons had been pre-positioned so that the people at Cam Ranh hospital could defend themselves. Whoever was in charge of security there should have been shot.

☆
CHAPTER 6

April 1967

Fired

It was a welcome trip to get back to Nha Trang. I had been gone too long and had gotten lazy, but I was as tan as I'd ever been. I was looking forward to smoking a big joint and eating as much lobster as I could before I would have to return to the field. I was also looking forward to getting paid, and knew I would have a lot of money because I hadn't received a cent in four months. When I got to the Delta compound and my team room, everybody was away; they, too, had returned to Nha Trang but were off doing some other training. I put away my bags and went into town for a seafood feast.

I consumed more lobster and beer than I should have, and decided to take a walk to burn off my full belly. As I was passing one of the many homes on the way into town, I noticed a couple of officers and enlisted men from the project standing in the street drinking beer and having a good time. I walked over to them and said hello, but they all turned their backs on me and walked inside the building. I didn't know what I had done to make them act that way, so I went to find Stamper to learn what was going on.

I went to the Hilton, but it was closed. I couldn't find Stamper, so I went to the Playboy Club, where I ran into Dave.

He told me that Sergeant Major Dunaway had closed down the Hilton Club and had relieved Sergeant Major Garfolio. Dave said that the sergeant major and several other NCOs had been drinking a lot and had gotten one of the waitresses to take off her clothes. On a bet, one of the NCOs put the willing waitress on the bar and had dinner. Just as he was finishing, Dunaway walked in. He ordered everybody out, fired the waitress, and closed the club. That is what I heard. I don't know if it's all true.

The next day, B-52 had a new sergeant major. As my bad luck would have it, the new man in charge was Sergeant Major Johanson, who had been my dog lab NCOIC. I didn't know of anyone who liked him. He was arrogant and treated every student as if he were worthless. Now he was my sergeant major. But I couldn't find out why the Delta people were angry with me. I went back to my bunk and crashed. Something was up, and I wasn't happy about it, but there was nothing I could do about it just then.

The next morning, I went to finance to collect my pay. The pay clerk handed me about half of what I calculated I should have received. When I asked what was going on, the clerk said that Mess Association dues had been taken out of my pay. Since I'd been in Khe Sanh and then the hospital, I saw no reason why I had to pay, so I went to see the new sergeant major to complain. Because he had just taken over, he wouldn't see me, but he left a message that I was to see Childers at the Mess Association.

I had a bad feeling about talking to Childers because of our last meeting and because everyone had told me how difficult Childers could be. I walked into the Mess Association building and told the person at the desk I was to report to Childers.

Before I could turn around, Childers was standing behind me in a threatening way. "What the fuck is your problem?" he said. I then told him I didn't think I should pay for something I didn't use. He said that as long as I was assigned to 5th Group I would pay, no matter where I was. "Everybody pays," he said. Ignoring his look of disgust, I took a step back to avoid his bad breath. Then I walked out of there as fast as I could. Before I reached the B-52 compound, I met Stamper, who told me to report to Sergeant Major Dunaway. An immediate feeling of desperation overcame me. I asked Stamper what was going on, and he told me he didn't know.

I went to Sergeant Major Dunaway's office, waiting for whatever was going to happen. Carrying a swagger stick under his arm as he always did, Sergeant Major Dunaway came out of his office and asked if I was Cornett. When I said yes, he put his swagger stick on my shoulder and said, "You're out of here." He then handed me orders assigning me to 1st Brigade, 101st Airborne Division.

With my tail between my legs, I went back to my room to gather what little I had. I didn't even have to out-process; my records were already being sent to my new unit. Dave had heard about what had happened, and he came to my room to see if I needed any help. He said he had been told to take me to the airport because a flight to Phan Rang was leaving in about thirty minutes. It was a great feeling to be loved.

I loaded my few belongings in the jeep. We got to the airport in record time, and waiting there was Master Sergeant Campbell. I couldn't believe my eyes. I thought now it was his turn to make me feel like shit. Campbell came over to me, put his arm on my shoulder, and told me to report to my new unit, keep my mouth shut and my eyes open, and learn how to survive. After six months, if I wanted to return to the project, he would help me. I couldn't believe what I was hearing. Campbell, helping me? I got on my aircraft and began a new journey. I would miss Nha Trang and the great food, but I would be back.

Looking back on this thirty years later, I realize that I was considered to be dangerous and could have caused people to die because I didn't know what I was doing. The men of B-52 were old professionals who knew each other and what to expect from each other. I, on the other hand, was young, unpredictable, and ignorant in the practical matters of war. Although it was a tremendous loss of face for me at the time, they did me a great favor. As time went on, I would learn. I became not only one of the best but one of the few who would stay in Vietnam to fight. I would not sit in the rear.

CHAPTER 7

April 1967

1st Bde, 101st Airborne Division

The flight didn't take but fifteen minutes. Once inside the terminal, I found the representative of the 101st, who made arrangements for me and about sixty other people to go to the replacement station. It seems I wasn't the only person to be sent from 5th Group to the 101st. I think the 5th Group cadre were hoping we would all get killed. On the other hand, the 101st had been taking a lot of casualties, and replacements were needed. Having been fired, belittled, and not ever having served with a conventional unit, I was having a bad time. I didn't know what to expect, except death. I remember even thinking that Dunaway might have called one of his buddies and told him to put me where I would most likely get wasted. I thought somebody didn't like me and must have told Dunaway I was expendable. To this day, I think it was Childers, because of the way I talked to him.

Again I had to process in, but I didn't have my records. The clerk who was taking care of me had originally been assigned to the 5th SF Group but had had a run-in with Childers. Small world. He made out a temporary record for me and sent a tracer out for the originals. Since the replacement company was looking for a medic, that was where I was assigned.

A clerk from the replacement company picked me up at the processing station and took me to my new unit. The first sergeant was Sergeant First Class (E-7) Jackson. He was a big black man who looked fat and out of shape, but later I was to witness his strength and agility in handling troops who came out of the field thinking they were badasses. He welcomed me and told me that I had my own dispensary and that support was supplied by the hospital at Cam Ranh Bay. There were doctors assigned to the 101st, but I never met one.

I was also to provide medical classes for people new in country. The course was part of the brigade's "P" (proficiency) training, which every soldier new to Vietnam and the brigade had to undergo. It gave the new soldier time to acclimatize and to adjust to the malaria tablets they had to take every day. In the past, new soldiers had been sent directly into the field, only to end up being medevacked because of heat injuries. Someone smart decided soldiers couldn't just sit around for two weeks, so a program was set up that would not only fill the downtime but save a lot of lives. Classes were taught on patrolling, ambush, booby traps, enemy weapons, and medical subjects. Also, the trooper was given instruction on how the brigade operated and "lessons learned" while the brigade had been in country. The soldier was issued his weapon (M-16) and would "zero" (shoot his weapon at a fixed target, adjusting his sites to end up with a tight three-shot group on the target) the weapon before he went to the "forward area." All of the classes were taught by NCOs who had already served a tour with a line company. Even the training wasn't without danger. Those kids carried loaded weapons with them everywhere they went. On one occasion, a soldier jumped off the back of a truck with a loaded weapon, hit the ground, and dropped his weapon, which discharged, killing the man behind him. Everybody on the truck panicked, and none of the cherries knew what to do. The soldier who had accidentally fired the weapon was in tears and wanted to kill

himself. He was immediately escorted away and taken to
headquarters. I found out later he was sent back to the States.
He wasn't the only person to get in trouble. The NCO in
charge was fired because he had failed to ensure that all the
weapons had been unloaded and were on safe. When I arrived
on the scene, about one minute after the incident occurred, the
wounded soldier was already dead. I put the body in a body
bag and took him to Graves Registration, where all of our
dead were prepared for return to the USA.

Along with the training duties, it was my privilege, as the
medic, to burn shit. That was the start of my day, the ceremonial dousing with fuel and the lighting of the honey bucket!
After my chores were done, I held a sick call. Usually the only
people to show up for sick call were those waiting for orders
who didn't have to attend P classes; soldiers not in class had to
take part in work details, like filling sandbags or policing
(cleaning) the perimeter, unless they were sick. Of course,
sometimes I had a person with a real reason to show up on sick
call, like VD. After sick call, the first sergeant held a formation
to count heads, pass out orders for R & R or for return to the
Land of the Big PX, etc.

After a week of conducting P training, I was becoming
bored with the routine and decided to accompany one of the
"cadre" (an instructor) looking for a training site for stream-
crossing class. We found one near the town of Phan Rang, on
the edge of a place called "the strip."

The Strip and Moon

The strip was a group of several makeshift buildings made
out of tin—bars, whorehouses, tailors, cleaners, and souvenir
shops for the American troops. After finding a suitable spot
for stream crossings, we tested it out by crossing the stream
for a couple of cold beers and the companionship of the
women who lived there. It soon became routine that after

every stream-crossing class, the cadre would stop for a beer or two. For local entertainment, the only alternative to the strip was the Red Cross Center, where we could play cards, watch a movie, or stare at the only round-eyed girls we could hope to see up close. Every unit had a club for its troops when they came back from the field. We REMFs (rear echelon mother-fucker) were allowed to go to them, but were never welcome, so I spent what free time I had at the strip. It was required that a soldier have a pass to go to the strip, but that never stopped me.

Occasionally, I would get caught and receive an Article 15. At the time, an Article 15 was a slap on the wrist that meant you gave up some money or rank to pay for some infraction that wasn't worth a court-martial. Only after the war did Article 15s become a problem when seeking promotion, a stripe or two. I wouldn't realize that until much later.

After several trips to the strip, I developed a friendship with one of the local girls, a young woman named Moon, and in my opinion the best-looking girl in town. Not to mention that she knew how to please me. Moon was always happy and wanted to help her family, and we took advantage of each other and the situation. Moon eventually asked me to be her partner in the bar, and I agreed, buying a stereo with huge speakers and supplying her with liquor and cigarettes. Her whole family lived with her, so in a way I was helping all of them.

As a medic, I knew firsthand that VD was one of the biggest problems with our soldiers, so I also provided treatment for *all* the girls on the strip, and after my arrival cases of VD from the strip grew extremely rare. I felt I was doing a service not only for the soldiers but for the army, the girls, and the community. I had medical cards made up for the girls showing the last time they had been checked and/or treated, and all the Vietnamese started to call me *bac si* (doctor). It goes without saying that very soon I could go into any bar on the strip and didn't have to pay for anything. Whatever I needed, whether hiding from the military police or having someone thrown out of a bar, all I had to do was ask. I was beginning to speak the language better, and the Vietnamese liked me for that even more. It was embarrassing to me that I frequently heard soldiers say to the Vietnamese, "You're so stupid, you can't even speak English." This in a culture that was two thousand years old before Christopher Columbus learned to pee outdoors.

Every time I went to town, Moon would try to give me money from my share of the profits, but I told her to put it back into the bar. Now when I think about it, I wish I had taken the cash, because I would have been rich. Even so, Moon's bar became the best place on the strip: she had the best-looking girls, the best food, and a wide variety of liquor. Most of the other bars served only beer and Vietnamese liquor. It wasn't long before Moon started having live entertainment.

Bull's-Eye

Even with the attractions of the strip, I wasn't happy being a REMF, and I was about to volunteer to go to a line (combat infantry company) unit when I met Rey Martinez, who was standing at the back of my medical class, watching my presentation.

My class on battlefield medicine was different because I tried to make it interesting enough that the soldiers *couldn't* fall asleep even in the hot, stuffy tent. After all, my class might save their lives. My standard procedure was to make all the second lieutenants (men who might lead an infantry platoon into combat) sit in the front row so they could see everything very clearly. I would then go through all of the material that was boring and mundane—water discipline, malaria, immersion foot, etc.—all the while trying to inject humor into the subject to keep the students interested. Then I showed them the technique of a simple tracheotomy, how to stop bleeding, and how to protect a wound. Then we progressed to other subjects such as heat injuries and VD. But I saved the best for last. Every soldier was issued a can of blood-volume expander called serum albumin. Everyone had to know how to administer it; medics were not always around to help people who'd lost a lot of blood, so infantry soldiers might have to administer the serum albumin at some time. Because of the thick consistency of the albumin, a large needle was necessary to administer it. When people are wounded, bleeding is usually profuse, so it was important that those soldiers know how to find a vein and insert the needle to intravenously administer the blood expander.

As that part of the show opened, I would roll up my shirtsleeve, ready my left arm by tying it off above the elbow with a piece of surgical tubing, and, using my teeth for assistance, I would then produce an extremely large syringe with the biggest needle I could find. I would insert the needle, untie the tubing, and draw blood. I would lecture the students about the difference in color between arterial and venous blood. I would explain how people, when seeing blood—copious amounts of blood and the ravages that the human body undergoes when traumatized by metal—go into shock. After filling the syringe, I would pull out the needle, with blood still coming out of my site of insertion. Then, looking at the officers in front of me, I told them it was now their turn. Then I would swiftly throw the syringe and needle at a dartboard hanging on the wall. Naturally, upon hitting the board, the blood-filled syringe would explode, spraying blood all over the place. I then told them that would not be the last time they would see blood. Three or four people fainted *every* time I did that class.

I finished my class one day and wandered over to a soldier wearing a camouflaged, tiger-stripe bush hat. He introduced himself as Rey Martinez, a member of the 1st Brigade's long-range reconnaissance patrol detachment, called Lurps for short. I asked him what they did. He said that the platoon worked in six-man teams, outside the normal range of friendly forces, doing recon work for the brigade. The teams consisted of two weapons men, a radioman, the team leader, the assistant team leader, and a medic. It sounded like Project Delta and just the thing I wanted to get involved in. And Martinez looked like he had his shit together. I didn't like being in the rear while other guys were fighting; that was like sitting on the bench and not being able to play. I asked how I could become a member of his organization. He told me that I had to volunteer and that being a medic would make it really easy to be accepted. I had other things to do that day, and we didn't have a lot of time to talk, so we agreed to meet for a beer after work.

The Interview

After finishing my duties for the day, I met Rey at the NCO club to discuss my future. When I arrived, he was already at the club with a ground pounder named David "Mad Dog" Dolby. Not long after that, the LRRP detachment first sergeant arrived and joined us for drinks. Master Sergeant Smith was tall and thin and had a look of wisdom about him. Rey had put on sergeant (E-5) stripes to get into the NCO club and was naturally very surprised to see Top Smith there. He was uptight and embarrassed that Top Smith had busted him impersonating an NCO. Top said that Rey's "borrowing" the rank was okay because that day he had put Rey in for promotion to E-5; then he bought us each a beer, and we all toasted Rey's promotion.

As the night went on, I convinced Top Smith to accept me into the organization. Mad Dog Dolby had also asked Top Smith about joining the LRRP detachment, but he was later not accepted because of having to go to Washington to receive the Medal of Honor. Dolby is still the only Medal of Honor hero I know. To meet him you wouldn't have known his actions had earned him our nation's highest award for valor. He spoke quietly and never bragged about what he'd done in May of 1966 while serving as a machine gunner with the 1st Cavalry Division on Operation Crazy Horse. His platoon was ambushed by a company-size NVA unit emplaced in bunkers with multiple small- and large-caliber machine guns. With almost his entire unit wounded or dead, Mad Dog took over what was left of the platoon and, firing an M-60 machine gun from the shoulder, made repeated one-man assaults on the machine-gun bunkers (the enemy kept reinforcing the bunkers through undergound tunnels) and single-handedly destroyed the enemy and saved the wounded. He never talked much about it that night but later told us the story when I got to Lurps.

The rest of the evening was spent drinking, conversing, and enjoying each other's company. That night, for the first time, I felt that I had finally found a home.

Hired

The next morning, I went to the replacement company commander and asked for a transfer to the LRRPs, but he claimed that I was too valuable to be let go at that time. Later that morning, Rey came by to visit me on his way to take a written test at Cam Ranh Bay to qualify for training as a helicopter pilot, and I told him what my company commander had said. He assured me that Top Smith would take care of the situation. Sure enough, the next day I received orders to the Long-Range Reconnaissance Patrol Detachment, 1st Brigade, 101st Airborne Division. My company commander was pissed off and told me to expedite my leaving "his" area.

When Rey returned from taking the test and was heading back to the forward area at Duc Pho, he picked me up from the replacement company and took me to my new home. His first words were: "If you're going with me, get your shit packed, 'cause we have to beat feet to Duc Pho." He was visibly upset, very uptight, and not the same person I had met five days earlier. But I happened to have been packed and ready to leave. All I was waiting for was a flight to the forward area. Normally, Replacement Company would manifest an individual on a flight to his destination, and I told Rey we had to get on the manifest to go up north. It was already afternoon, and most manifested flights left in the morning hours. He insisted we didn't have time and would have to hitch a ride on the first plane going to Duc Pho. I loaded my duffel into a rear-area Lurp vehicle, and we were driven to the flight line at Phan Rang. On the way to the airstrip, Rey and our Lurp driver started talking about a Lurp team that had been hit hard that morning. There had been casualties and a KIA (killed in action) in the contact. The details had been sketchy, and no names had been attached to the wounded and dead. From the conversation as I understood it, not just any team had been hit, but the one Rey was assigned to.

As luck would have it, a C-130, the first aircraft preparing to take off for Duc Pho, was just getting ready to leave. Rey started talking to the crew chief and somehow got us on the aircraft. It was flying to Chu Lai first and would stop at Duc Pho on the way back. On the flight to Chu Lai, Rey was pretty quiet, and I could see he was upset. I felt he needed to talk, so I started asking him questions about his team. After a while, he loosened up and started talking.

He told me the team leader was S.Sgt. Vincente Cruz, who was from Guam. According to Rey, Cruz was a very capable leader, cool under fire, and had a lot of heart. The senior scout was Sgt. Derby Jones, whom Rey thought of as an older brother. Initially they had been on different teams, but they had pulled a lot of missions together. According to Rey, Derby was solid, the kind of man I'd want with me when the shit hit the fan. S.Sgt. Larry Christian had come into Lurps with Rey in December 1966. They'd begun on different teams, but both had recently been assigned to Cruz's team. Sp4. David "Fireball" Dixon was the medic. As a medic, he had been used on different teams, but he and Rey had worked a lot together. He described Fireball as on the wild side, to put it mildly, the kind of man who liked to wear a claymore strapped to his chest. Fireball claimed he would never be taken alive. That said it all. The junior RTO (radiotelephone operator) was Sp4. Elmer Kolarik. A Michigan native, Elmer was tall, quiet, dependable, and had a dry sense of humor. Because Rey was the senior RTO, they had shifted an RTO from another team by the name of PFC Sid Tolson. Sid had just turned seventeen years old, but he was mature beyond his years. He was a man the team could count on.

It had been a tight team, Rey said. All the teams were tight, he emphasized, and even though the detachment might reconfigure a team as needs arose, the platoon's having only four to five teams made everybody close, like family. Rey also said that as a medic, and because of the shortage of them in Lurps, I would be moved from team to team as the missions arose. That meant that I would be getting more than enough "bush time."

Listening to Rey talk about his team, and seeing the emotional involvement he had in their well-being, I realized that the feeling of brotherhood that existed among the men of the unit was strong. That was what I had always wanted. I felt like I had found a home. From the outside, I had seen that kind of brotherhood in Delta, but I had never earned my way into it. The talk of casualties also made me vividly aware of just how dangerous the job I had volunteered for could be.

☆
CHAPTER 8

May 1967

Foul Dudes

When we arrived at Duc Pho, we hitched a ride on a truck heading toward the 1st Brigade's forward rear area. Because Lurps were attached to the brigade's headquarters company for administrative purposes, I had to process in with it. The first person I met was the first sergeant of Headquarters Company, a man who was commonly referred to as "Patch Pockets" (dick head) because he seemed to have every badge a person could earn in the army sewn onto his fatigues. I immediately concluded that I had run into another Childers. Rey had warned me that the guy was an REMF and to remember that we took our orders only from Top Smith. After Patch Pockets's briefing about spit-shined boots and clean haircuts, I was ready to get out of his presence.

Rey then took me to "Lurp Hill," and I reported to M.Sgt. Lloyd "Top" Smith. He welcomed me to the detachment and introduced me to the commanding officer, Lt. Daniel McIsaac, a former NCO who had gone through OCS (officer candidate school) and been commissioned. Top Smith and Lieutenant McIsaac were pretty somber, and because Rey was with me, the day's events quickly became the topic of conversation. They had a tragic story to tell.

Cruz's team had been inserted the previous day into the western edge of the Song Ve Valley. Having been inserted into a B-52 Arc Light carpet-bombing zone, they had been extracted on "strings" (ropes) four hours into their mission. They were resupplied on another team's LZ, and then reinserted into another RZ (recon zone), onto a bare hillside that offered no cover or concealment. The team had laid dog (waited quietly) in the only vegetation available, in a dried-out streambed halfway down the hill mass. The situation had rapidly deteriorated.

Unknown to the team, it was surrounded by the NVA that night and attacked at first light. The only warning the team had was that one of the enemy had cocked his rifle bolt just prior to the attack, and the distinctive sound saved the team from instant annihilation. In the first few seconds of heavy enemy fire, Fireball Dixon was killed, and everyone else on the team was badly wounded except for Larry Christian.

In a heroic and determined counterattack born of desperation, Derby Jones and Larry Christian saved the team and their lives. Fighting against a forty-man enemy element, the two Lurps, using full-automatic M-16 fire, grenades, and M-79 grenades, attacked the ambush continuously, leaving the enemy reeling from the viciousness of the two-man assault. Changing positions constantly, Derby and Larry tried to make the enemy think that the two-man attack force was larger than it actually was.

In a display of bravery, Derby Jones attacked back into the overrun team's position and secured the med bag that Fireball had been carrying. He performed lifesaving first aid on all of the wounded, then dragged Fireball's body and wrapped it around the only working radio to protect it. He secured the team's ammo and redistributed it between himself and Christian. All of that while being wounded himself.

Sgt. Derby Jones was put in for the Distinguished Service Cross for the bravery he displayed in the defense of his team.

The requested award was later downgraded, and he was awarded the Silver Star. S.Sgt. Larry Christian was awarded the Silver Star for his part in the action.

That was one hell of a welcome and an eye-opener on how life could go horribly wrong for a Lurp team. As we left the Lurp TOC (tactical operations center), I was introduced to some of the other Lurps. The first person I met was Allen "Teddy Bear" Gaskell. The first word out of his mouth when he saw me was "Lurch." From that day forward, that was what everybody called me. Teddy Bear was small of build, with deep blue eyes and a dry wit. I found out he had been in the LRRP detachment longer than anyone currently in the platoon, and was all of twenty-one years of age. Later on, I came to see that TB was one hell of a good Lurp in the bush. Some of the other Lurps I met were Ron Gartner, Rudy Lopez, Larry Beauchamp, Walt Bacak, Ron Weems, Pappy Lynch, Jim Cody, Bruce Redmer, and Gene Sullivan.

A couple of days later, the LRRP detachment was given a mission to secure a small hilltop (Nui Cau, Hill 163) that strategically overlooked the brigade area. Located to the northeast, it also overlooked the beach where supplies came ashore from ships supporting the brigade's mission. The Lurps were to eventually move onto the hilltop, securing it while pulling reconnaissance missions in the brigade's area of operations. A team consisting of Ron Gartner, Jim Cody, Rudy Lopez, Gary Fandel, and Lieutenant McIsaac would be inserted by helicopter on the hilltop. Two engineers with a mine detector would accompany the team. Positions built by Marines on the hilltop had been the site of heavy fighting three months previously. A heavy team (twelve men) led by S.Sgt. Waldo Bacak would walk from Lurp Hill and link up with the team, clearing a trail down from the hilltop. I was a member of the heavy team with Bacak.

As the team was coming down off Nui Cau, one of the engineers tripped a booby-trapped mine, killing both engineers and severely wounding Jim Cody, Ron Gartner, and Rudy Lopez. Lieutenant McIsaac and Gary Fandel were unharmed because they had stayed on top of the hill while the linkup was being made. Under Lieutenant McIsaac's orders, we held in place at the base of Nui Cau; he was afraid we might set off booby traps. McIsaac and Fandel rushed down from the hilltop and provided first aid; then they brought in a medevac to evacuate the dead and wounded.

I couldn't believe it. I had been in the unit three days, and already there had been one killed and seven wounded. What the hell have I gotten myself into? I thought. If that attrition rate continued, my job as a medic was really going to prove useful. I already had mixed feelings about what I had done, leaving a real cushy rear-area job to put my life in harm's way. As time went by, I would come to appreciate my decision. The old saying "When the going gets tough, the tough get going" was really applicable in the LRRP detachment.

A few days later, another trooper came into the LRRP detachment, James Walker, alias Limey, who was born and raised in England and was one ornery cuss. He'd brought his bravado halfway across the world with him. Limey's idea of a good evening's entertainment was to fight, and he didn't care with whom or how big his opponent was. I thought I was going to end up hating Limey because he was so cocky. So to get Limey on my side, the first thing I did was to try to knock him out. His jaw was as hard as his head, but I did manage to knock him down; then I sat on him and told him we could take our relationship one of two ways: we would get along, or one of us would kill the other. We became the best of friends. Still, every once in a while after a few beers, we would end up trying to knock each other out. When people from some other organization tried to break us up, Limey and I would end up knocking them out. If everybody left us alone, we would get tired and pass out. On occasion, Limey and I would have beer-drinking contests. We would each take a can of beer, bite the top off, and drink the beer as fast as we could. Whoever was fastest could give the other guy a punch in the shoulder. I won most of those contests but not without a few cut lips. As luck would have it, Limey and I ended up on the same LRRP team.

Every battalion in the brigade had its own recon unit: Tiger Force, for 1/327; Recondos, 2/502; Hawks, 2/327; but the Lurps did most of the dirty work for the brigade. We were used as bait, raiders, and anything else someone didn't want to do.

Because the Lurps had recently lost two teams, they had been recruiting and reorganizing, and new people were coming into the Lurp platoon. They came from other units and had one thing in common: They were all volunteers, driven by a sense of adventure, who wanted to serve with an elite unit. We were a little cockier, and each of us ended up with a nickname. The term Foul Dudes was coined by S.Sgt. Ronald Weems, who had come to Vietnam with the brigade in 1965. He had done a lot of line time and had helped organize the sniper platoon for the 1st Brigade. He was a first-class ass-kicker and a badass.

"Foul Dudes" reflected our personalities, and we were all rebels. We were alienated from the headquarters company, and Patches specifically, and that made us feel special. One time, while all of us were loaded, a new guy by the name of Land ate a Lurp ration dry, then consumed a large quantity of water. The Lurp ration rehydrated in his belly and swelled. Suddenly, he was on the ground in the throes of agony and moaning. Everyone was in hysterics, claiming he had just finished eating his boot, and they all expected me to do some high-speed lifesaving first aid. Instead, I got down close to his face and ad-libbed, "Don't let it bring you down!" Suddenly, all the Lurps were rolling balls of laughter. I told everyone laughter was the best medicine for any kind of ailment. All of a sudden that became the first "High Saving

Step"of the Foul Dudes, and it served us well in all aspects of the war.

During the retraining of the Lurp detachment, I was asked to help with the instruction in first aid and as a training aid for Lt. Dan McIsaac, our OIC. His class was on close-quarter killing. The LT (pronounced "ell tee") drew large circles on my body to indicate *where* a person could be killed with a blow or a knife, then proceded to demonstrate on me *how* to kill someone. After the class I went to shower, and people who had not attended the class were giving the lieutenant's diagrams funny stares. They probably thought I was trying a new camouflage technique. We had classes on patrolling and map reading, also taught by LRRPs. For a while, the detachment felt like Special Forces. But we were teaching ourselves instead of teaching indigenous personnel.

Leaving by Foot

One day, a sergeant first class (SFC, E-7) arrived at the detachment. Because of his rank and prior service with Special Forces, he was supposed to take over one of the teams. He was also going to be teaching a weapons class, but while we were all in line for chow, with the E-7 standing alongside Top Smith, a shot rang out, and everybody hit the ground except the new man, who had shot himself in the foot. I ran over to him, and he didn't say a word. By the time I took off his boot and saw that he didn't have any bleeding, his shock was starting to wear off, and pain was setting in. He had a perfect hole, right through the top of his foot and out the bottom. After placing a field dressing over the wound, I took him to the brigade field hospital, but I never got to ask why he left Special Forces. Perhaps he had met Master Sergeant Childers.

When I got back, Top said the sergeant first class had been standing with the muzzle of his rifle resting on the top of his boot when the weapon went off. Top thought the guy shot himself on purpose because he didn't want to be a Lurp. He had said as much to Top Smith when he processed in. He was close to retirement and wanted out of Vietnam. Well, he got his wish. I don't know what Top wrote as an after-action report, but that was the last time we saw or heard from the sergeant first class.

First Raid

Around the first week in June, the LRRP detachment was given a mission to raid a Viet Cong village that was suspected of being the base for several high-ranking Viet Cong political officers. The village was located on the east bank of the Song Ve, which gave the valley its name. We would be operating in five five-man fire teams and a headquarters controlling element. I would be the raiding force medic attached to the headquarters element with Top Smith, Rey Martinez, Larry Christian, and some other men whose names I can't remember at this writing. We were to carry our LBE (load-bearing equipment) fighting gear and take as many prisoners as possible. A reporter would be attached to the headquarters element to observe the LRRPs while we raided the village. Before we left on the raid, some of us recorded messages on tape to be sent to our hometown radio stations. I said hello to my family and told them everything was fine and that I couldn't wait to get home.

We were transported by trucks to the airfield and loaded onto the waiting helicopters. The reporter rode on our helicopter, clicking pictures all the way to the drop-off point. The village we were assaulting had not been prepped by gunships or artillery; it was to be a surprise raid.

The village sat on the east bank of the Song Ve, surrounded by tall coconut palm trees. We inserted without incident, but as soon as the helicopters left, firing broke out all over, and the ell tee called for gunships. We all found cover and started returning fire. There were spider holes all around the village. Larry Christian and I occupied one together, and, back-to-back, we fired into the village and anywhere else we took incoming from. But as I was firing toward the village, I saw the reporter running toward it. I yelled at him to come back, but he ignored me. I heard the gunships coming, and about the same time, I saw the ell tee throw a red smoke grenade into a courtyard to mark where the enemy was—right where the reporter had gone. Larry and I jumped out of our cover and ran after him. Just as the gunships started opening up, I saw the reporter crouched behind the mud wall of one of the homes in the center of the village. He was taking pictures of the gunships that were firing at him! I covered Larry as he ran to the reporter; then Larry covered me as I ran to their location. I grabbed the reporter and yelled, "What the fuck are you doing?" He said he had some great shots. I explained the significance of the red smoke to him. He thought the smoke had been thrown to cover our movement into the village, so I pointed out that one of the gunships had fired a rocket into the center of the village, almost hitting us.

I grabbed the reporter by his shirt, and we all ran out of the village with minigun rounds chewing at our heels. The three of us dived into the first spider hole we could find and tried to get as small as possible. Spider holes were made for small people, but we all made it into one, the reporter rammed in on top of Larry and me. Gunship fire felled a palm tree and provided more cover for us. It seemed like hours before the shooting stopped and we were able to crawl from our hiding place, but in reality, only minutes had passed.

When we moved back to get extracted, I briefly mentioned to the ell tee what had happened. I heard later that the ell tee had really dug into that reporter's shit because he could have gotten us killed. The ell tee said he didn't care if the reporter had gotten hit. That was the last time we had news media accompany us on a mission. I found new respect for our ell tee because I knew his concern was not only for the mission but for his troops as well.

It had been a really successful mission in that we grabbed a bunch of prisoners, one of them a high-ranking political officer. No one had been hurt, and we'd all performed well.

Second Raid

Because of the success of the first raid, the LRRP detachment was ordered to perform another raid. I can't remember the name or location of the village, but I still wake up at night thinking about it.

The mission would be the same, the taking of prisoners. I was once again the chief medic and was assigned to the headquarters fire team. Lieutenant McIsaac would be in charge of the fire team and the whole raid. His two radio operators would be Rey Martinez and Pat "Mother" Henshaw. Clay Wentworth and John "Big Chad" Chadwick would round the team off, providing firepower and support.

The only equipment we had to carry were our weapons and radio and my aid bag. We lifted off around 1400 hours, then flew NOE. We arrived at the village and, with the exception of a herd of water buffalo, it appeared deserted. As the four helicopters and four teams were approaching the village to land, one of the door gunners observed someone, weapon in hand, running for the tree line. Trying to drop the running figure, the door gunner opened fire with his M-60, but the figure disappeared into the overgrowth. The door gunner then turned the hot weapon on the village, stopping only when we had to get off and would have been in his line of fire. We swooped down into a dry rice paddy. The helicopters took off and assumed a racetrack orbit some distance from the village we were raiding. They would await our call for extraction, and they wouldn't have to wait long. We were to check the village, capture some prisoners, and leave immediately.

On line, we moved toward the village, at the ready. As we entered the tree line, we started taking incoming fire. The enemy had been taken by surprise but was quickly mounting a defense. Outside one of the hootches (homes made of bamboo and straw with dirt floors) we came to were two rucksacks that looked to be VC. As we got closer to the hootch with the rucksacks, two young women who had been herding cattle and were caught in the open paddy when we landed were between us and the hootch. Weems, one of the fire-team leaders, told them in Vietnamese to stop, but they kept moving. Weems then grabbed one of the girls and put her on the ground. The older girl went to her belly, and both girls started praying for us not to kill them. Another Lurp and I reached the hootch with the rucks and proceeded to check it carefully. We could hear a child crying from inside. I yelled into the hootch, *"Lai dai!"* (come out), but the crying grew more intense, almost to a scream. I looked inside where a child, a girl about two years old, was clinging desperately to what must have been her mother, who was sitting up in the corner of the room with her arms around the little girl, as if trying to protect her from harm. There wasn't any visible blood, only a small hole in the mother's head. She was dead. A stray round had killed her. I pleaded with the child to come out, but the more I talked the more terrified the child became.

In a crouch, I moved into the hootch as another Lurp covered me; I didn't know if the owners of the rucks were still inside, waiting to blow us away. There were two other small rooms in addition to the room with the dead mother. Most hootches had a trapdoor in the floor that concealed an area that could house an enemy. That hootch had a trapdoor, but after carefully opening it, I found that it contained only pottery filled with rice. There was nothing in either room. By the time we finished checking the rooms thoroughly, the other guys had checked the rucks that were sitting outside. They contained demolitions and things that a man living in the jungle needed to survive.

Meanwhile, the platoon's mission to capture prisoners had deteriorated into a running gun battle. With the enemy resistance gaining strength by the minute, Lieutenant McIsaac decided to extract us while we still had the chance to do so. Using the gunships to suppress some of the fire coming against us, he called in the slicks to land in trail formation where we had inserted minutes earlier.

We ran back out of the tree line and jumped into the helicopter for extraction. As I was getting into the helicopter, Rey Martinez slid clear across the helicopter and out the other side. Clay Wentworth helped him back inside. By that time, the enemy was shooting at us with a heavy machine gun (.51 caliber), and tracers were flying everywhere, several of them coming in one door of the helicopter and going out the other. One round smacked heavily right above my head. As we started to fly clear of the village, the wood line we were flying over came alive with AK and RPG fire. Suddenly, my helicopter started bucking and shuddering terribly. The pilot turned around and gave us the thumbs-down; we were going back down. We all interlocked arms and prepared for the crash. Our pilot was very good and was able to control the helicopter until we slammed into the ground. Fortunately it stayed right-side up, and nobody was hurt.

Before the helicopter came to a full stop, most of us had already exited the aircraft, because we were worried that it would blow up. We were still receiving incoming from the wood line, and we immediately returned fire, setting up a perimeter around the downed helicopter. The only cover we had was the rice paddy dikes, but we had plenty of firepower with the helicopter's two M-60s and our individual weapons. Our pilot told us reinforcements were on the way. Then the rest of the helicopters swooped down, dropping off the other three teams. The incoming had slackened somewhat, suppressed by one of the gunships, and all we could do was wait for attack or rescue. To our east was a village that seemed abandoned, and the fire we were receiving came from the west. The only trees were in the direction of the incoming fire and in the direction of the abandoned village. So we were in the open and ripe for the picking.

After a couple of minutes, we heard the rescue helicopters. They were gunships only, and we would still have to wait for extraction ships, but at least we had plenty of firepower. After an hour the gunships had to leave, but by then the approach of the pickup ships was audible. The extraction went without incident. The rear had sent a CH-47 to pick up the downed copter, and it was the first thing out. We followed without another shot being fired at us.

After returning, cleaning our weapons, and taking a shower, the day's activities sank in, but I could still hear that child's screaming and see that dead woman. I thought about that child without a mother, and it disturbed me.

Two-man Relief Mission

It was a new day, and I was going to really get acquainted with my new team leader. His name was Walter "Waldo" Bacak. He was five feet ten inches tall, had receding dark hair, and was missing one front tooth, which he liked to display. He had been through Ranger School and was one crazy son of a bitch, someone I would want with me when the chips were down.

After about two minutes of conversation, Bacak said we'd been assigned an important, classified, two-man mission. The mission was to relieve the thirst of our Lurp platoon. In the two-and-half-ton truck (called a "deuce and a half") he had acquired from Headquarters Company, we headed for an army supply depot run by the 25th Infantry Division by the airstrip at the base of Nui Dang. When we got there, we found a convoy was entering the gates of the supply depot, so we fell right in line with them. While the other trucks were being loaded, Bacak pulled up to where pallets of beer were being stored. He jumped out of the truck, went to the back, and lowered the tailgate. Spotting an unattended forklift, he got behind the wheel, drove over, picked up a pallet of beer, and loaded it onto our truck. A pallet of beer consisted of about one hundred cases of beer. Bacak took the forklift back to where he had found it, returned to the truck, and told me to drive out of the compound. I thought for sure that someone would stop us at the gate, but no one did. Bacak waved at the guard as we went through, and our mission was accomplished. No one else had beer that day but the Lurps. More than likely he knew, but Top never asked how we got the beer. Our detachment commander, Lieutenant McIsaac, was the only officer who guessed how we got the beer, but he never said anything about it. He just told us to be careful. I don't think we ever finished all of the beer, at least not that night.

The Perfect Mission

Two days later, we had to go on a real mission. It was supposed to be for three days. Bacak's team consisted of Bob McKinnon, James "Limey" Walker, David Wofford, Paul Dufresne, and myself. Lieutenant McIsaac would also be with us on the mission.

People today have a hard time believing how much we carried to the field. I put C-ration cans in a sock and lined the inside of my ruck with them. If I ever took a round in the back, it would have to go through my C-ration cans first. I normally took one case of Cs and about four Lurp rations. I was a growing lad! I had two bladders of water, two pounds of C-4 plastic explosive, fifty feet of detonation cord, two claymore antipersonnel mines, a "goody pack"—a heavy-duty plastic battery bag that contained coffee, sugar, cream, cocoa, hot sauce, and chewing gum—my poncho liner, and, last, my M-5 aid bag that sat on top of my ruck. We weren't lucky enough to be allowed to carry rain gear, like a poncho. On my LBE harness and belt, I had two water canteens, one knife, four fragmentation grenades, two smoke grenades (one green, one red), and one white phosphorous grenade. In two ammo pouches, I had eight loaded magazines for my M-16. I also carried a sawed-off M-79, with a shotgun round in the chamber, strapped to my web belt in an old antenna case. I had two bandoliers of M-16 ammo in magazines and a bandolier of M-79 HE rounds draped over my LBE and body. Everybody carried a map in a plastic bag in the left pant-leg pocket and a compass tied to a parachute cord around the neck and tucked inside the shirt or in the right shirt pocket. In one pocket I carried a signal mirror, and in the other a strobe light. By the time I had everything in my ruck and on my person, someone else had to help me up.

At first light we lifted off, and after about fifteen minutes of flying time, we dropped down onto the top of a ridge; then, without anyone getting off, we lifted once again. We made a couple of similar false insertions before reaching our insertion LZ. The chopper couldn't land because the pilot couldn't tell how high the elephant grass was (sometimes it grows as high as twenty feet). We were told to jump. But when we exited a helicopter while wearing hundred-pound rucksacks, then fell twenty-some feet, we had a tendency to hit the ground hard. On that mission, though, the grass was "only" about ten feet tall. I hit the ground with a thud and waited for the helicopters to leave the area. The helicopter rose into the air, then disappeared to make another false landing.

We lay dog in the grass for about five minutes before moving into the tree line. We moved slowly because "Charles" (the VC, from "Victor Charlie") sometimes laid booby traps in the elephant grass or tree lines that surrounded them. Every step

we took was carefully made as we maintained 360-degree observation. We moved about three klicks (kilometers) before
making a rest halt. Bacak wanted to rest the team and study
the map before moving on, and the pause also gave us time to
chow down. While I leaned back on my ruck, I opened a can of
C rations and began to eat. Bacak was trying to capture a
dragonfly and succeeded. He made a noise to get everyone's
attention, then put the dragonfly in his mouth and pulled it
through the space created by his missing front tooth. All of the
insides of the dragonfly oozed out of his mouth and onto his
chin. He then took one finger and pushed the slime back into
his mouth. I suddenly lost my appetite. A couple of minutes
later, we moved on. I was glad.

Two klicks later, we were sitting on top of a hill that looked
down into a valley containing a small village surrounded by
rice paddies. Lieutenant McIsaac had found a large boulder
on the side of the hill with an excellent view of the village
below, and the boulder was well camouflaged by the foliage
that surrounded it. We took turns listening to the radio and
watching the village through the binoculars.

The first day we didn't see anything move into or out of
the village. But after an uneventful night, the ell tee had the
first watch in the morning, and he called me over to verify
what he was seeing. Over a two-hour period, we observed
about twenty men, wearing black, moving into the village.
They moved slowly and only a few feet at a time. After the
twentieth person entered the village, no more activity was
visible. At that point Bacak and the ell tee decided to call artillery on the village, and a reaction force was alerted and
standing by to enter the village after we finished pounding it
with artillery. The first round was a WP (white phosphorous)
round for adjustment, followed by HE (high explosive) that
leveled the village. We were then told to move to our extraction point as soon as possible. The ell tee wanted to wait until
he saw the reaction force move into the village, but his request

was denied, and we left the area without ever learning what was found there.

While we were on the move to the extraction point, we heard small-arms fire coming from the direction of the village. We were lifted out without incident, none of us ever firing a round or having one fired at us on that mission. It was the perfect mission.

The Friendly Neighborhood Barber

The brigade had finished an operation and was getting ready to relocate to a different area of operation. Some of the battalions and the Lurps were on stand-down, and Mad Dog Dolby and a friend of his had come by for a visit one evening. Several of us were sitting around doing a bowl on Lurp Hill, and Dolby had just finished telling us about the battle for which he had been put in for the Medal of Honor. Suddenly, a large flash appeared from the direction of the beach. The flash became a huge mushroom cloud–shaped fireball. I thought Charles, out of revenge for the morning's activities, had dropped an atomic bomb on us. Rumor said that a forklift driver had dropped something sensitive in the ammo dump, and the dump went up, taking him with it.

The next morning a few of us decided to go into town, and I stopped to get a haircut by one of the locals because I liked the way they massaged the scalp and cut nose and ear hair. I always fell asleep while the barber performed his duties, but I tipped well and thought that the next time I went into the village I would get excellent service. After my haircut, we went to eat and down a couple of beers; then it was time to return to base camp before curfew.

We had no sooner hit the base camp than we started receiving incoming rockets, mortars, and small-arms fire. We had our weapons with us but not nearly enough ammunition for my satisfaction, so I ran to our ammo bunker and grabbed as many bandoliers of ammo as I could carry. Our area sat on the perimeter with only concertina wire and claymore antipersonnel mines for defense. It was getting dark, and the night was overcast, so visibility was limited to about one hundred meters. The artillery was putting up flares and HE. We had a few hand flares, and we sent them into the air as well. It looked and smelled like a Fourth of July fireworks display. But even with the flares, it was difficult to see the perimeter clearly.

On our side of the perimeter, there was nothing but rice paddies that the enemy could use as cover, and we had mined the area with claymores and booby-trapped those with M-26 hand grenades, and when one went off, we could see bodies moving through the wire toward us. For what seemed like hours, I fired clip after clip, and threw every grenade I had. Just as I was about out of ammo, I saw and heard gunships flying to our rescue. As quickly as the war started, it ended: I watched as VC ran across the rice paddies with gunships firing them up. When it was all over, it was too dark to make a sweep of the perimeter, but we could see bodies still in the wire. We watched them all night, just waiting for one of them to move. First light revealed ten or fifteen bodies in the wire, one of them the barber who had cut my hair and probed my ears to trim the hairs there. It would be many years before I again let a stranger cut my hair.

Bait

That morning we were told that intelligence said about eight hundred NVA were moving through our area of operation, so we Lurps were tasked to sit on top of a hill as bait. We inserted onto the hilltop and immediately started putting out concertina wire, claymores, and trip flares while making as much noise as we could, because we wanted the NVA to know where we were. I didn't like the idea of being bait, especially with eight hundred troops wanting to eliminate us, and the weather was turning to rain, which I hated even more. How would we be extracted and how would help get to us if we were attacked? During the two weeks we spent on that hill, I probably slept only eight hours. Unfortunately, we received many missions on which we were used as bait. Fortunately, Charlie was too smart to take the bait.

Hide-and-Seek

After we were extracted, we were resupplied and sent back into the field. Because the eight hundred NVA hadn't taken the bait, we were to try to determine where they had gone. Tired and not really wanting to go back, I thought about ways to avoid the mission, but I would have been given a lot of crap from the Foul Dudes if I hadn't gone.

After several false insertions, we were let off in a small jungle clearing and moved quickly into the wood line. I was nervous about looking for eight hundred NVA. It's one thing to sit in a location and watch, but when you have to move and find the enemy, that makes for a new ball game. Bacak's team—point man Ernie "Dirty Ernie" Winston, Limey Walker, Bob McKinnon, Bacak, and myself—made the first contact. I was the rear security, tasked with making sure we were not being followed and sanitizing the team's trail. After we moved a couple of klicks into our area of operation, Dirty Ernie spotted a fresh bunker complex. It was well camouflaged, but Ernie was a master scout, a real hound dog who had a scent for the enemy. We waited for a couple of minutes before moving forward to check out the bunkers.

Whoever had occupied those bunkers hadn't been gone long. We carefully looked for booby traps, but could not find any; the enemy had left in a real hurry. The bunker-village complex was large enough to hold eight hundred people. It had underground tunnels that went from bunker to bunker. It also had a small hospital that had been recently used. We found bandages, and there were blood spatterings everywhere. Bacak called in a spot report, and we all hoped we would be pulled out of the field. Instead, we were ordered to pull back and observe the bunkers until daybreak, at which time we would be extracted. Bacak took us to high ground with good observation of the bunkers below us. Our landing zone was only two klicks away and all downhill. The night went fast and without incident. The next morning we were extracted and ready for some beer.

Hors d'Oeuvres

After our normal cleanup and showers, it was time to party. The only problem was that we were all broke. Fortunately, Bacak found a couple of very large, black, and extremely ugly beetles at the shower point and told us not to worry; we would party that night. Since the first day I met Bacak, I had known that he was resourceful; whatever he wanted, he knew how to get.

We went to a local beer tent owned by 1st Battalion, 327th Infantry, 101st Airborne Division, where a tableful of paratroopers was playing poker. Bacak walked up to them and, without reservation, took one of the beetles from his pocket and threw it onto the table. All those big, bad paratroopers jumped back from the table with looks of fright. One of them told Bacak to "Get the fuck out of here!" With forethought, Bacak had tied a string to one of the legs of the beetle. As soon as the beetle hit the table, Bacak apologized to everyone and pulled the beetle back into his hand. Some of the people at the table stood and stepped back, while the rest of the people just ignored what had happened.

Bacak then made a proposal to the players: "How much to bite the beetle in half?" All of the players looked at each other and said nothing. Bacak threw the beetle back onto the table and said, "How much to eat it?" One man said five bucks, one of our guys said ten; then a black guy threw in twenty bucks and said, "Put up or shut up!" Bacak waited until he thought there was enough money on the table for all of us to party. Then, like a connoisseur of fine wine looking over a good vintage, he surveyed the beetle, trying to find just the right place to take a bite. In the meantime, more money was accumulating on the table. Just as I was beginning to think he wasn't going to eat the beetle, Bacak glanced one more time at the pot of money and took a bite, a smile on his face. He finished off the beetle, still chewing as he picked up the money. We partied most of the night, all on Bacak's meal.

Fourth of July

Morning came quickly, and my head wasn't in the right place. Bacak walked into my bunker and said I was going out as the medic on Christian's team. He told me to behave, because Top was going along. Christian's team that day would consist of Christian, Rey Martinez, Jaybird Magill, Paul Dufresne, Top, and myself.

In order to deny the enemy use of the Song Ve Valley, not long before this a massive relocation program had been carried out by the 101st Airborne against the civilian population of the valley. The Lurps had participated in it, and called the operation the Cattle Drive. Once cleared of all civilians, the Song Ve Valley became a "free-fire zone." Anyone operating in the valley was fair game because he was considered the enemy. Our area of operation (AO) was in the western edge of the valley. We were to look for enemy forces infiltrating back into the valley.

At last light on 2 July, we were inserted into a small opening on the jungled side of a mountain. It was not visible from the valley floor, so we were probably inserted without being seen. We moved by contouring the side of the mountain until we found a point from which we could observe the valley without being seen.

The area was alive with the sounds of birds and chattering monkeys, and the smell of exotic flowers hung in the air. Surrounded by green triple-canopy foliage, we had all the cover we needed. It was hot and humid, but the cover of the jungle furnished shade and occasionally a breeze that brought some coolness with the scent of flowers. We could see the valley below us, and the abandoned road that ran the entire length of the Song Ve Valley. A river meandered alongside the road. Just to the north were the remains of a destroyed bridge that had spanned the river. On the east side of the river was a small village from which all the people had recently been relocated. The eastern edge of the village was bordered by a tree line, which abruptly ended at some dry rice paddies extending into the distance toward some hills to the east. The west edge of the village crowded the bank of the river. Heavy vegetation grew on both banks of the river. Contouring the river on the west bank was a good-size trail. The river flowed northeast in the middle of the valley, which was littered with unused rice paddies. The road headed straight north and disappeared into a narrow valley.

The first day and night we didn't see anything and didn't expect to, because the 1st Brigade had just finished relocating the entire population from the valley. It was 3 July and getting dark; the sun had gone down behind the ridge we were on. The sunlight was still visible on the ridgeline on the other side of the valley. There was enough light to allow us to watch the valley and observe a couple of figures on the west bank of the river traveling south on the trail, heading in our direction. They were a good distance from us and difficult to make out clearly because of the dense vegetation along the trail. As they drew closer, they passed through an open area on the trail, and we could see they were a large group moving with caution and very slowly. It was a company, about ninety people, on the move. Some had on black PJs, and some were wearing North Vietnamese pith helmets and blue uniforms. It was dusk when they stopped downriver from the destroyed bridge. After a couple of minutes, they sent a seven-man squad across the river to recon the village. They crossed the river in a staggered and spread formation. They were very professional. That was one of the few times I actually got to see the enemy when he was unaware of our presence.

Top called in a SALUTE (size, activity, location, unit, time, equipment) report. We had artillery on call and the ability to call in gunships, but by the time the gunships could arrive, it would be too dark for them to do anything.

These people moved with precision and took all necessary precautions while the whole company crossed the river and moved into the village below us. Top was going to call in artillery but, after thinking about it, decided to wait. The enemy would have figured out where we were after the first round hit, and because of the closing darkness, we wouldn't be able to observe our artillery work out. There wouldn't be a reaction force or any way to be extracted. So we waited.

The company of VC was going to spend the night in the deserted village. After darkness totally overcame the day, we could see the enemy building cooking fires inside the hootches, where they were well concealed from the air. It was a scary situation but at the same time exciting. Top decided to have the artillery pound them first thing in the morning—hopefully before they decided to move. That was a long night.

It was the morning of the Fourth of July, 1967. Before first light, we watched the enemy light their cooking fires. Sleeping the night before had been impossible because everyone was anxious for the morning's events. Top Smith had coordinated everything with the artillery and an infantry platoon reaction force, which would already be in the air, waiting to be inserted when the artillery stopped. The artillery would be shooting a TOT (time on target), in which a battery (six guns) or multiple batteries are fired at the same time, with the rounds arriving on target at the same time.

Top Smith would be calling the shots, and Rey Martinez would be on the radio; Rey, a former artilleryman who had a lot of experience in the use of artillery, would be doing the communicating with the redlegs (artillery). Soon it was light, but still difficult to see. Everyone in the rear was ready. Top had picked a spot two hundred meters from the village for the spotter rounds. Top looked at Rey and told him to fire. Rey gave the word over the radio, then turned to Top and said, "On the way." Two willy pete (white phosphorous) rounds exploded exactly where Top had asked for them. Top said, "Left two hundred, fire for effect." Rey passed that message over the radio, then turned to Top and said, "On the way." It seemed like hours before the rounds hit, but in reality it was only minutes.

Top had the binoculars and could see the enemy milling around right after the willy pete rounds had hit. Then it seemed like the whole village came alive with people running everywhere. The artillery hit all at once, and the village disappeared under an orange fireball and black-and-gray smoke. Bodies were flying in the air along with the hootches. Being so far away, we all disassociated ourselves from the matter of reality. People were dying, and we all were cheering. But I wasn't thinking of those people's deaths, not until years later. In a matter of ten minutes, a hundred rounds must have been put on that village and the surrounding area. It would have been cool to watch the infantry move in, but we were ordered to move to our extraction point.

We moved as quickly as we could without sacrificing safety. As we approached the LZ, we heard the choppers coming in. The same choppers that had brought the infantry were extracting us. Everything went like clockwork, and Top Smith was the reason. As we lifted high enough to see the remains of the village, we saw bodies lying on the open ground. We saw no movement.

Top relayed to us that the infantry had said we'd done a good job, and that they would finish cleaning the area up. We were flown back to Duc Pho, and Top went over to artillery to congratulate them on a job well done. He was also hoping to find out if the infantry had said anything about a body count. When Top returned to our area, he said no information had been passed on. It was a memorable Fourth of July because we had done well what long-range recon was supposed to do. Limey and I drank warm beer, toasting each other for bringing death and destruction on the enemy. Eventually we passed out from exhaustion.

After the events of the Fourth, 5 July seemed mundane. The only memory I have of it is Bacak breaking in two new men to our unit by taking all of their money. He bet the new guys he could piss over a two-and-a-half-ton truck. He could do that only after consuming a great quantity of beer. When his bladder was about to burst, he was ready to prove his ability at long-range, indirect urination. He made one of the new people stand on the opposite side of the truck to witness that he cleared it. Bacak got about four feet back from the truck, pulled out his penis, grabbed it tightly to build up pressure, then let go. The stream of urine flew not only over the truck but onto the new guy. After a few moments of triumph, Bacak collected the money from the new guys and bought them all a beer or two. It was, we all said, a God-given gift, and Waldo Bacak knew how to use it well.

Chu Lai

Rey Martinez and Eddie Mounts received orders for MACV Recondo School in Nha Trang and left us to our fate for a few weeks. Rey was unique because he was a born leader and didn't know it. He never had to push someone to do something; he would merely ask that it be done, and it would be done. While he was gone, the brigade moved its operational

base to Chu Lai. Operation Wheeler was started in the middle
of September and ended the last days in November. It was
monsoon season, and a wet, miserable time.

Losing Our Heads

Because of the shortage of brigade helicopter assets, the
Lurps were having trouble acquiring long-range recon missions. Brigade decided to base the Lurps out of battalion fire-
bases, which were normally located on hilltops. We would be
under operational control of whatever battalion we were assigned to, and we would perform walk-off recon missions or
anything else the battalion commander wished to use us for.
We were placed under operational control of the 2/327 Infantry Battalion, whose firebase was west of Chu Lai. Several
days before we arrived on the hilltop, lights had been spotted
in the late hours, every night, at the base of the hill on which
the firebase was located. The day before we arrived, the battalion commander had dispatched his recon element, the
Hawks, to investigate. The Hawks hadn't made it two hundred
meters outside the wire of the firebase before becoming em-
broiled in a firefight and killing two of the enemy. The day we
arrived on the hilltop, the battalion commander gave us the
mission of investigating the lights, because the Hawks had
been tasked with the security of the firebase. Justifiably, the
Hawks felt we were stepping on their turf, but we were only
following orders.

Stone Dead

We took two teams, Bacak's and Danny Williams's. Bacak's
team consisted of Bob McKinnon, Limey Walker, David Wofford, Paul Dufresne, and myself. Danny Williams's team consisted of John Hines, Wolfman Kraft, Jimmy McCormack,
Fred Wyche, and George Sullens. We left the firebase early in

the afternoon and patrolled to the bottom of the hill without any problems. It was raining, and there was a heavy mist, almost a fog, at the bottom of the hill.

Everybody was leery about the mission because the day before, the Hawks had made their contact before they had reached the bottom of the hill. Nobody was saying anything, but we knew some angry enemy would probably be waiting for us. We were exposed most of the way down the hill, so once we reached the cover of the jungle, we felt a lot better.

We patrolled until we came upon a clearing that led into a rice paddy. Then someone up front spotted a couple of Vietnamese in the rice paddy. While we were watching, a couple of minutes later there was an explosion. Apparently the two men had accidentally blown themselves up while planting booby traps to kill Americans. Now they were fertilizer. Tough luck!

Bacak decided not to go forward any farther but to pull back a couple hundred meters and watch. That made us happy because we didn't have to cross the clearing and the rice paddies. Just before dark we moved into our night defensive position (NDP). Our night layover site was about two hundred meters from a trail we had been paralleling. We formed into our defensive security wheel in the heavy vegetation. Our radio watch consisted of everyone in turn having to monitor the radio for an hour. My radio watch came after Limey's. On the other side of Limey in the defensive wheel was McKinnon, and next to him was John Hines. It was a wet, cold night, and there was a feeling in the air that something was going to happen. Hines had brought a canvas tarp out into the field, covering himself with it in an attempt to stay dry. But that broke a strict taboo on a Lurp team: we didn't bring into the field ponchos, canvas tarps, or any other material that might make a noise. I couldn't sleep because of all the racket Hines was making with his tarp. Limey said something to Hines about the noise he was making, and promptly went back to sleep. I lay there trying to find a comfortable position, trying to avoid the rain falling on my face and the mosquitoes buzzing in my ears.

I was lying on my back with my weapon across my chest when shots rang out, and green tracers (glowing bullets from enemy ammunition; ours were red) flew over my body and hit Hines. He fell over Limey, and all hell broke loose. I grabbed Hines, rolled him onto his back, and checked to see if he was breathing and had a pulse. He was stone dead. I yelled at Danny Williams that Hines was gone. Hines had been on radio watch and had been sitting up when the incoming fire had swept through our area. Bacak yelled for a "mad minute" (all the team members fire their weapons on full automatic, covering their preassigned areas of responsibility from the defensive wheel), and everyone on the heavy team complied. Limey couldn't find his weapon because I had rolled over onto it. Williams decided to throw grenades through the thick vegetation. The first one got through, but the second one bounced off a bush and landed really close to us. Fortunately, my rucksack took most of the shrapnel. Bacak yelled that we were not to throw any more grenades, then started calling in 81mm mortars, which were set up on the firebase.

The first round was white phosphorous and landed about fifty meters from us. Too close for comfort, I thought. Then he started working the area around us with HE (high explosives). Saturating the sides of our position with mortar rounds, he moved the fire like an artist with a paintbrush. During all this time, we could hear and smell the enemy around us. During a lull in the mortar fire, the enemy moved in close, and Bacak called for another mad minute. My weapon jammed, as did those of four other people. Afterward, I reasoned that during the night most of the weapons had accumulated moisture in the chambers, causing the rounds to sweat and thus jam. The only weapon firing effectively was Limey's World War II–era M-3 .45-caliber grease gun.

Contact was made with the firebase, and the Hawks were

being sent as a reaction force to assist us. But in the darkness the Hawks couldn't locate our exact position. So we were to fire straight up into the air using tracers so the Hawks could link up with us. But only Limey's grease gun and one or two M-16s could fire. And Limey didn't have any tracers for his weapon. My weapon jammed again. So there we were, in triple canopy; we couldn't throw grenades, and most of the weapons were jamming. For a moment I thought that we were all going to end up as casualty statistics. And all around us was the enemy's distinctive odor of smoke, *nuoc mam* sauce, and body odor.

Bacak called for another mad minute, but after three rounds my weapon jammed again. I swore that if I lived, the first chance I got I would find a weapon that didn't jam every time I needed it. Fortunately Bacak did a good job with the mortars, and we didn't take more casualties.

We were there all night, waiting for the enemy to take advantage of our poor situation, but they never attempted to penetrate our position. At first light the reaction force moved into our location. I wrapped Hines in the noisy tarp that had protected him from the rain but not from the bullets that took his life. As we moved Hines to the extraction LZ, we came across a bomb that had been dropped but had not exploded. The enemy had been working on it, trying to dismantle it for its explosives. Engineers were called in to explode the bomb while the reaction force provided security.

I rode back to Chu Lai on the helicopter with Hines and escorted his body back to Graves Registration. Limey went along with me and recovered the tarp that Hines's body was wrapped in. The rest of the team had walked back uphill to the firebase. That night Limey burned the tarp. By then Rey was back from Recondo School, and we told him what had happened to Hines. That same night we had a memorial for him. The loss of life isn't felt until after the heat of combat. I'd always thought of myself as being indestructible until I watched someone get hit during a firefight. Only after taking Hines's body to Graves Registration, a body full of life just hours earlier and now only a lifeless carcass, did I realize not only how vulnerable I was but how gut-wrenchingly lonely it is to die without family. At least the Vietnamese had their loved ones around them. Not to say that makes death any more acceptable; death in combat is never acceptable, but the comfort of family during tragic events is undeniable. Commanders who really knew their troops could identify with the grief that we felt.

A couple of days later, LRRPs were tasked for several missions that were supposed to last only six days. The whole operation took more than fifty.

10–20 "Body" Count

Rey Martinez had scrounged several cases of LRRP rations, dehydrated food packets. If plenty of water was available and you had hot sauce, they were the best rations for the field. Water would turn out not to be a problem because it rained from the day we left until the day we returned. The only alternative to LRRP rations was C rations, which came in cans containing food and condiments. I carried both. I prepared my ruck with about a case of LRRPs and a case of C rations. I put my C rations in a sock according to the order in which I wanted to eat them; then I lined the back of my ruck with the sock. On missions in which we sat around while being used as bait, everybody became gourmet chefs by trying to mix and match meals, condiments, etc. We could make everything from pizza to mulligan stew.

The missions we performed during that period included everything from long-range recon, "static deployment" (staff talk for "bait") on top of hills waiting for the enemy to attack, providing security, and search-and-destroy patrols.

Bacak's team was tasked to recon a road that intelligence thought the VC were using to supply troops. It was more an oxen trail than a road. We walked off the top of a firebase at midmorning. The rain had stopped for about an hour, long enough for us to move into the bush without having to worry about not seeing or hearing what was to our front. When the monsoon season hits, the rains feel like an ocean of water has been dropped all at once. We couldn't see into the distance, and we couldn't hear the sounds that normally would warn us of the enemy, for instance, the noise a piece of dry wood gives off when stepped on. The only thing the rain did that helped us was to carry the scent of the enemy. I could smell a VC within a hundred yards.

That day, the water faucet didn't turn on until we were close to our objective. The road we were to watch ran east and west, the vegetation being on the north and south sides of the road. We stopped at a small hootch on the north side of the road. With the rains starting up again, we quickly set up in a linear ambush, with an M-60 covering each end of the line and claymores set at both ends of the ambush. We lay hidden in trees, and brush that gave us excellent cover. Chickens were running around the small hootch, so Bacak felt confident we would be seeing something. Night fell over the bush, and from my position in the middle of the ambush line, I tried to focus on the hootch on the other side of the road. The driving rain made it almost impossible to see. Of course, I had learned long before not to look directly at something I thought I saw in the dark. Instead, I maneuvered the beam of whatever light I was carrying so that the object I was trying to see passed through it. If the object was still moving, then something was out there.

My radio watch was quiet. I passed the radio to Limey, who was next to me. He must have really liked me, because every time I turned around, he was there.

The rain never let up, and all of us were soaked to the bone. I was just about to doze off when Limey started pinching my arm and pointing toward the hootch. I tried to focus on what he was seeing but had a difficult time making anything out. We woke everyone up and waited to see what Bacak wanted to do. I immediately became nervous with anticipation.

Suddenly one of the claymores went off and chaos exploded—M-60s firing, everyone on full automatic, hand grenades exploding, then silence. We didn't receive one round in our direction. Bacak told everybody to get on line and move through the kill zone. There must have been fifteen to twenty bodies lying dead on the road, but no weapons. Upon closer examination, we realized we had just killed a troop of gibbons, huge primates that looked like and walked like small VC going through the jungle. I let Limey take credit for the body count.

We were compromised and had to move out of that area before the real enemy found us. I didn't like the idea of moving at night with the rain falling so hard that I couldn't see anything except the man in front of me. But we walked until first light; then Bacak called for extraction.

Bloodsuckers

We were extracted, all right, right to the top of another hill, one already occupied by members of our platoon. That was really depressing because we were all looking forward to a shower and clean, dry fatigues. Everybody looked upset. We were greeted by Williams and his team, who had been on the hilltop two days or so, and looked like it had been longer.

I don't think Bacak liked the idea that Williams thought he was in charge. Williams briefed Bacak, and Bacak passed the word on to us. We would be sitting on that hill for at least two weeks while the brigade worked out in the valley below us. At least we didn't have to walk.

After two days on that hill, I wished we were back in the jungle. Over the next two weeks, I learned every bad habit everyone had. Limey and I got into a wrestling match over his chewing his gum. I won, but he kept chewing. The monsoon never let up, and at night we hunkered down in bunkers with mud-and-water floors, so I did most of my sleeping while sitting on my ruck. At night when the rain stopped, the jungle sounds would start up, sounding like a symphony, each insect, bird, and animal choreographed into a perfect concerto of music so rich it defies description. One small lizard had a call that sounded like a bird saying, "Fuck you! Fuck you!" I could hear the rain start in another location, and the closer it came to us, the louder it got. It would rain hard for hours, then suddenly just stop.

We made several patrols around the bottom of our hill but never saw anything except leeches. Small creatures resembling red worms, leeches quickly swelled to a much larger size by sucking our blood. It didn't matter what we did to protect ourselves, leeches found a way to our skin and, for the first couple of sucks, remain undetected. But I learned fast to sense their presence. It was amazing how fast they responded to body heat. If we'd been moving and we stopped, they would home in on us, inching along the ground like a Slinky toy undulating down a stairway, by extending themselves forward from tail to head, then repeating the process. Or they dropped onto us from the surrounding foliage. In water, we could test them by placing a foot into the edge of the water and watching them swim swiftly toward it. The only way to remove the leeches was to squirt them with insect repellent or burn them off with the end of a lit cigarette, but it left one with an open wound that was susceptible to jungle rot and other diseases. To treat the wounds, I went through a lot of antibiotic ointment, which seemed to help if used regularly and the wound was kept clean, which wasn't always possible. For that reason I carried many different items in my M-5 kit—IVs, suture sets, drugs, and bandages, and all arranged in the med bag according to my needs.

One thing we did that became a ritual was to cook. Each of us had his own secret recipe for preparing C rations and LRRP rations. I used to mix them both, taking the cheese and beef in spice sauce from the C rations, then mixing them with beef and rice along with lots of hot sauce. The worst thing about eating was having to go out into the rain to find a place to take a dump. Not only were the rain and the mud problems, but leeches were attracted to the exposed butt and to the hot excrement that was left smoking on the side of the hill. I would check my behind three times after taking a dump without finding a thing, but as soon as I got back to the bunker, I could feel the little suckers. Then I would have to search for the beasts again. Eventually, higher decided it was a waste of manpower and time for us to just sit on top of that hill, so they moved us to the firebase of the 1st Battalion, 327th Infantry. Looking for signs of people in the area, we were to work the valley below the firebase.

Artillery to the Rescue (As Usual)

A few days before we got there, Tiger Force had been dispatched to the base of the hill on which the 1/327th was entrenched. They were to recon the immediate area, looking for trails and any information on the enemy that would help in the defense of the firebase. They hadn't even reached the bottom of the hill before contact was made. The commanding officer didn't believe that the contact was real and told the team leader to bring back proof of the contact. A crazy Indian by the name of Sam Somora was a member of that Tiger Force team. When the team came back to the top of the hill, Sam was carrying two sandbags and gave them to the commander. The officer opened the bags up, and two severed enemy heads fell out. Visibly shaken, the commander went nuts, and Sam was shipped out on the next helicopter available. The same helicopter that picked up Sam sliced off the head of a soldier running to retrieve the mail from the helicopter. The guy didn't stay low enough to the ground as he approached the waiting helicopter.

The next day we were assigned to scout the area where Sam had made contact.

Life at the firebase was strange because every day, at the same time, a sniper would take shots at anything that moved. The first time the sniper fired, he wounded one of the artillery cannon cockers, but after that no one ever got hit again. Even so, we were sent to find the guy, who would shoot only when the rain had stopped in the early afternoon. It must have been his lunch hour, so he thought he would practice on the hill full of GIs. Anyway, hoping not to be detected, we left the hill during the rain. At the bottom of the firebase was heavy foliage, so once we reached the bottom, it was easy to move without being seen. Nearby, a small village sat in the middle of rice paddies, its tree line bordering the paddies. We knew approximately where the sniper was shooting from because it was about the only place a man could fire a weapon and not be detected. We moved to a location that would allow us to watch that area, but not so close that we could be seen or heard.

Like clockwork, the rains stopped, and from a rice paddy hobbled a tiny elderly man carrying a weapon bigger than he was. Without any concern for his being seen, he picked a spot on top of a small knoll and positioned himself so that he could fire at the firebase. He was shooting from more than five hundred meters, so his shooting the cannon cocker must have been one hell of a lucky shot. We watched him position himself, then fire the first round. He reloaded, but only one round. We watched him fire a couple more rounds, but it seemed that he didn't have any particular target in mind. He probably couldn't see that far. When he was finished, he got up and started slowly walking back to the rice paddy he'd come from. We picked that moment to expose ourselves. He heard our movement and turned away, dropping his weapon and starting to run, but Limey fired a burst over his head, and the old man fell to the ground. I couldn't waste the old guy and neither could anyone else on Bacak's team, so we captured the old guy and took him and his weapon back to the firebase—my first prisoner of war. We turned the old guy over to the 1st Battalion people, and that was the last time the firebase was sniped. For a while anyway.

That afternoon we did receive incoming rockets, one of which struck the artillery center. Charlie must have been mad because we took the old man. The direct hit wounded one soldier. So the artillery lowered all of their guns and fired into the tree line where the rockets had come from. Then gunships were called in, and they showered the tree line with minigun firepower and 40 mm cannon. When all was said and done, we were sent to check on the damage and see if any bodies could be found. We walked into the torn-up tree line under the watchful eye of the gunships hovering above us like mad hornets. There weren't any bodies to be found, but if someone had been in the area, the most we could have found would be blood trails, because an area of about one hundred meters long and a hundred meters wide had been leveled. I have to praise the artillery people who, in the middle of a rocket attack, lowered their guns to fire back at the enemy. They didn't stop firing until they were told to. Those guys were the bravest guys I've known. The sad thing was, under the rules then in effect they couldn't get the combat infantryman badge, and there wasn't a badge that commemorated that they had been under fire and performed their mission with great courage.

During the same rocket attack, I was in a corner of a bunker, trying to get as small as possible. I had flashbacks of Khe Sanh, and heard again the shouts of Marine artillerymen returning fire on the enemy. I can't really say enough good things about the bravery of artillery people.

After we returned and reported, we were given time to pack for another mission. We would be going in with a team led by Top Smith. Top and his team were inserted on the side of a hill that overlooked a narrow valley. We were inserted on the other side of the valley and farther down. Our mission was to watch the small valley for NVA movement. The valley was narrow and had a "village" of three or four hootches. In the center of the valley was a field of crops tended by three or four men. What was strange about the village was that there weren't any animals, children, or women. From my team's vantage point, we couldn't see much other than the small figures working in the field; Top Smith's team was close enough to distinguish faces, and they could see that black-clad figures were bringing packages and bundles from the village and putting them into the ground, in the middle of the crops. The Vietnamese would walk out and, before doing anything, look around as if they were afraid of being seen, then lift a trapdoor and deposit whatever they had into the hole. After a while, an empty-handed black-clad figure would walk to the same trapdoor, retrieve one of the bundles, then disappear into the jungle.

Top Smith decided to call artillery on those people because a line company was moving into the area, and it was making enough noise that the people in the fields could hear them as well as we could, and we were about three klicks away. Soon the tiny figures were running into the village, so Top Smith called in the big guns, and the village disappeared in smoke and fire. From where we were sitting, all we could see was explosions and people running. But we could feel the ground shake as the artillery rounds slammed into the terrain. We watched as the hootches were leveled and the crops in the field were blown away. After the artillery stopped, the line company swept through the area, and we watched as it checked the ruined hootches and the fields that held the trapdoors. They must have found a lot of supplies that the VC wouldn't be using anymore. But before we could find out for sure, we were told that we were to be extracted once the company was finished with the village.

Superspade

It had been close to forty days since we had come out in the field, and everybody was ready to go on stand-down. Lester "Superspade" Hite's team had thought up a plan to get out of the field: the oldest one in the books—capture a prisoner! They captured two prisoners and watched stupefied as the prisoners departed on a helicopter.

A few days later, Superspade's team observed a Caucasian walking with a platoon of thirty to forty Vietnamese. Lester lived up to his nickname; he was one of the most courageous people I ever had the privilege to meet. Superspade got close enough to see that the Caucasian was either a Russian Special Forces soldier or an East Bloc adviser. Once the people in the rear heard about the Caucasian, they wanted Superspade to take him prisoner. Superspade was all for snatching him, but the reality was that Superspade's team consisted of only twelve men, and the Caucasian was surrounded by forty VC who wouldn't want to lose him. But if it had been possible, Superspade would have done it.

The weather was very heavy rain, and the darkness of the night was crawling up on Superspade's team, so he decided to wait until morning to see what the VC might do. While watching the VC platoon disappear into a growth of vegetation, Superspade sent two men to locate an overnight spot. The two men found a suitable place that overlooked the area, and Superspade decided to spend the night there. About an hour after darkness, Superspade told everybody to pack up because he felt uncomfortable in that location. They moved about four hundred meters in the rain and darkness before they found a place Lester was comfortable with. Before they had departed the previous area, Rey Martinez and a couple of the other Foul Dudes had put out booby traps.

Hite's team had no more than sat back on their rucks when they heard the booby traps explode, followed by a one-sided firefight. Superspade had saved the day; if he hadn't moved from that area, all their names would probably have ended up on the war memorial in Washington. His intuition was just one of the reasons he was called Superspade.

Booby Traps

Superspade and his team joined my team on top of a hill from which we were to observe a junction that 1st Brigade line companies were sweeping toward. Staff Sergeant Weems was the man in charge, because he had the most experience. Our mission was to locate the enemy and call in artillery on his position. The Marines had occupied the hill before us and had left the area around our perimeter covered with concertina wire and multiple booby traps. Weems had a .50-caliber machine gun brought in, which we used for sniping and target spotting. The weapon had a range of over a mile, and we could adjust our aim by watching the tracers fly toward where we were aiming. We spent a lot of time digging foxholes and preparing our defenses.

Close to our hill was a hilltop firebase that sat in the middle of the valley below us. Anything and anybody going through the valley had to go around or over that hill. Early in the predawn morning, we were awakened to the sounds of the firebase in the valley being attacked. It looked like the Fourth of July once again. As we were to learn later, the firebase had been attacked by a large VC battalion. The attack lasted until Puff the Magic Dragon* appeared on the scene. Puff caused the attackers to make a swift departure. But my fear was that we would be next on the NVA hit parade. I didn't sleep at all that night, nor did anyone else. Every sound I heard, I thought it

---

*The AC-47 Dragon ship, a World War II–era, twin-engine cargo and transport aircraft refitted with three 7.62 mm Gatling guns. With a cyclic rate of fire of 6,000 rounds per minute, Puff (a.k.a. Spooky) was a powerful and frightening ground-attack weapon system.

was the enemy. Finally daylight appeared, and at least we could see the perimeter. As daylight overcame the darkness, F-4 Phantoms arrived and bombed areas all around the firebase and our location.

The crew of a helicopter bringing us supplies told us they had spotted some "indigenous personnel" checking out our perimeter. Weems took a team to check out the report but didn't get far because of all the Marine booby traps they encountered as they went; we didn't know where the Marines had put all the traps.

After a couple of days, Top Smith joined us and took a team into the valley, with Rey Martinez walking point. We patrolled to where three valleys came together. We ran across trails that had been used often by a lot of people carrying heavy equipment, and we decided to parallel the trail that lay at the base of our hill. After going about half a klick, we took a burst of AK fire. I thought that for sure someone had gotten hit, and the first person to come to mind was Rey. But we had taken only that one burst, and then nothing. Top Smith called for me to come forward because Melton had been hit. He had been lucky, because the round must have hit a rib and been deflected down, exiting his hip and blowing out a huge hole in the process. Top called in a Dust Off (medevac) and gunships. The Dust Off was shot at as it took off with Melton.

Top Smith decided we were too small a unit to be patrolling in that area; he felt that if we continued, we would be ambushed. If the enemy had balls enough to fire on a Dust Off in the presence of a gunship, we had no business being there. We distributed all of Melton's equipment and his radio and moved back to the top of our hill, setting out more booby traps as we went. As soon as we got to the top of the hill, God opened the faucet, and the rain came down in bucketfuls.

When we got to the top of the hill, Ernie Winston had to take a dump. Of course, in the blinding rain and what with all the Marine booby traps and our own, he tripped a booby trap and flew through the air better than Air Jordan, head over heels, followed by a stream of his own excrement. He wasn't seriously hurt, but he smelled very bad for the next couple of days.

A couple of days later at the same junction we had previously attempted to reach, an infantry company came in contact with a dug-in, waiting enemy. Even from our vantage point, it was difficult to see what was going on because of the fog after the morning's rain. But we could certainly hear all the firing. Our gunships couldn't do anything because they couldn't see. We were monitoring the frequency the infantry company was on, and soon they had casualties and were requesting a Dust Off. As the fog lifted, the gunships and the Dust Off were moving in, but as the Dust Off was coming in for a landing, it was shot out of the sky. We saw the tracer rounds hitting the aircraft and causing it to crash. Of two gunships, one was shot down, and the other flew out of the area. Once again the infantry company was alone. Finally, pairs of F-4 Phantoms arrived and started dropping devastation on the enemy below. As soon as two jets dropped their load, they were followed by two more. The angle of their attack on the target brought them directly over our hilltop. They were so close we could clearly see the pilot's helmet. The release point of their bombs was directly in front of us, and we could see the retarding fins on the bomb popping open. The noise of the aircraft was more deafening than that of the bombs they were dropping. As the bombs struck the ground and exploded, waves of energy and force radiated outward from the detonation point. To this day, I am thankful for our having air superiority in Vietnam.

One lone enemy machine gunner was firing at the F-4s as they dropped their deadly arsenal. Through it all, the lone enemy gunner continued to fire. We almost had a cheering section for this guy. He was really brave to withstand all the firepower that was being thrown his way. Then one of the jets flying over our heads was hit and left with a trail of smoke behind him. The clouds were moving back in and the jets had just a small hole through them to enter and drop their load. Finally, one of the jets was able to "suppress" the enemy machine gun, and a Dust Off was able to get the infantry wounded out. The whole show had been a remarkable display of skill and bravery by the pilots and of courage by the enemy.

A couple of days later, while we were still in the field, the skies became black and a warning was sent to us to be prepared for a big blow. We could see the black clouds coming our way, with lightning flashing and striking the ground. Once the black shroud was over us, the jungle became calm; then all at once the wind picked up with a force such as I had never seen before. Lightning was striking all over the top of our hill, and the wind seemed to be trying to blow us off it. The wind was strong enough to pick up the .50-caliber machine gun, which was on a tripod with sandbags anchoring it, and blow it over the hill. Lightning strikes were so frequent, they lit up the dark sky. The storm went on for hours as we hugged the bottom of our foxholes while praying not to be hit by lightning. Just prior to the storm's full force hitting us, we received a radio transmission informing us that an enemy force had been spotted at the base of our hill. But given the conditions, no one even thought about the enemy because we were so preoccupied with surviving the storm. It would have been interesting to see those little guys try walking up the hill in that wind. If the enemy *had* been able to get to the top, we would have been eliminated; we didn't have radio contact with anyone.

During the storm, one of our men fell asleep on his air mattress and floated downhill, never waking up until he hit the wire. He lost the air mattress, which had been the envy of everybody in 1st Brigade LRRPs. As far as we knew, it was the only air mattress in LRRPs anywhere.

Some of our brother LRRPs had to go to the forward rear

area (Chu Lai) to take care of administrative things, and I watched as they lifted off with smiles on their faces. I had wanted to go too, but one of the medics had to stay behind. I was picturing them in the rear, drinking cold beer, when suddenly ground fire from the base of our hill started hitting their helicopter. The helicopter headed down the valley like a wounded bird, spitting black smoke from its exhaust. But before it could hit the ground, the pilot managed to get control, and the aircraft gained altitude. We found out later that they had made it to a camp on the outskirts of Chu Lai. Jaybird Magill had been aboard, and he said later that everybody on the helicopter had gotten religion, and some of them had had to change their pants when they got to Chu Lai! But later Derby Jones, who had also been on the helicopter, told us about how brave everyone had been while the ship was going down. We laughed so hard, I'm sure the enemy heard us.

A couple of days later, we were helicoptered off that hill and set down on a steep hilltop where Marine S.Sgt. Jimmie Howard had earned the Medal of Honor. The top of the hill was narrow, and the Marines had built bunkers that, by the time we got there, were falling apart. We hadn't been on top of the hill for more than an hour when we received our first incoming. The mortar rounds hit the side of the hill but never landed on the narrow strip we occupied. That night it rained so hard the decaying bunkers we were huddled in filled with water and forced us to sit on our rucks outside the bunker until daybreak. The next night we were mortared again, but that time we called in artillery on the spot where we thought the incoming was coming from. When morning came, so did the sun, and we could finally dry our things, which had been wet since we first went to the bush. A couple of hours later, we were extracted back to Chu Lai. Naturally, we all thought we were being choppered onto another hill.

When we got back to our rear area, Murphy, our truck driver, had cold beer and steaks ready for us. It was a most memorable day. With full stomachs, and a little drunk, we were taken to the shower point to scrub off all those days of sweat, shit, and leeches, not to mention the stench. When we got back to our hootches, we were told we would be going out again in the morning, so we resupplied our rucks and replenished our ammo and decided to make the most of our one day of rest and recuperation. We went into town and found a beach house that a couple of Marines had mentioned to us. We figured out later that the Marines wanted us to get our asses kicked, because the little beach house was operated by the White Horse Division; that is, it was a Korean facility. When we walked in, quite a few Koreans were drinking, and all of them were watching us. We didn't know at the time that we were only the second group of Americans to enter the establishment; the first group never got a drink.

Lurps not being sensitive types, we found an empty table and sat down. The waitresses wouldn't come to our table, so I went up to the bar to order our drinks. Rey followed me to help carry the beer to our table. Just as I finished paying for the beer, a short, stout Korean approached me from behind and to my left. I could see him out of the corner of my eye. I turned toward that hero, who, at the same time, took a karate stance and, with a loud yell, smashed a newly opened beer can sitting on the bartop, spraying me and everybody else close to me. Well, that startled me to the point that I hit the stupid guy with every ounce of power I could put into the punch. I hit him so hard that he flew into the arms of his buddies, who had gathered around for the show. Then all of the other Lurps came to my rescue. The Korean I had hit got up, shook his head to clear it, looked me in the eye, and smiled. I thought, Oh shit! and just knew we were going to war with the Koreans. As it turned out, the ROK I'd hit was just out of the field like us. The Korean had thought we were air force pukes, but when we told him we were bush rats, we couldn't buy a beer for the rest of the night.

Of course, it was difficult to communicate, because none of

The Foul Dudes in 1967, waiting for helicopters. Facing the camera are Rey Martinez (left) and "Brother" Weems. (Author's collection)

The author at Chu Lai, where he was one of the Foul Dudes, October 1967. (Boss Weisberger collection)

Major Minter, June 1969. (Author's collection)

The author at Da Lat, 197(
(Author's collection)

A display of captured weapons at Da Lat, September 1971. (Author's collection)

Author in Da Lat with AK squad following a mission. (Author's collection)

Author with Captain Phong in Don Duong during a mission in 1970. (Author's collection)

them spoke English and none of us spoke Korean. As the night went on, we used hand signals to talk. Soon we were singing songs and toasting each other. The drunker we got, the more beer cans we smashed.

It was late at night when we finally headed back, but we were stopped by a Marine shore patrol accompanied by a Marine officer, who started to give us problems about where we had been and the reason we were out so late. Pizza Joe Remiro started yelling at the MPs, saying something like, "Let's kill them." They left us alone.

The next day, after just one day out of the field, we were sent to support the 1/327th Infantry firebase. It goes without saying that as soon as we landed on the firebase, it started to rain. We were to provide security for the battalion firebase at night and patrol during the day.

Soon after arriving on the firebase, Top Smith took a team out looking for a sniper who had been potshotting the artillerymen. Ernie "Dirty Ernie" Winston was walking point. Dirty Ernie was a colorful character. He had come over with the brigade in 1965. He had been trained as an engineer and spent a lot of line company time. He was always modifying and carrying "exotic weapons." For example, he had modified an M-14 by chopping the barrel and the stock. Every time he fired that thing, it threw a flame out ten feet in front of him and was so loud it would have blown out the eardrums of anyone alongside him. Really impressive! He had also modified a twelve-gauge shotgun in the same manner. One time in Duc Pho, we had been out on an operation, and we had captured some prisoners. We were taking small-arms fire from a tree line adjacent to a hootch complex. Dirty Ernie was carrying that shotgun in a homemade scabbard on his web belt. Already firing his M-14 from a kneeling position, Dirty Ernie decided he wanted to bring his shotgun into play. Pulling his shotgun out, Dirty Ernie torched one off. The shotgun's barrel peeled back damn near to the chamber! It numbed his left hand clear up to his elbow, and the pellets from the round sprayed into the arm of a woman prisoner Dirty Ernie had been guarding. We surmised later that while Dirty Ernie was kneeling, the barrel, poking out the bottom of its scabbard, had rammed into the mud, plugging it.

After having checked the area and finding nothing, Top stopped the patrol to take a break just prior to ascending the hill on which the firebase was located. Dirty Ernie had continued a little way up the hill and was sitting down, leaning against his rucksack, looking back downhill from where he had come. A sniper hidden in a wooded draw took a shot at him, hitting him in the knee. Dirty Ernie was fortunate, because if his leg hadn't been bent at the knee he would have been hit in the chest. It was Winston's tenth Purple Heart. He was medevacked out of the field but spent just two days at the hospital. He was back before Top's team came out of the field, but Lieutenant McIsaac ordered him back to the hospital. Ernie went, and we never saw him again. He was later killed in action while working with Tiger Force in the A Shau Valley.

After Top and his team returned, we spent many days pulling guard and filling sandbags. One day Rey went to the TOC (tactical operations center) on the firebase for a team leaders' meeting and also to pick up "sundries" for us, including beer. On his way back, we got mortared, and Rey came flying into our bunker with a look of extreme relief that he had made it back without getting hit. The only problem we had was that each beer exploded when we tried to open it!

The VC had made a direct hit on the fire direction center, causing some dead and wounded. Again, the artillery guys were out in the open, returning fire against the unseen enemy. Rey said that we would be used as a blocking force for one of the rifle companies and that we were going to be airlifted in without rucks. I liked that idea because I could carry more ammo.

About this time, one of the men on George Sullens's team

came to me and said that Sully had bad jungle rot on his feet. I talked Sully into letting me look them over. I saw that he had jungle rot not only on his feet but all over his body, so I put him on profile and gave him medication. I also told Sully that he wouldn't be going to the field until the jungle rot was better. But as soon as he found out about the blocking mission, he went to Rey Martinez and complained about my putting him on profile. Rey interceded on Sully's behalf by going over to talk to Top Smith and Lieutenant McIsaac. Rey then came over and talked to me, and I told him about the severity of Sully's jungle rot and how humping in the bush would only make his condition worse. Rey explained that the ell tee said Sullens could go and that we would be in a fixed position, waiting for the enemy to come to us.

It was 1 November 1967 and a beautiful, sunny day. After all of the rainy days, the sun was a welcome sight. But while we loaded onto our waiting helicopters, Pizza Joe Remiro and John Chadwick were being transferred to Tiger Force. We lost a lot of good people at that time.

As we flew to our insertion point, we dangled our feet outside the helicopter, and I watched as the earth moved so fast below me that I couldn't focus on any one thing. Flowing below me, the landscape looked like a sea of green with just an occasional patch of blue supplied by rivers and streams. The area was predominantly paddies, with islands of vegetation among them. Finally, our landing zone came into sight, a dry rice paddy nearly hidden by the trees that surrounded it. We landed without anyone shooting at us, moved quickly, and reconned the immediate area. Then we came to rice paddies that were still being farmed. They were flooded with water, and little sprouts of rice were sticking above the surface. We lay down facing south, with rice paddies to our front, using the paddy dikes as a shield from potential enemy fire. On the far side of the rice paddies was a large island of vegetation that bent south, and around the bend of the island was a good-size village. Directly across the paddies from us, about 150 meters distant, were some hootches in the tree line that bordered the rice paddies. Most of the hootches were built of palm, but there were a couple of permanent buildings made of cinder blocks.

We soon received word by radio that the push had started and the infantry company was moving in our direction. In the distance we saw people running from the direction of the infantry company's advance. They were quite a way out when we were told to open fire, and we hit several of the running bodies. Then all of the runners disappeared, and for a moment I thought our job was over. About ten minutes later, another group started to run across the rice paddies, this time closer and with visible weapons, but pushing civilians in front of them. But they were running from the village, right to left and away from us. We were told to open fire again. We still had not received any enemy fire. Once we stopped firing, the people in the rear (of course) told us to check out the area we had just fired up. None of us wanted to walk across that open rice field, and we thought the order stupid, but Lieutenant McIsaac said he had been given an order. Anger welled up in me. We would be in the open, and we had just fired up a large group of people. Exposing ourselves in the open would give them the perfect opportunity to pay us back.

The order of march was Rey Martinez's team, with Beaver on point, followed by Rey, then Sullens, Gunther Bengston, and Doc Kraft. McKinnon's team would trail Rey's team. Walking through the water-filled paddies, occasionally using the dikes to stay out of the water when the dikes ran in the direction of movement, Rey's team had gotten about halfway across the paddies when we suddenly received massive enemy fire from the hootches directly across the paddies from us. My team was providing cover for the teams moving out. We fired everything we had at the village. I saw Rey, Sullens, and Bengston fall when the enemy opened up. I thought they were all hit.

As we returned fire, Doc Kraft ran to the aid of George Sullens. It turned out that Rey hadn't been hit, and he was firing at the hootches directly opposite where he had gone down. The enemy was doing a good job of keeping his shots low to the ground, so the only way to move was to low crawl. Boss Weisberger and I ran out and picked up Bengston, who was hit in the neck and bleeding profusely. We pulled Bengston back to our dry, flat land and proceeded to give him a serum albumin IV. While Weisberger, under my instruction, inserted the IV, I inserted a trach tube in Bengston's neck to keep the airway open. Thank God, no major arteries had been hit.

While Boss and I were working on Bengston, Doc Kraft and Rey had been working on Sully out in the open paddy and under fire. Sullens died. A burst of rounds had hit him in the chest, and he was probably dead before he hit the ground. Bengston would be okay with the trach in his throat. The firing from both directions was still intense. It was difficult to work on Bengston because of the rounds hitting all around us. It was a miracle that no one else got hit. While all of that was going on, anger continued to build up in me. Why would we walk across an open field, exposing ourselves to anyone who wanted to kill us? In the past we always had cover or used well-known techniques to minimize the possibility of being exposed to enemy fire. I blamed the ell tee, and in the heat of the moment I yelled at him, "Whose fucking idea was this bullshit?" Later Lieutenant McIsaac pulled me aside and told me higher had ordered our move across the paddies. I understood that meant we had to do it, but that didn't make me feel any better, nor did it make the order intelligent. Idiocy from above is still idiocy. One dead and one wounded for nothing.

The firing was still intense when we called for a Dust Off. Greek Dokos, Dirk Sasso, and Rey had retrieved Sully's body from the exposed wet paddy and eventually loaded him into the Dust Off. Boss Weisberger and I loaded Bengston into the Dust Off. The crew chief of the Dust Off helped us load our men as enemy rounds struck the aircraft repeatedly. The pilot was screaming at us to hurry as bullets riddled his helicopter. We literally threw our people on the chopper as it was lifting off. The door gunner almost got left behind, and his .45 pistol fell to the ground from his holster.

With all the firepower coming from the village, there must have been a large force in it. We couldn't lift our heads more than six inches above the ground. I still can't believe none of us got hit while carrying our men to the chopper. Finally gunships arrived, and the incoming fire came to a halt. I was lying with my head below the dike, watching Teddy Bear making coffee. I couldn't believe it; no matter what transpired, there was Teddy Bear drinking coffee with a smile on his face. I couldn't help but laugh, and the laughter drained away a lot of my frustration over the day's events. After the gunships finished their mission, we extracted and flew over the village and the area from which we had received fire. We had made the enemy pay for the loss of our friends; there must have been twenty bodies lying in the open, looking very dead.

We were flown back to the firebase to continue to pull security. We had no sooner gotten off the choppers than a sniper started taking potshots at us. When he was finished, mortars started pounding the firebase. That evening the rain returned. We all sat around telling stories about Sully and how we missed him. Sully was a guitar-playing, country-singing cowboy. He was good enough that he could have made a living at it as a civilian. He liked to write songs that described our daily lives, inserting our names where it always seemed to sound just right. The two of us had spent many hours entertaining the platoon. It was a long, sad night, one that returns to me even today.

A week later, we went on a mission to observe a village that was suspected of being used by the enemy as a base area. We were to find out if that was a fact or just a rumor. My team was sent to watch the village. Lieutenant McIsaac would accompany our team. I still harbored mixed feelings about him from when Sully had gotten killed. We were inserted about two klicks from the village and made our way to a tree line from which we could watch a road that led into and through the village. The road had rice paddies along both sides, and a couple of people were working in them. We were in the only area a person could hide in and reasonably expect not to be seen; all the area around the village was open. We watched all night and for a couple of hours the next morning before we decided to move into the village.

As soon as we left the tree line, shots were fired at us from a single-shot weapon. The two people working in the fields started to run, and we opened up, shooting at the village from where we had received the incoming. One of our guys had shot both of the people working in the fields, and the one farthest from me started screaming. We had stopped receiving incoming, and McIsaac wanted to check the people in the rice paddies. McIsaac and Boss Weisberger went to the Vietnamese who was screaming, and Limey and I scrambled to the person closest to us, an old woman who didn't have a weapon. She was shot in the leg, and was lying there in fear and not saying anything. I felt really bad, and I gave her a shot of morphine, bandaged her wound, and told her in Vietnamese that I was sorry.

Then I heard a shot from where McIsaac and Boss were standing by the wounded Vietnamese. One of them had shot the man, killing him. Boss later related that he felt the man had been yelling for help from his friends. Boss several times asked the man in Vietnamese to be quiet, but that caused him only to yell louder. They'd seen movement from the direction of the hootches and received incoming rounds.

<h1 style="text-align:center">★
CHAPTER 9</h1>

November 1967

Operation Wheeler was over, and our platoon was sent back to Phan Rang by way of a navy LST. It was not a fun cruise; it seemed that almost everyone on this navy vessel was drinking, but the officer in charge wouldn't let the Lurps indulge. So we played poker all the way to Phan Rang. I lost my ass. Bacak won and decided to drink even though we were told not to. So the captain jumped all over Top about Bacak, and Top got on Bacak, putting him on restriction for two weeks after we returned to Phan Rang.

On the "cruise" down the coast toward Phan Rang, that LST got pretty small. An entire infantry battalion was on the ship along with all the trucks and equipment. There was a mast with a crow's nest on top. We climbed up there at night and smoked, relatively safe from discovery. The view was great, and the roll of the ship could really be felt from up high.

A somewhat humorous incident occurred on our cruise. One of the navy crewmen had a pet monkey. We were all playing with it one day, and it got on Harvey "The Beaver" Bieber's head. Beaver had a pack of marijuana cigarettes in his shirt pocket that had been put together by the Vietnamese to resemble a pack of American cigarettes. Perched on Beaver's head, the monkey reached into his shirt pocket and started taking those marijuana cigarettes and eating them. We

150

all thought it was really funny because of the expressions on Beaver's face and the monkey's. That went on for quite some time when suddenly the monkey went rigid, let out an awful screech, and fell off Beaver's head, stone dead. We all felt really bad for the monkey, and when we told the navy crewman what happened, he was pissed. He carried on about us being callous, inconsiderate, and having killed his monkey. We ended up having to compensate for the monkey's death by giving him some money and, I believe, some Lurp rations.

When we arrived in Phan Rang, the tide was out, and it was too shallow to off-load our equipment, so we had to wait. It was hot, so we used the LST as a diving board and took a dip in the sea. Top got raked over the coals again because we went swimming. That poor guy took a lot of shit over our behavior. The navy kicked us off the ship, which was what all of us really wanted anyway.

As soon as we returned to Phan Rang, everything started to change in the unit. Rey and a couple of the other original Foul Dudes would be leaving on extension leave, and we lost Ell Tee McIsaac. Our new commander was named Lieutenant Kinane, and we were fortunate in that he turned out to be a good officer. But the "personnel turbulence" was a terrible waste: it took a long time to find an officer who would take care of the unit; then the army, in all its wisdom, transferred him somewhere else. McIsaac wanted to stay with us, and a lot of guys had extended to maintain the team's integrity, but it was no use. Even the unit designation was to change in order to reflect the whole 101st Division, which was joining the 1st Brigade. We would be leaving in a few days for Phan Thiet.

Before we left Phan Rang, I had to find Moon and let her know where I was going. But first I needed some courage, so Weems, one of the Lurps, took me to an opium den. He said that would make my head right to say good-bye. The opium den was a hospital for addicts and a getaway for GIs. Paradise is the stuff of dreams, and in that smoke-filled room, dreams were created to escape the reality of war.

We entered the room, joining several older Asians who were lounging around, either waiting to dream or already in another world. After waiting for those in front of us to go through all the customs and formalities that were required before we could partake in that den, it was my turn to smoke from the pipe of escape. I bowed to the old, thin man who would be my pathfinder and guide me through my first experience with that wonder drug.

I lay down, resting my head on a small wooden block used as a pillow, watching with fascination how the old man prepared my dream. From an ancient tin cigarette can, the old man produced a small piece of a black, hard substance and pinched a piece the size of a pencil eraser from it. With the skill of a diamond cutter, he placed the small piece of opium on the end of an instrument that resembled a probe. On the table between me and the old man were a long bamboo pipe, a lit candle, a smooth rock, and a water glass turned upside down. The old man took the probe with the opium on the end of it and held the opium over the candle. He carefully turned the probe so as not to burn one side too much. As the opium became hot, it swelled, and the old man took it from the fire and shaped the glob on the smooth rock. After the opium was shaped to the old man's satisfaction, he pushed the opium into the pipe. Then he put the glass over the candle, handed me the end of the pipe I would be smoking from, and put the end that held the opium over the glass. I was told to slowly draw from the pipe in one long inhalation, trying to suck into my lungs every molecule of smoke to ensure that I received the full benefit of the narcotic. After five pipefuls, I withdrew to allow the drug to send me on my dream. Slowly all hostility left my mind, and a peaceful feeling of total euphoria overcame me. All fears disappeared and were replaced by a feeling of compassion and a sense of tranquillity.

We left the opium den with grins on our faces and a sense of a mission accomplished. We then moved to my bar. After I told Moon that I was leaving the neighborhood in the next few days, she asked me to stay the night. I agreed but first I had to go with the old Foul Dudes to visit each bar for a drink and to say farewell to all the girls we had known. Of course, every bar on the strip was busy; the whole brigade must have been partying that day, and guys were standing in line to make sure they got laid before heading back to the bush. That ritual certainly never bothered me; for some guys, it would be their last intimate moment with a woman.

The first place we stopped for a drink, we immediately sensed something was wrong with the way the people in the bar were acting. Everybody in the bar was watching something going on in one of the rooms where the girls usually provided sex for the boys, but not with everybody looking on. Curiosity got the best of me, and I went to see what was going on. One of the GIs was holding a knife to the throat of a girl, and another GI was having sex with her. She was terrified and clearly not a willing participant. I went back and got Rey so he could also see what was happening. That scene bothered Rey and me, but everybody else in the bar was either participating or watching, and no one was helping the girl. When the GI finished, he took the knife, and the next guy got on the girl. Another example of the ugly American.

Rey and I decided to end the party. With a couple of other Lurps covering our backs, I took the guy with the knife, and Rey took the guy on the girl. They were surprised and didn't struggle much. Of course, I had hit the knife wielder with a full bottle of beer, so he just crumpled to the floor. At that, the girl jumped up off the bed and pounced on top of the other guy. If she'd had a knife, she certainly would have killed him. I let her beat on him a while until the military police arrived and pulled the girl off. I told the MP the GI had raped her and a couple of the other guys had, too. By that time, the bar had cleared and only the Lurps remained. I suggested to the MP that they make the guy pay for all the men he had allowed to rape her. I took the guy's wallet and counted his money. The cheap son of a bitch had a couple hundred dollars, but he had to rape that girl. The asshole was an REMF to boot! I gave the money to the girl and the bar owner and left everyone happy. I told the MP that I would be glad to bear witness to the guy's action that day. They took my name and unit, but that was the last I ever heard about the incident. They probably took him to his unit and let him go. Too much paperwork.

After a few more beers, we decided to return to Moon's bar and smoke a joint. The safest place was on the roof of the bar. The day's activity had brought us down again, and all we wanted to do was be mellow. It was a way to bond with men who would be my friends for the rest of my life. After a few tokes of the joint we were smoking, when we were at the right mental level, we returned to the bar to enjoy ourselves.

After only a couple of drinks, we were all dancing together. I did a spin, with a beer bottle in my hand, and caught Doc Kraft in the mouth, and he began bleeding like a stuck pig. That marked the end of the drinking, and we staggered back to the homestead to crash. As soon as we got there, I took out my aid bag and got my suture set. I sewed up Kraft's lip and passed out.

The next morning I got up with a hangover and faced the sight of Kraft's lip. I had put the stitches in fairly well, but I finished the procedure with a huge bow. Fortunately it takes only a couple of days for lips to heal. When I removed the sutures from his lip, it had healed without a noticeable scar. Even so, I'm sure Doc Kraft will remember our dance for a long time. I'm still amazed how drunk we were and how easy it was for us to come and go without being stopped by security. On several occasions when we were restricted to our areas and not allowed to go into town, we slipped through the perimeter and partied the night away, then slipped back through the fences the next morning at first light without being detected. If we could do it drunk, that shows how easy infiltration was for the VC.

The next day we were flown to Phan Thiet to recon for the brigade. Just then was when I decided it was time to find a new home and to take my extension leave. My wish was granted, and after only one week in Phan Thiet, I received orders to fly back to the World (USA).

Before I left for the States, the whole 101st Airborne Division in all its glory arrived in our new base camp in Bien Hoa. Of course, there had to be a ceremony. Division wanted soldiers new and old to the conflict to stand in review for our new Napoleon, Major General Barsanti. So I had to stand in formation and watch the short man act like Patton and give a recently arrived soldier a Bronze Star. Of course, the reason the man was getting the medal was infuriating. He was being awarded it because the general asked him why he was in Vietnam and the soldier replied he was in Vietnam to kill Communists! When I thought of all the men who had given their lives and received only a Purple Heart, I lost respect for the man giving the award away and also lost respect for the value of the medal. Hell, I had been in Vietnam for over two tours and hadn't received even a Good Conduct ribbon. Come to think of it, my conduct might have had something to do with that.

My flight was out of Camp Alpha, in Saigon, a place run like a basic-training unit. We had formations three to four times a day, and when we received our flight papers, we were inspected by an NCO for proper haircut and proper uniform. We flew on civilian airlines but couldn't wear civilian clothes. Except, of course, for the officers, who could wear whatever they wanted. I complied with the NCOs' requests, thinking First Sergeant Patches was probably the one who made the rules at Camp Alpha. Another rule was that no one was allowed to drink before we got onto the aircraft, so they said. I had a few in town before I reported to Camp Alpha for formation.

My flight back to the USA. took me through Alaska. I couldn't see much because it was dark at two o'clock in the afternoon. As everyone off-loaded the aircraft, we had to stand in line to be strip-searched for drugs and whatever else we might be smuggling back to the USA. They even checked our anuses. I don't know how many people were caught with contraband, but everybody who got off the plane got back on after the search.

We finally arrived at Tacoma, Washington, where, as in Vietnam, it was raining. Once again, all enlisted men had to first be inspected by the in-processing cadre at Washington before we could kiss civilian soil. I went through more stress in- and out-processing than during the war. But, good soldier that I was, I complied with all the standards and finally was freed. I then went to the civilian airport and booked a flight home, to Culver, Indiana. I went to the first pub I could find in the airport. The first thing I noticed was all the military police walking around, not to mention all the strange-looking people (Hare Krishnas) hanging out in the airports and passing out books. If the MPs hadn't been around, I might have eliminated a few of those people.

The flight took three hours, and I landed in Chicago, then caught a flight to South Bend, Indiana. Once in South Bend, I called my dad and almost gave him a heart attack; my family didn't know I was coming home.

I waited two hours in the airport lounge before my dad arrived; by that time I was becoming intoxicated, and it showed. My dad being the old soldier he was, and more than happy to see me, joined me for a couple more. An hour passed before he finally got me out of the bar. Along with a big spread of food, everybody was at home waiting to see me. I had forgotten how good a cook my mother was. I was greeted by my little brother, Michael, and little sister, Vicky; my older sister was married and was living in Chicago. The night went fast because I was falling asleep from intoxication and fatigue.

The next day I went shopping in town. I didn't own any civilian clothes worth looking at. Besides, it was winter, and the only civilian things I owned were made for warm weather. My mother was getting her hair done while I tore through the only clothing store in town. I bought everything from shirts to shoes, and I probably spent several hundred dollars. Thirty years ago that was a lot of money. That night, looking like a yuppie, I went into town to see if I could find someone to talk to. Well, the night was a waste.

Because I thought my eyesight might be getting bad, I decided to have my eyes checked and made an appointment with an eye doctor, a local veteran my father recommended. After the examination, the doctor asked how long I would be in town and invited me to go with him on his boat. That afternoon, carrying a case of beer for emergency supplies in case of an unexpected drought, we hit the lake and water-skied and drank until I was blind. But as we left the boat to return home, the doctor tried to put the make on me. I spent the rest of my time at home with my family and learned to appreciate them more, especially my mother. I tried calling Lana to let her know I was in the USA but couldn't get in touch with her.

Soon it was time to return to Vietnam. The trip back to Nam was filled with nightmares, but I couldn't wait to get back to where the women liked me. I also reviewed the options for what I was going to do when I got back to my unit. The boys would be disappointed about my low-key trip home, so I decided not to tell them.

Oddly enough, departure to Vietnam didn't require clean haircuts or strip searches. Before I knew it, I was back in Bien Hoa. By the time I got back, 1st Brigade LRRPs were in Song Be near the Cambodian border and were about to be disbanded. Some of the Lurps had been given the option of going to the newly formed division "LRP" Company (F Co., 58th

Infantry) for long-range patrol. The recruiting was more liberal, or so I thought: a man who'd been a cook when I left had become a Lurp. I didn't recognize anyone except Rey and a couple of the other Foul Dudes who were left from the old days. Even Top Smith had left. I was ready to find a new home for the time I had left in Vietnam.

Fortunately, the P-training first sergeant wanted me in the same job I'd had before I had joined the LRRPs. The day after I returned from leave, I reenlisted for duty in Germany. I would have to serve out my extension before receiving orders to Germany. Working at the replacement company made it possible to go into town as much as I wanted. So as soon as I had the chance, I went to Phan Rang to find Moon and see if she wanted to open a place at our new location. But the strip was a ghost town by then, and I learned that my bar had been destroyed by a riot. I lost everything, including Moon.

I reported to my new job with P training at the rear base for the 101st Airborne Division, at Bien Hoa. It served the same purpose that P training had for brigade. I ran the medical dispensary for the training company. Rey had stayed with the 1st Brigade Lurps, and when they were disbanded at Song Be in early February, he went to division Lurps. F Company's area was right down the road from our area, and it happened that they were passing through on their way north, to Phu Bai. We had a minireunion right there at Bien Hoa.

Brother Weems, Superspade Hite, Rey, a friend of his named Victor Cisneros, Teddy Bear Gaskell, and several other Lurps and I decided to do some rappelling one evening. The 101st had recently taken over the 173d Airborne's base camp at Bien Hoa, where there was a rappelling tower for training. So one evening we went to the rappelling tower, climbed to the top, and smoked several bowls of good dew. After catching a buzz, I decided I would go on the ropes first. Rey and Weems had rigged a double-strand rappel, but I decided I wanted a single strand and to "smoke it" down. So, with a

Mary Jane brain arrest, I did something really dumb by untying the knot for the double strand but not retying the single strand to the anchor bar. Nobody noticed what I had done, and the ropes were there and looked ready to go, so I started leaning back to form a good L position.

Surprise, surprise! I fell thirty-five feet to the ground with a thud. Weems had tried to stop me from falling by grabbing the rope, but I was too heavy, and he tore up his hands. Rey said that I had the presence of mind to get my body back to the wall of the platform, leaving fingernail marks all the way down the wall.

Thinking I was dead, everybody ran down the tower. Rey walked over to me, and all he could say was "*Wow!* Some fall, dude." I thought I had broken my hip, but in fact only sprained both my ankles. Weems was pissed because he had to come up with an excuse for what had happened. We decided to tell the people in charge that we were practicing our rappelling when the rope broke. Weems's hands were badly rope-burned, but he never showed them to anyone but me. With lots of ointment and care, his hands healed in no time.

That was the last time I smoked and rappelled. It took about two weeks for my ankles to heal to where I could carry a ruck.

CHAPTER 10

June 1968

It had been about six months since the Foul Dudes had gone north with division Lurps. Ernie Winston had been killed with Tiger Force, Teddy Bear Gaskell had been shot through the ass, and Jaybird Magill had been with him. Doc Kraft and several other Lurps had been busted in rank and sent to line companies by the chickenshit headquarters hierarchy in division Lurps. And Rey had been railroaded out of division Lurps with less than three weeks left in country. Of all places, he got assigned right with my company. His job was to greet cherries (new guys in country) arriving in Vietnam to serve with the 101st. He picked them up at the airport and "cadred" them through P training until they left for their combat units. Life in the rear was great, and we had become a bunch of REMFs.

A couple of days after Rey got to the training area, we all went to the NCO club to watch the first round-eyed women any of us had seen in a long time. Derby Jones was coming through on his way home on extension leave, and we wanted to celebrate with him. With Derby was Joe Hooper, a friend of his who was going back to the USA to receive the Medal of Honor. We were all sitting at a large table, Derby, Joe Hooper, Victor Cisneros, Tom Riley, a friend of Rey's from division Lurps who was killed in action a few days later, and myself.

Because of the female singers, who were from Australia, the club was full. The beer was flowing, and we were all having a good old time. I didn't know it just then, but a table with eight or so REMFs was behind and to the right of us. And one big fat NCO there was buying beers, taking a couple of gulps, then throwing the cans to the front, hitting people in the head. Those were the days of heavy metal cans, and they really hurt when they hit. The guy was a typical bully, and everybody at his table thought that he was cool. Well, every time he threw a beer can, it sloshed Rey with beer as it spun over his head. I didn't know that was going on because Rey was behind me and to my left as we faced the stage. Rey later told us that he looked at the guy after the NCO had thrown cans a couple of times and that the whole table had sneered at him and given him the finger.

Well, after a couple of repetitions, Rey got up with a full can of beer and walked over to their table. He told the NCO to stop throwing things, and the fat NCO made the mistake of swinging at Rey from across the table. Rey stepped back and, with a baseball throw, let the idiot have it between the eyes. The can split the guy's head from eyebrow to eyebrow, and he went down like the ton of shit that he was. None of us at our table knew that was going on because we were watching the big-breasted women to our front. The next thing we knew, there was a big commotion behind us; Rey was down on the floor, and that whole table was trying to kick the shit out of him. Rey had punched several guys and was covering himself with one guy he'd grabbed by the ears. Before it was all over, the whole club was fighting, and while the fight ensued, the girls and the music never missed a beat. They kept on singing, "Oh, when the saints come marching in, Oh, when the saints come marching in." Brawling to music was exhilarating! The best part was, every time the bully got up, somebody would nail him and back on his ass he'd fall. When the party was over, the only guy who looked like he'd been in a brawl was the bully, his face covered with blood, his eyes swollen shut.

One evening, after the workday was done, Rey and I drove in my medical jeep to the NCO club. As we were pulling out of the dispensary, a cherry came over and told us somebody was lying alongside the wall of my dispensary and might be hurt. We got out of the jeep and walked around the dispensary and found a young Airborne trooper lying there, crying his eyes out and calling for his mother. Mucus was running from his nostrils and dripping off his chin. He was a mess. At first I thought there might be some medical problem and started assessing him, but all I could get out of him was, "I want my momma; I want to go home." Rey and I tried the good-cop, bad-cop routine on the kid. Rey started yelling at him to get his sorry ass up, threatening him with death, trying to shame the kid, and telling him that the only momma he had was 101st Airborne. All that did was make the kid cry harder. I tried the nice-guy approach, but it didn't make a difference. This kid was scared about Vietnam and everything to do with it. Talk about lack of self-esteem. I couldn't believe the army had not only drafted him but sent him to Vietnam. I went up to the company commander's office and told them they had a problem. We watched as they tried the same approach we had attempted. I'd never seen anyone quite like that, and we left the area grateful we didn't have to deal with it.

A week later, Rey and I went to the NCO club to celebrate Mark "Wolverine" Thompson, one of the Foul Dudes who was going home. The Lurps had really appreciated Wolverine because he was good in the field and cool under fire. After the club closed at midnight, we were all driving back in my jeep. Victor Cisneros, a hometown friend of Rey's, Wolverine, a black sergeant named Homer, and Rey were in the jeep. As we were approaching the training area and my aid station, 122 mm rockets started impacting in our area. I stepped on the gas so we could get to our bunkers at the dispensary. Then I heard Rey yell that one of the rockets had made a direct hit on a barracks full of people new in country. About that time, we hit a pothole, and Rey went flying out the back of the jeep, and Homer bailed out to get Rey. I yelled at Rey to go check for wounded and that I would grab my aid bag and join him and Homer. The rockets were still impacting as I grabbed my gear and headed to rejoin Rey. Cisneros and Wolverine, who were pretty hammered from drinking, made it into a bunker.

Earlier that evening, Rey had picked up about sixty new replacements who had arrived from the States. When the rockets started slamming into the area, instead of hitting the ground as instructed, the new people had rushed out of their barracks for the bunkers outside. One of the 122 mm rockets hit directly in the doorway of their barracks, catching a mass of soldiers exiting the building. I ran to the destroyed billets, looking for wounded. As I approached the barracks, I came across a couple of bodies in front of the building. One had been decapitated, and the other had lost most of his chest. The chest wound died as I worked on him, spitting blood in my mouth with his last gasp of expelled air.

Rockets were still raining down, but we could hear people screaming from inside the rubble in front of us. There wasn't anyone else around to help with the wounded. Rey, Homer, and I pulled out about twenty people from the smoldering ashes that were left from the direct hit on the billets. After the rocketing stopped, other people stepped in and helped Rey and me with the dead and wounded. It took most of the night to get the wounded medevacked; the dead remained lined up outside the destroyed building in which they had met their deaths.

Rey told me later that when he ran into the first body he couldn't see well because of poor lighting. While working on the wounded man, he thought he was standing in mud until he realized he was standing and kneeling in the man's intestines. Rey couldn't do anything for the young man because the whole left side of his chest had been blown away. The second person Rey worked on had taken several large shrapnel holes through his legs, and one large fragment had all but taken the guy's right knee off. The young man kept asking Rey if he was going to lose his leg. Rey jerked his own shirt off, ripped the sleeve off at the shoulder, and wrapped the knee tight, then lied to the man and told him he had a million-dollar wound and would be going home. He didn't have the heart to tell him the knee and leg were hanging on by the skin at the back of the knee and that in all probability he would lose his leg. While Rey was finishing up the man with the leg wounds, one of the cherries grabbed Rey and led him to a casualty who was unconscious. The young man was bleeding from the ears, nose, and eyes. Rey couldn't find any penetrating wounds, but the guy wasn't breathing. Rey cleared the man's airway and started mouth-to-mouth, and was blowing in air when suddenly the wounded guy violently regurgitated up a huge amount of blood into Rey's mouth, causing him to swallow most of it. That started Rey vomiting, and when he finished, he started resuscitation again. Rey got the man breathing and restored a somewhat erratic pulse by the time we loaded him on the helicopters. Unfortunately, they lost him on the helicopter ride to the hospital.

After we loaded all of the casualties into helicopters, Rey and I went back to the comfort of my aid station for some rest. But before we could get comfortable someone was knocking at the aid station door. An overweight young lieutenant was standing on one leg saying he had been hit by shrapnel from the rocket attack. I helped the officer to my examination table to look at his wound. He had a large cut on the top of his big toe and nowhere else. I asked him what he was doing when he got the wound. He said he was running for a bunker when he tripped on some PSP, cutting his toe. All he wanted was a bandage and a record of my treatment for his wound. He wanted to take the paperwork to his aid station and have his medic submit him for a Purple Heart. I thought Rey was going to kill the guy. I cleaned his wound and saw that he needed a couple of stitches. So without giving him anything to numb the toe, I put about five stitches in it. He had tears in his eyes before I was finished with him. We had four killed and sixteen wounded that night, and most were in critical condition. Rey and I had provided all of the first aid for the wounded. I kept thinking about all those bodies lying in front of the destroyed billets and how they deserved a Purple Heart, not that guy. Hell, I'd been wounded in Khe Sanh and never received anything except getting fired from Special Forces. I finished bandaging the guy's wound while Rey lectured him: Rey said *he* could get the ell tee a Purple Heart, but that Rey would have to shoot him. Rey had a glazed, wild-eyed look and was serious. The lieutenant must have realized that he was in way over his head, because he left the area as fast as he could without any paperwork.

The next morning the company commander and a staff officer met with Rey and me to talk about what had occurred. The staff officer voiced the opinion that those 122 mm rockets were short rounds and had been actually aimed at the airfield. We disagreed with him and told him that on the launch-target line the only damage the rockets could have done was to make holes in the vicinity of the runway. It was not anywhere near aircraft or refueling storage tanks. We told the staff officer that the rounds were intended for the P-training area and that someone must have paced off the correction from the other "stray rounds." We also brought up that all of the bunkers were built without having direct access from inside the building. The bunkers looked great and were all "dressed right dressed," but it was putting the troops in danger to have them exit the building, then run around the outside of it to enter the bunkers. We were bluntly told to mind our own damn business.

I had the responsibility of taking someone to identify the four dead. Since they were from the troops Rey was in charge of, we had a formation and asked if anyone knew the four men who had been killed. A large number of new people had been through AIT (Advanced Individual Training) together in the States, and they had been sent as one big group to Vietnam. One private made the unfortunate mistake of volunteering that he had known all four men. He hadn't realized we needed someone to ID the bodies. Rey, the private, and I drove to Long Binh Graves Registration, where the bodies were being held. There the attendants unzipped the body bags one at a time for the kid to ID. They hadn't been cleaned up yet, and they looked very gruesome and smelled horrible. Rey and I were used to seeing bodies, and more important, they weren't our friends. The naive young private had been in Vietnam less than twelve hours, and he was identifying four of his friends. He was a mess. He had 364 days to go in Vietnam.

Feeling sorry for the kid, Rey and I decided to take him under our wing. He was an 11B, an infantryman (a.k.a. bullet stopper) and for him, the war was just beginning. We took him to Saigon and got him stinking drunk. Then we had him smoke a couple of bowls. He got so fucked up, he passed out in the back of my jeep and wet himself. That evening, the sun was going down as we pulled up to the new barracks the cherries were in. We backed the jeep to the door and unloaded him. Then, with his feet dragging, we carried him to his bunk, took off his boots and wet pants, and covered him with his poncho liner. In a loud voice, I told everyone in the barracks that the man was under special care and special training and to let him sleep. For the rest of the time that he was in the training company, Rey and I took extra-special care of him. When Rey marched them to their classes, he sat with the cherry in the class and passed on all the minute details associated with the subject that was being taught. Everything we both had learned, we tried to pass on to the kid, from how to organize his LBE for comfort and expediency in an ass-kick; to trusting his intuition; to how to walk, how to look, and what to look for; to how to prepare great meals with C rations. Rey gave him a Marine K-bar knife before he went north to the forward area. He was a good, decent young man, and I hope he survived the Vietnam War.

I had already forgotten about what had happened the night before until I went to the billets and there was the smell of ashes, gunpowder, and most of all, death. The people who died in that billet never had a chance to survive; the people who didn't get wounded had a rude awakening to the life they were about to endure. The faces in my medical class that day were listening to *everything* I said. Not one person got dizzy from practicing intravenous infusion on his partner. I had a difficult time sleeping that night, and even with the aid of beer and smoke, I couldn't get certain faces out of my mind. In the past, I'd been able to forget the dead and wounded. Now they were all catching up to me and living in my dreams. I started wondering what I could have done better to aid some of the wounded I had worked on, and whether I had just caused more harm than good. At that moment, I knew I had to get out of the area or I would go crazy.

Rey was getting out of the army, and he wanted me to go with him. I told him that I had just reenlisted and had to serve my extension before I could leave the country. But Rey informed me that with the division having taken over the personnel section, he had a friend who could take care of my reenlistment paperwork, and I could ETS (i.e., get out) with Rey. It would cost me my pistol.

Two weeks later, Rey and I were on our way to California, to get out of the army. We decided to smuggle some smoke back to the United States because stateside smoke wasn't of the quality that was available in Vietnam. We put envelopes of grass into empty ammo bandoliers and taped the bandoliers around our waists. We also put envelopes into the pants where we bloused them into the boots. We were lucky because there weren't any strip searches when we arrived in the United States. Customs looked only at our baggage. I had some good pictures of some of the VC we had wasted, but the customs people took them, and I couldn't get them back.

We out-processed through Oakland Army Terminal and had been given all of our back pay, plus travel pay and pay for any leave time we had coming. Rey's buddy had taken care of us. We were out of the army!

We took a cab to San Francisco International Airport. Crash Clark, who had served with 1st Brigade Lurps, Division Lurps, and had been with Teddy Bear Gaskell when he'd been shot through the ass, was with us. On arriving at the airport, we pulled up curbside. As we were getting out of the cab, I noticed one guy because of his clothing and long hair—also that he was very interested in us. I flashed that he was Lurping us, and had picked up on his vibes, but then completely put it out of my mind. We entered the airport and checked in with the airlines we were flying with. It was the Fourth of July, and the airport was like a ghost town. After checking in, the three of us proceeded to the nearest bar in the terminal. As we walked down to it, I noticed the same guy again, and he was with several other individuals. They all wore the same garb, which could be described as hippie dress. There was no doubt they were interested in us.

We entered the empty bar and took a table. There were two older businessmen at the bar and the bartender, who was sporting a Nehru jacket over a very colorful shirt: hippie dress but on the upscale, trendy side. The bartender was reading a paper and a little reluctant to serve us. One of us ended up going to the bar and buying some shots of whiskey and beer chasers. We had our private toast for getting out of the army and Vietnam alive. We started reminiscing about what we had been doing a year ago, which brought Rey and me to the Fourth of July mission in the Song Ve Valley. We made a toast to that. Finishing our beer, we walked out of the bar and the terminal to smoke a bowl. As we were coming out of the bar, we ran into the same hippies we had seen earlier. We went and smoked our bowl, then returned to the bar. On our way we ran into the same hippie guys, and by then we knew these guys wanted something from us.

We sat down at the same table we had used earlier. We ordered another round of beers and were enjoying them when the hippies (five of them) entered the bar and sat at a table next to ours. We were making small talk when the hippies interrupted our conversation. They wanted to know if we had just gotten back from Vietnam. It was pretty obvious we had, because we were thin and deeply tanned. We told them we had. They asked us if there was good pot over there and we told them yes. These questions were asked with disrespect. We could feel it in their mannerisms and the vibes we were getting from them. Finally they got down to what was really on their minds. "Well, how many babies did you fuckers kill?" asked the smallest one of them. Another one quipped, "I bet you killers only wasted children and women." "How does it feel to murder people?" added another. Three of the hippies were good-size guys about our age, with the easy life showing in their belt line. The other two were smaller, about Rey's size, but made up for it with their big mouths. We could tell they had done this before and enjoyed it. They were patrolling the airport looking for men recently returned from Vietnam. They had nothing better to do on the Fourth of July.

We were taken aback by the sudden attack. We had just smoked a bowl and were pretty laid back. Finding his tongue, Rey spoke up, telling them we didn't want any trouble and to leave us alone. This only redoubled their attack, and they scornfully told us we couldn't cope with someone's standing up to us. This was enough, and anger welled in us. One of us said, "Yes, we killed lots of babies, and you are next." Finally I smacked one of them and the fight was on. It was three against five, and they didn't stand a chance. All the frustration, sorrow, and anger of the past year we took out against those five people.

We beat on them like a bad dog on a street, giving them an ass-kicking they richly deserved. The bartender called the cops, who promptly showed up, and we were fingered by the bartender as having started all the trouble. But we were saved by the two older gentlemen at the bar. They had watched the whole episode and intervened on our behalf. Nobody was arrested, but we were all kicked out of the bar. Thanking the two older men, we offered to buy them a drink, which we did at another bar in the terminal. It turned out they were World War II Marine veterans. We really appreciated what they had done for us. We ended up staying in the bar all day long. One of us had a late flight out, so we decided to stick around and keep him company. Canceling several flights home, we spent the Fourth of July, 1968, drinking ourselves into oblivion.

My father picked me up at South Bend. I was so drunk I don't remember the trip home. The next morning, I awoke with a huge headache, surprised to find myself at home. A note on the night table next to me told me to pick up my mother from the hairdresser. I made breakfast, then went to pick up my mother, who introduced me to her seamstress, Monica Idonaswala Lewdnski, and she looked like a sure thing: Monica had been a contender for Miss Indiana. About five feet six and with dark brown hair, she was built like a movie star. She also sang with a local band on occasion. She was a very talented woman, and I fell in love at first sight. Or maybe it was lust.

When we got home, my mother said that Monica seemed to like me, too, so she invited Monica for dinner the next Friday. I couldn't wait until Friday came, so every day I sent flowers to her place of business. To pass the time until Friday, I volunteered at the local VFW to help build its new clubhouse.

Finally Friday arrived, and I was to pick up Monica at her home. She lived on a farm, but I wasn't familiar with the countryside, and I searched for an hour without success. Finally, I found a small gas station and called her. She said she would meet me at the gas station. I hung up the phone, and before I could get out the door, Monica was standing in front of me; she lived right behind the station. Dinner with my parents went fast, and soon it was time for Monica to go home. After all, she had to work in the morning; all I had to do was drink. I took her home and got my first round-eye kiss in over two years. I was in love and couldn't wait to see her again. We made a date for the following night. While she was at work the next day, I went out and bought a used Corvette. After all, I had ten thousand dollars with me.

That evening I picked her up from work and took her home. I spent the next twenty-five days in her presence.

I had been home long enough and needed to find a job. My sister had set up an appointment for me with the comedian Joey Bishop for a job interview out in California. My sister's boss knew Joey personally, and Joey owed him a favor. I had always wanted to be a stuntman, and that was the perfect opportunity. I called Rey, and he said he'd give me a place to stay. The night before I left for California, Monica and I made love for the first time. It was at that time that I gave her a ring and asked her to marry me. She accepted. All was right with the world.

Before Rey had left Vietnam, he had ordered a new 1968 Firebird 400. He picked me up at the airport in his new car. We cruised around in style for the next two days, all over southern California. On the day before my interview, we picked up the suit I was going to wear from the cleaners. That day also, Rey received a telephone call from his half brother, whom he had met only once before. They agreed to meet that evening to get reacquainted. His half brother came over, and we went out to have a beer. We were in Downey, California, and picked the first tavern we saw. It was a bad pick, one that would have serious consequences in my life.

The little bar was crowded. We bought a pitcher of beer and went to the rear of the bar, which was quieter and had some empty tables. The three of us sat around and talked. After a while, wanting to give Rey and his brother some time to themselves, I wandered back out front and sat at the bar. The lady bartender was good looking, and the more beer I drank, the better looking she got. She was really friendly and started flirting with me, telling me how she hated her boyfriend and was looking for a change in her life. Forgetting we were back in the United States of America, not Vietnam, I asked her if she smoked grass. She said she did but couldn't because of her boyfriend. I told her I could take care of her boyfriend if she would come with Rey and me after she got off work. She didn't say anything because she had to serve more customers. Throughout the night, we conversed when she wasn't busy. Several times during the evening, I went back and checked on Rey and his brother.

Around closing time, I went back and sat down with Rey and his brother. We finished up the remaining beer and started walking out of the bar. Later Rey told me he could sense that things were just not right. We could smell an ambush; a bunch of guys were congregated by the doorway. I couldn't figure out what the hell we had done, because we really hadn't had much contact with anyone in the place. As I exited the door, someone on the outside swung at me, and the fight was on. Pretty soon Rey and I were punching it out with a bunch of guys, and Rey's brother was just trying to defend himself. But after we started hurting a couple of them, suddenly a lot of handguns came out. We understood very well: they were all off-duty cops. Of all the places to have a drink, we had chosen a cop bar. The bartender had told the cops about my offering her grass, and those guys didn't like our looks. The one with the gun to my head put handcuffs on me and took me to where they already had Rey against the brick wall of the tavern. One particular asshole cop grabbed Rey by the hair and was rubbing his face hard into the brick wall. With his hands behind his back, Rey couldn't defend himself. The cop was giving Rey a hard time because he was Mexican, calling him a spick. Rey tried to get at him, but there were several cops holding him. Rey was yelling at them and carrying on, saying that they were dogshit and we'd killed better men than them. The cop got very close to Rey's face, talking shit all the time, when Rey suddenly spit into his face. The next thing I know, one of the cops hit Rey with the butt of his gun, causing Rey to go down. Then an older cop, a sergeant, intervened and actually saved our asses. Being handcuffed, we were helpless, and most of those cops were punks. And there is nothing worse than a punk when he has the advantage.

They put me on the ground next to Rey and started to search us. Rey was clean, but I had a bag of smoke and a loaded .22 pistol in my back pocket. I had carried a weapon everywhere since I had gotten to Nam; I felt vulnerable without a weapon. The cops then took Rey's key from him and opened up the trunk of his new car. The cops found all of the grass we had brought back from Nam. They were going to confiscate Rey's car until I told them the grass was mine and Rey didn't know anything about it.

The cops took us to the L.A. County jail. Rey was released when I confessed to being the owner of all the smoke and the weapon. Rey's poor brother had gotten the dogshit pounded out of his ribs. They turned him loose because he really had been innocent. Since that night, Rey has never seen his half brother again. One month back in country, and I was looking at a couple of years in jail for the same grass we smoked freely in Nam.

The cops had taken all of my money, so I couldn't get a lawyer, and Rey's parents lived in a trailer, which they couldn't use as bondable collateral. My only recourse was to call my father and ask for help. That was one of the toughest phone calls I had ever had to make. My father had been bragging about me to everyone in Culver; now I was a drug addict and a dangerous person.

Fortunately, I have great, understanding parents. My father got hold of a friend of his whose son worked for a law firm. On my second day in the L.A. County jail, my lawyer visited me. By then I was sober and feeling like a lowlife, and I wasn't feeling much better when he told me he was a corporate lawyer who had never worked on a criminal case. Again, luck was with me; a good criminal lawyer owed my lawyer a favor and helped him with the case. But it was two weeks before I went to trial, and for two weeks I sat in jail with some of the lowest people on earth. Of course, all of them were innocent. I heard enough stories there to write a book. Finally, after all the beans I could eat, it was time to go to trial. I bought a suit, cut my hair, and shaved to look good for my court appearance. The trial was quick because my lawyer convinced the judge that the case was built entirely on an illegal search and seizure. Which was true. Not to mention that the cops who had taken us into custody had been drinking and had never read us our rights. The bartender had been called to testify against me, but when she got up on the stand she didn't recognize me. Anyway, the judge dismissed the charges. The prosecutor wanted to refile against me, but I told my lawyer I would go back into the army if they would leave me alone. The prosecutor agreed, and within an hour of my release from the L.A. County jail, I was back in the army, going to Germany. I had to spend only one more day in L.A. before leaving the country.

I was too embarrassed to call Monica and tell her what had happened. I figured I would wait until I got to Germany and see how she felt about me. All I wanted to do just then was to get out of the States. I had disappointed my family and felt like a lowlife. I spent a sober day waiting for my flight.

☆
CHAPTER 11

August 1968

I had reenlisted for the airborne unit in Germany, the 509th Infantry Battalion, 8th Infantry Division, located in Mainz, Germany. Rey had served with this same unit in 1966. In the fall of 1968, the Germans didn't like Americans, mostly because of Vietnam. After two weeks in Mainz, I was ready to return to Vietnam. I put in for Nam and waited to see how long it would take to get back to the country that understood me. I was a medic, and there was always a priority for medics in Nam. While in Germany, I ran into a couple of old Lurps who'd become MPs. We spent some time together, but they were different; they wanted to forget Vietnam, and I wanted to return. It seemed to me that, by then, even the military personnel were against our being in Vietnam.

It took longer than I expected to get back to the only world that would accept me for who I was. But I spent the months while I was waiting wrestling for the army. I had won the European championship and had the opportunity to go All Army, but orders came in for Vietnam, and wrestling was forgotten. Before I left, I called Monica and asked her to set a date to marry me. She said as soon as possible. I didn't have any leave left, so I told her as soon as I became eligible for R & R, I would let her know.

I was assigned to MACV as an adviser to Regional and

Popular Forces (RFPF; we called 'em Rough Puffs). I was to be a member of a Mobile Advisory Team (MAT). These teams were introduced in late 1967 to stop the Viet Cong from harassing villages in the countryside. By training the local people to defend themselves against the Viet Cong, the MATs helped to provide the security the villages needed to survive. The MAT teams came under the supervision of the District teams, and the District was monitored by the Province teams.

Before going to my permanent duty assignment, I had to attend adviser school in Di An, a small town outside Saigon. The school was two weeks in duration and consisted of language training, weapons training, and lectures on the customs of the Vietnamese and of montagnards. How I was chosen was a mystery to me. It was at Di An that I met S.Sgt. Douglas Baines Scherk. Scherk and I would be inseparable for the next two years.

I met Scherk during in-processing at Di An. We were the only E-6s in our class, the rest of the students being lieutenants or captains. After in-processing, we were given quarters, and Scherk and I ended up roommates. That evening we sat around drinking, and I discovered that Scherk had also come from the 101st Airborne Division, and we shared a lot of the same problems. Scherk had to come back into the army to avoid the law as well. His problem was more about family than drugs, although he did smoke grass, which was another common bond.

S.Sgt. Douglas Scherk was born in Atascadero, California, into a military family. His father retired from the military and ended up teaching at one of the California universities. Scherk joined the army as soon as he graduated from high school. After all of his training, he was sent to the 101st Airborne Division and spent a year with one of the line companies. He didn't like the 101st, but he didn't want to leave Vietnam. He extended for the Advisory Command, and that was how he got to be where he was.

Scherk was about five feet nine inches tall and weighed about 150 pounds, and he was slim, with thick, dusty blond hair. Women loved Scherk's looks because he was handsomely rugged and very quiet. I, on the other hand, was six feet four inches and about 190 pounds and stood out like a sore thumb. Scherk was infantry and knew his craft well. There wasn't a weapon he couldn't take apart and put back together. He was also an excellent shot. He made the instructors look stupid. I, on the other hand, had the language down and could speak it well enough to pass the course exam before I took the class. So I helped Scherk with the language, and he helped me with weapons. Later on during our tours, whenever Scherk and I were around other Americans, we spoke Vietnamese so that no one could understand us. When going to local Vietnamese resturants, though, we wouldn't speak the language until we received the check. It was amazing what people would say when they thought you didn't understand the language. The Vietnamese women would talk about how good-looking Scherk was. When we started to leave, Scherk would speak to them in Vietnamese and thank them for their kind thoughts. This would make him even more attractive to them. In times to come, Scherk and I would go through a lot of hardships and share memorable adventures.

It was a quick two weeks, other than having to go to the dentist to have my wisdom teeth extracted.

Scherk and I graduated at the top of our class and had our choice of assignments. We both chose Darlac Province. He was assigned to a mobile advisory team outside Ban Me Thuot, close to where I was assigned, Lac Thien, where the past president's palace was. I lived in a Mnong montagnard village called Buon Dham in a remote area of Darlac Province. The montagnards didn't trust or like the Vietnamese, and for good reason. In early 1968, because of death threats to their leader, Eban Hbut, a couple of companies of montagnards left Vietnam and set up camp in Cambodia.

In late 1968, the Vietnamese were afraid the montagnard companies would side with the Communists and attempt to overthrow the government of South Vietnam. A plan was devised to eliminate the montagnard companies. A meeting was to be set up between the montagnard leader and the Vietnamese leaders, ostensibly to work out a solution to repatriate the montagnards back to the South. In reality, the Vietnamese intended to kill the montagnards. The Vietnamese poisoned all the wells in the Darlac Province in hopes of ridding the country not only of the montagnard companies but of a lot of the civilians as well. The plan backfired once the Americans found out about it. Unfortunately it was too late for the civilian population of Lac Thien. The wells had already been poisoned, and hundreds of civilians died. The Vietnamese tried to convince the people it was done by the Communists, but too much pointed at the South Vietnamese government. The leaders of the montagnards stayed in Cambodia until early 1969, when, under the watchful eyes of the Americans, the companies returned to South Vietnam's highlands. The companies were given Special Forces advisers and everything they needed.

Mobile advisory teams were supposed to consist of five men—two officers and three NCOs of various job skills—and an interpreter, usually from the *buon* (village or hamlet) we would live in. The officer in charge (captain) made plans or implemented plans from the higher. Our captain, Robert Stewart, from Alabama, was a short man, thin, with a bushy mustache, who had been an artillery officer before becoming an adviser. When he spoke, our interpreter had a difficult time understanding his southern drawl. Our other officer was Lt. William Digs. He stood about five feet ten inches tall and had an athlete's build. He was out of ROTC and thought he knew everything. His job was to observe and to delegate minor tasks; they really didn't matter, but that gave him something to do. Our senior NCO was SFC John Holt. Unlike the ell tee,

Holt was heavyset and liked to eat and drink and not much else. His job was like that of a first sergeant; that is, he was to make sure things got done. Then there were the guys who really worked, like the weapons sergeant, S.Sgt. James Good. Staff Sergeant Good was from Columbus, Georgia. He was a good old boy who worked hard and played hard. He had been Airborne but was injured and taken off jump status. He never forgave the army for making him a leg (non-Airborne personnel). Good walked with a limp and had a hard time walking distances, but he never gave up or asked for help. His job was to implement the defensive perimeter, train the popular-force cadre, and be the guy who had the tactical and defense answers.

Then there was the medic, me. My job was sanitation and medical care for the civilian population and the team members. A typical day for me was to have a sick call early in the morning. After sick call, if there weren't any patients I had to take to see a physician, I would assist the weapons man by providing medical support and helping him with his training schedule. Normally we would be done by noon. I would then chlorinate the wells and set traps for rats around the village or clean the existing traps of rats. Other than the ell tee, everybody got along well. The captain made sure to control the ell tee, while Good and I made sure the sergeant first class had beer and that the job got done to district's standards. Good and I were the only men on our team who spent time talking to the people and helping with their problems.

Buon Dham was a village of about one hundred people. It sat on the edge of a lake and was surrounded by triple-canopy jungle. It was a beautiful area. The jungle contained numerous species of monkeys and birds. It also contained tigers, elephants, water buffalo, and other wildlife that provided food for our small village.

The homes we lived in were made of bamboo and elephant grass. The floors were dirt. In areas of heavy rain, the homes sat on stilts, which kept them dry during the monsoon season. The village meat animals were pigs and chickens for the most part, but occasionally dogs and cats were sacrificed, then eaten. The religion was animism. The people sacrificed animals for worship, then ate them. Not long before, some of the people had been cannibals. On the occasion of any kind of holiday or wedding or death, a sacrifice was called for; the bigger the sacrifice, the wealthier the people were. There would be a party every night at this village. Sometimes we advisers were invited, and sometimes we were not.

The montagnards had holy people who worked as healers. First came the sacrifice. The animal that was going to be offered as a sacrifice was held over the person the sacrifice was made for; then the priest or the person performing the sacrifice cut the throat of the animal and drained its blood into a bowl. The bowl of blood was held over the lucky person, who was then offered a drink from the bowl. After that person was finished, the bowl was passed around, offered to the oldest person first. The remaining blood was added to the sacrificed animal, and then it was cooked for the ceremony. While the sacrifice was being made, the person presiding over the ceremony chanted ancient verse.

After the sacrifice and while the food was being prepared, we would drink from a jug of *nampai*, a home brew made from rice or corn. While the rice or corn was cooking, a ceramic pot resembling a huge vase or jug was lined with banana leaves, leaving enough space at the top of the jug for partially cooked rice or corn. Once the rice or corn was added to the jug, more banana leaves were put on top of the rice or corn and the top was sealed with mud. The jug was then taken and buried for whatever length of time the maker wanted. From my experience the period ran from less than a month to usually no longer than six months. I have had some that was a couple of years old, but that was from really large containers. A normal jug was no more than two and a half to three feet high. The longer the container stayed in the ground, the higher the alcohol content of the brew. Once the jug was ready to be drunk from, the owner dug it up and removed the mud plug. He then added water to the jug and inserted a large straw. The taste of *nampai* varies from sweet to gagging. I liked the sweet. Corn-based liquor was normally sweeter than rice liquor. After the jug was tapped, the host or a friend sat behind the jug and added water as people drank. One of the old people's favorite jokes was to add water while a guest wasn't looking to make the guests drink more. If it was good *nampai*, I wouldn't mind; I have passed out in many a montagnard house after drinking great *nampai*. Once in a while, the host would add Vietnamese rum to his jug; then it would take only a couple of cupfuls before I got sick or drunk.

My first night at Buon Dham, I was introduced to the chief and elders, including the medicine man. Because I was considered to be a medicine man, I was offered more respect than the other members of my team. To the Mnong, people with the ability to preserve life or to heal someone were more valuable than those who took lives or taught how to take a life. They would sacrifice animals to save someone's life. I spoke only Vietnamese at first, so our interpreter had to go with me to social functions, and he told me only what he wanted me to hear. After a couple of months, I could understand most of what was said and didn't really need the interpreter, but we had become good friends, and he still accompanied me to all the functions. Sometimes he invited only me and not the other team members. The first couple of months, I was becoming used to the people and their customs and stayed as an observer as I tried to learn more about those wonderful people.

My interpreter, Enug, was a montagnard. The people of the *buon* called him Bobleem. Bobleem was large for a montagnard, standing about the same height as our lieutenant, a little taller than the captain. He had lost one eye while serving with

Special Forces. He spoke pidgin English and could speak French and Vietnamese. When we had to deal with Vietnamese, Bobleem interpreted while I sat back. I could speak Vietnamese fluently and understood everything that Enug told the Vietnamese. Enug didn't know I spoke Vietnamese as well as I did. I didn't want anyone to know how well I spoke until I knew what people would say if they thought I couldn't understand.

One thing I learned quickly was that the Vietnamese thought the montagnard was an inferior human being. They treated the montagnards worse than animals. The government officials in Lac Thien were Vietnamese, and all the montagnard villages (*buons*) came under their jurisdiction. Government funds and aid went to the local Vietnamese people first. Whatever was left over was given to the montagnards.

Our team's higher was called District and was in our chain of command. District had its own compound with Vietnamese guards and security. District was located across the road from Buon Ya, just south of Lac Thien and north of Ban Me Thuot. Our headquarters ("Province") was located in Ban Me Thuot, about forty miles southeast of Lac Thien and fifty miles south of Buon Dham. The MAT province headquarters was quartered in a place called the Bungalow, a beautiful teak A-frame building where Teddy Roosevelt had stayed when he was hunting in the area. Six months after I came in country, a soldier cooking in his quarters somehow burned the Bungalow down. Another landmark destroyed by the Americans.

My village had once been occupied by the French. At that time, the montagnards had been treated so badly that they revolted, killed all the French in their area, cut off their heads, put the heads on pikes, and displayed them around the perimeter of the *buon* for all to see.

The largest tribe of montagnards in our province was the Rhade, who thought themselves to be the upper class of the montagnards. They also thought of the Mnong as inferior, but not to the extent that the Vietnamese did. The Rhade were better educated and lived a more modern lifestyle, but they still made sacrifices and lived in bamboo homes. They did wear more clothing. The Mnong had worn loincloths for probably thousands of years. The only time they were found in more modern clothes was when someone gave them the items to wear. Very few Mnong could read and write. I never met a Vietnamese who could speak a montagnard language; just about all montagnards could understand Vietnamese. They just refused to speak it. After living with the Mnong for a couple of months and hearing them speak only Mnong, I started to pick up the pleasantries of the language, because I made an effort to learn as much as I could.

After the training was over, the rest of my team would retire to their hootches or go to town to associate with the other Americans or with the Vietnamese. Because I went out of my way to learn the language and customs of the people, I was invited to all the ceremonies, even in other *buons*. My first sacrifice, a chicken, was for being a friend of the people. During the ceremony, I was given a brass bracelet with markings to show my importance to the people. As time went on, I was to receive more sacrifices, eventually even a water buffalo, the highest honor. Before I left Buon Dham, I had over two hundred bracelets.

Only one road ran between Ban Me Thuot and Pleiku, and went through Lac Thien, and most of it was mud during the monsoon season. The district commander was a black major whose name I can't remember. He was a tall, thin man who seemed afraid of everything and everybody. I think he sometimes believed one of his own people was going to try to kill him. The major was responsible for the numerous MAT teams spread all over the Lac Thien area. He never visited our *buon*, but he required our captain to report to him once a week or to submit a situation report. We could reach Ban Me Thuot and our district boss by radio. My captain scheduled his supply runs at the same time as his reports to the district chief. If he didn't go, he made sure one of us took his report to the district commander. Our captain's only concern was that report and pleasing the major at District.

After I'd been in country for two months, I wanted to get a leave or R & R to return to the States to get married. I couldn't get R & R to Hawaii, which was the only American-port R & R, because the officers had first choice of the R & R locations. I requested three weeks' advance leave to my home so I could get married. I first had to get permission from the district commander. That took about two weeks, but he did finally approve my request. I flew out of Ban Me Thuot to Saigon, then on to Oakland Army Terminal, arriving early in the morning. I was expedited through the system so I could be home for most of my leave rather than being stuck at Oakland doing paperwork.

As I was leaving the Oakland army compound, hundreds of people outside the compound were waving banners and signs, yelling at everyone who walked through the gates. I was wearing my uniform and looking like a good Airborne trooper. As I went through the gate, someone threw a tomato and hit me in the chest, ruining my appearance. The crowd was shouting obscenities and calling me a baby killer. Of course, that had happened on my last run through there, but not on such a grand scale. The military police had to escort us through the crowd to waiting taxis.

All of us in uniform were devastated by what had just happened. The taxi driver, who was sympathetic to us, said that protesters had been outside Oakland for weeks harassing every GI who passed through those gates.

With the tomato smeared all over my uniform, I was a mess, so when we reached the airport I went to the latrine to clean it off. I had an hour before my flight was to leave, and the day's experiences were wearing on my mind, so my next stop was the airport bar. There I found a couple of the guys I had shared the taxi with already having cold brews. But the atmosphere of that bar was cold: a lot of people were there, but they had their noses in the air. The waitress wouldn't wait on us, and when I went to get the drinks the bartender acted as if he couldn't see me until I screamed at him to make sure I got his attention. It was a united front from everyone in the bar against every soldier who represented our involvement in Vietnam. I was seeing red, and if I'd had a weapon, somebody might have gotten hurt. It seemed like hours before my flight was ready to board, but finally the time came. I couldn't wait to get out of that place, but I was afraid of what I might find at home. If it hadn't been for the thought of Monica, I would have turned around at Oakland and returned to Vietnam.

I arrived in Chicago early that afternoon and had to wait thirty minutes before my flight to South Bend, Indiana. For fear of people giving me problems, I didn't go to the bar. I sat looking out at the runway, avoiding civilians.

My father, mother, and Monica met me at the South Bend airport. Monica had a warm hug and a hot kiss for me when I entered the terminal. They were the first people I saw who did not seem to be turned off by the sight of me.

My mother and Monica had everything ready for our wedding. All I had to do was show up. That night I wanted to be alone with Monica, but my family and her family had different ideas. We had a big dinner and talked about the upcoming event, the women in one room, the men in another, all shooting questions at me about the war and what I was doing. I was still upset over the protesters at Oakland, and I poured out some of my hostility on the listening family. But they took it well. Being "family," they were sympathetic and hoped they could make it up to me. I said that the best way was to let me be alone with the woman I was going to marry. I went into the room filled with Monica's and my mother's relatives, took Monica by the hand, and told everybody we would see them later and headed for the local Holiday Inn. Monica didn't want to walk to the desk to register because they knew her, and she was afraid people would talk about her all over town. But they didn't know me, so I got the key.

It was a great night, but Monica had to work early in the morning, so we couldn't sleep in. When I woke up, I discovered that she had left me at the Holiday Inn without a ride home. As I called the taxi, I had a grin on my face; I had forgotten all about the protesters.

When I got home, I was still grinning. My dad recognized the grin and invited me to go with him to the local VFW for a brew. I told my dad the first thing I wanted to do was buy a car. I had a lot of cash and was tired of taxis and bothering other people for rides. My dad introduced me to a friend who sold Chevys. An hour later I left the lot with a new canary yellow convertible Corvette.

The VFW opened early, which was a good thing, since it was the only place my dad would drink. At that time, he was the commander and had the run of the place. The bar was in the basement, and a new building was being built on the old foundation, and a lot of people were doing handiwork on the building. I helped out for a couple of days until the building was done, consuming more time drinking beer than working.

Our wedding was on the first Saturday of my leave home, but a true honeymoon would have to wait until my return from Nam. Only family attended, a relatively small group of about twenty. The reception was held at the same Holiday Inn Monica and I had used on my first night home. Now she wasn't afraid of anyone seeing her with me.

The time went fast, and before I knew it, I had to return to Nam. I didn't want to go back now that I had found something at home, but duty called. I drove my Corvette to Oakland and put it in storage.

During the trip back to Vietnam, I blocked out everything around me as I thought only of Monica and how I would get home to her as quickly as possible. I left Oakland worrying about my car, my wife, and my life. I left cool weather at home and arrived in Saigon to heat and humidity that made breathing difficult. Before the first night was over, I was back in my *buon* thinking about how fast the three weeks had gone. Then Bobleem came to my hootch and invited me to a party and a welcome back. Thinking about the eight months I had left in Vietnam, I went with him; it felt good to be around people who treated me as one of them.

In the first two months after I returned to Vietnam, I wrote numerous letters home but received only one letter from Monica. I wrote my family, and they said they didn't know why she wasn't writing. Meanwhile, I was sending all my money home so that we could save enough to buy a home when I got out. Then one day I received a letter from my mother warning me that she had caught Monica with another man. It seems my mother's insurance agent had called to ask for me because Monica had taken out an insurance policy on me that didn't have a war clause. It was worth $250,000 and the premium was being paid out of the money I was sending home. The insurance agent needed my signature on some papers that would rectify that mistake. Without a war clause attached to the insurance policy, if something happened to me in Vietnam it would be worthless. The insurance agent hadn't been able to get hold of Monica to give the papers to her. So my mother went to her home and found her naked in the arms of another man. Of course, Monica was completely surprised by my mother's visit, but Monica's mother was there and acted like nothing had happened.

Clearly, Monica had thought I'd be coming home in a box, and she was going to benefit from my death. I found out later that she had been with the same guy a couple of nights before our wedding and the night after I left for Vietnam. It was good that I was in Nam; someone would have died if I had been in Indiana. My mother and father arranged to have the marriage annulled and the insurance canceled. Of course, I lost all of the money I had sent Monica, but I also lost my belief in love. From that point on, I didn't like people much anymore, and I made up my mind that Vietnam was home, vowing to stay there until I died. I threw myself into taking care of my village to the point of "going native."

The night after the big revelation, Buon Ya and district headquarters were hit by mortars and small-arms fire. No Americans were killed, but a lot of montagnards were killed and wounded. I was asked to help treat some of the minor injuries. The closest hospital was in Ban Me Thuot, and the only transportation there was by vehicle, because the Vietnamese wouldn't send the *buon* a medevac helicopter for montagnards, and the Americans wouldn't send a medevac because there weren't any wounded Americans. District had an FLA (field land ambulance), but it could transport only two wounded at a time, so I talked the district commander into letting us use the two-and-a-half-ton truck to transport the wounded to Ban Me Thuot.

To get to the hospital took us a couple of hours of slow driving, and when we arrived, the Vietnamese doctor didn't want to treat the wounded even though two children needed emergency surgery or they would die. I left the children there, went to the Bungalow and conferred briefly with the American doctor, then called the hospital and said that if they didn't treat the montagnards, medical supplies the Americans normally sent to the hospital would never come again. By the time I got back to the hospital the two montagnard children were in surgery. The aggravation and importance of the incident made me forget about the problems in my love life.

I stayed the night at the Bungalow and, in the morning, went to check on the people I had taken to the hospital. Except for the two children, all of the wounded I had brought were ready to go back to Buon Ya, and some of them had already left. I picked them up on the way back. When we got back, the village was having funerals for those who'd died in the attack.

The montagnards have a period of mourning. But first, the body of the deceased is wrapped in cloth and incense is burned. Food is prepared and set alongside the body to take to the next life. The mourning lasts all night, the women wailing and crying to show their loss. The men sit drinking *nampai* and talking about the deceased and all the good things the person had done in his or her lifetime. The next morning after a grave is dug, a procession follows the wooden casket to the grave. The body is put into the grave along with the person's favorite things, including his animals. After words are said over the grave, it is filled in with dirt and mounded up to create a hill that looks like a temple. A picture of the deceased is placed in front of the grave and flowers are laid all around it. After the funeral, everyone returns to the village, and a sacrifice is made in honor of the deceased. Then everyone drinks and eats until passing out or leaving for home. Usually the elders are the last to leave, drinking until the sun rises.

Despite my headache from the night before, I got up the next day and went to Ban Me Thuot to check on the two children. It was a good thing I did, because their IVs had run out, and the Vietnamese weren't about to replace them without a good reason. I went back to the Bungalow and talked to the doctor again. He gave me all of the IVs the children would need. Since I was afraid the Vietnamese would use the IVs on Vietnamese patients if I handed them over to the staff, I gave them to the parents and told them that when one was empty to make sure the nurse gave the children another. Then I returned to Buon Dham village and crashed for the rest of the day. It was amazing that the montagnards took so much abuse from the Vietnamese. Their lives paralleled (and probably still do) those of minorities in our country. No thanks to the Vietnamese, the two children lived and returned to the *buon* two months after the attack. The *buon* had a big welcome home for the children and a surprise for me.

Everybody in the *buon* brought a jug of *nampai*, and people from other *buons* came to the biggest celebration I would ever attend. A water buffalo was sacrificed in honor of the children and me. All of the jugs were put into one long line, with their owners sitting behind them dressed in traditional garb. In another corner of the celebration, eight or ten men with large brass cymbals of different sizes struck them with hard wooden mallets, making them ring out. Together they made harmony. I started at the first jug but made it to only the third jug before I had to take a break.

The party lasted three days and nights. After that celebration, I had met just about every montagnard who lived in Darlac Province. The downside of the celebration was that from that day forward montagnards from other *buons* brought all of their sick to me. My sick call increased from four or five people to fifty. Of course, some of the people just liked the medicine I handed out. After I gave an old man some cold medication, he left to trade his meds with another old guy because he liked their color better. That was when I learned to make the montagnards take the meds while I watched.

The time went fast while I was serving with that MAT team. The dispensary that I worked out of was too small to handle the number of people who were showing up, so I talked to some of the elders and proposed to them that I travel to each *buon* to the sick rather than having them come to our *buon*. That worked out well for the patients, but I ended up spending so much time traveling that I never got back to my own *buon* until well after dark. It wasn't a good idea to have a lone American driving down the only road late at night; sooner or later the VC would hear of my travels and try to eliminate me. The only solution was to get someone to help. I talked to the District commander, and he agreed that the six medics in the district would rotate the job of taking care of the sick.

When it came time to go on R & R, I got hold of Scherk at his *buon*, and we decided to go to Thailand together, because that was the easiest R & R to get and the cheapest. I met Scherk at the Bungalow. We had to find our own transportation to Saigon, so we went to the local airport and talked Air America into giving us a spot on the daily flight to Saigon. Once in Saigon, we had to go through Camp Alpha, the processing station, then on to Bangkok, Thailand. Most of the R & R flights were civilian carriers, and the one we took treated us well. After only a few hours, we landed in Thailand.

When we got off the plane, we were required to listen to a tour agency briefing. Of course they wanted us to stay at their hotels and take their tours. Scherk and I listened to their pitch, then dashed out the door to the first waiting taxi. We didn't care about money; we both had a thousand bucks and only a week to spend it. After haggling a bit with the driver, we worked out a deal for him to drive for us while we stayed in Thailand. He would pick us up in the morning, take us home at night, and act as an interpreter in between. As it turned out, we were lucky in our choice: the taxi driver knew the best places to eat, drink, and find women.

Our first stop was to buy silk suits. We were greeted at the door of the tailor shop by a beautiful young girl who handed us each a cold beer. After selecting the color and material for our suits, we were measured, then told we would have to wait about two hours before they would be done. We were then escorted to a large room at the top of the tailor shop where six recliners surrounded a teak table that held snacks, cold beer, and the biggest bamboo pipe I had ever seen. Also on the teak table was a large bag of Thai weed, the strongest smoke on earth. In one corner of the room was a large television set and a VCR. We sat in the recliners drinking cold beer, smoking Thai weed, and watching flicks until our suits were done. The suits cost us one hundred and fifty dollars but would have cost six hundred in the States. We paid, then left the tailors half-drunk, high, and horny.

On our way to the hotel, Scherk spotted a beautiful girl waving at us on the side of the road. It was love at first sight for Scherk. The driver didn't want to stop, but Scherk insisted and the driver complied. I got into the front seat so Scherk could investigate his newly found love. About ten minutes later Scherk screamed for the driver to stop the car. The driver did, and we saw that Scherk was about to punch his love. The driver stopped Scherk and made the girl get out of the taxi; Scherk had somehow discovered that his rare beauty had a bigger penis than he did. We continued on to the hotel while Scherk cursed to himself and spit.

At the hotel, we told the driver to pick us up in an hour. Scherk made a beeline to the bathroom and brushed his teeth at least ten times. We both cleaned up, putting on our new suits. We looked like a million bucks. Our driver was on time and took us to find real women.

Prostitution was legal in Thailand and regulated by the government, which saw that the women had medical checkups after having been with a customer. When a women was selected, the customer was shown her medical card.

We walked into an establishment that had a good recommendation from the taxi driver because it took pride in the honesty of its girls. Within the main room, the bordello had a glass-enclosed chamber in which were twenty to thirty very attractive women, each with a number on her dress. We picked the numbers we liked, and they were summoned. In 1968, the going rate for a day and night with a girl was thirty dollars. The price was less for a "short time." Scherk and I decided to rent two girls each for the week we would be in country. The girls liked the idea; they were all friends.

We left the brothel and decided to take in some Thai boxing, a championship match that cost as much as a girl did. Thai fighting is really brutal, in and out of the ring, and people ended up fighting more outside the ring than inside, but it was fun to watch, and the girls really got into it. After the fight, we went to a Thai restaurant and stuffed ourselves with the best food I had ever eaten. After stopping at a couple of nightclubs, we were exhausted and decided to retire to our hotel suite, where Scherk and I had adjoining rooms. We had a lot of fun that night and slept like babies.

Early the next morning, our driver picked us up and suggested we go to the beach. It was about an hour's ride, but when we got there, we learned we could rent a boat and scuba gear for five dollars a day. There could be nothing cheaper or more fun than that.

Once we arrived at the dock to rent a boat, the girls left to purchase food and beer. Scherk and I were given a quick familiarization with the scuba equipment. By the time we were finished, the girls were back and ready to go.

Resembling a Chinese junk without sails, our boat was a commercial fishing craft about thirty feet long. It came with a driver and had a charcoal grill on the deck. In the middle of the boat was a large hold for fish. But that day the hold was filled with beer and ice.

Scherk and I were the only people who wanted to dive, so we spent most of the day in and out of the water until we ran out of oxygen. We were diving in the Gulf of Thailand, in the clearest, cleanest waters I had ever seen. It was my first attempt to dive, but Scherk had some experience and knew what his limitations were. I, on the other hand, was full of testosterone and really had no business diving without instruction. The first time in I jumped into the water and my mask was ripped off my face, causing me to thrash in the water. After getting my mask back on, I found I was exhausted from finning to stay afloat while I adjusted my mask. I then submerged into the clear blue waters to look for all the beauty I expected to find.

Scherk swam over and motioned me to the surface, where he told me to stop breathing so quickly because I would be out of oxygen in ten minutes at the rate I was inhaling and exhaling. I submerged and was controlling my breathing fairly well, but when I tried to go deeper than about ten feet, I got a huge pain across my face, as if my sinus cavity were going to explode. I surfaced once again. Scherk also surfaced, this time with a look of frustration. I told him about my problem, and he advised me to breathe air into my mask as I descended. Once more I submerged. Everything was going well that time except that I kept floating to the surface. Scherk decided it was time to take a break and have a beer. When we got on board the boat, Scherk told me to put on a weight belt. We had a beer and decided to try it again. I stepped into the water that time and had no problems with my mask, but the weight belt was too heavy, and I descended very quickly—about one hundred feet down. On the bottom, I saw lots of round sea urchins with hundreds of long needles all over their bodies, but before I could study them, I had to deal with my rate of descent. That time I knew what the problem was, and I finned my ass off going back to the surface. I removed some weights from the belt and tried again.

Only then could I enjoy the dive, and the view was worth the work. We saw lobster running across the floor of the Gulf of Thailand. The bright and varied colors of the different species of life were spectacular. We didn't catch anything, but we really didn't want to.

Night was suddenly upon us, and we had to return to shore. While Scherk and I had been diving, the girls were cooking and preparing a feast fit for a couple of princes. After a wonderful meal, we decided we would return the next day and resume the festivities. I had no energy left that night, and as soon as my head hit the pillow, I was unconscious until the next morning. It was the only night I didn't think about sex.

We had left the hotel with the intention of not returning until it was time to leave Thailand. As soon as we found out the fisherman would rent us the boat for the three days we still had, the girls went for supplies. Scherk and I went to get enough oxygen to last us for the three days.

We dived every day, and ate, drank, and had as much sex as we wanted, anywhere we wanted, on the deck of our boat or in the warm seawater. At night over our charcoal grill, we sang songs, ate seafood, and drank German beer. Life doesn't get any better than that.

The time passed much too quickly for our liking. The day we left, our girls went to the airport with us, and we promised we would return on our extension leaves for thirty days. Scherk and I left Thailand with the best memories any young soldiers could want.

We arrived back in Saigon too late to catch the last flight to Nha Trang, so we would have had to wait until the next day if we hadn't decided to leave that day anyway. We stood outside the base exchange on the air base waiting for our ride to arrive. Eventually, an air force airman pulled up and walked into the base exchange without locking his vehicle. In those days, jeeps didn't require keys, and the only way to secure them was to chain the steering wheel to the floor. The airman was in a hurry and hadn't done that. We jumped in the jeep and headed for the main gate, where we were waved through without a glance. In no time we were on Highway 1, driving down the coastline.

The shortest drive would have taken us across territory that was closely monitored by the VC, so we took the scenic route and stopped only at Nha Trang to eat and relieve ourselves. The only bad part of the trip was from Nha Trang to Ban Me Thuot, where we had to go through the Korean sector of operation and were stopped to state where we were going. The ROKs had patrols out and didn't want us to be ambushed. We made it back to the Bungalow before dark. Then we had to decide what to do with our new vehicle. After a brief search, we discovered a supply sergeant who was more than willing to take care of it and make sure we got to use it whenever we were in town. He even drove us back to our districts. I really didn't want to be back in Nam, and I certainly didn't want to spend the night at District headquarters. Unfortunately, my transportation couldn't travel the roads at night.

At District, the perimeter was guarded by Vietnamese, and the only thing Americans had to do was serve radio watch. They never even left their tent at night to check the guards unless they were under attack. But, since I was a guest, I had to pull radio watch, and I was pissed. I relieved a guy at two in the morning for a two-hour stint. At about two-thirty, I heard mortar rounds hit the *buon* across from District. I woke everyone and told them, but the district chief, an artillery major and a very frightened man, yelled at me that the report had better not be a false alarm. I went back to the radio and waited for instructions. I thought District would investigate the report, but all they did was come into the radio tent and listen. No more rounds went off, so they returned to their bunks, telling me not to wake them again with a false alarm. I was amazed at the way those people acted. When my relief came, he assumed the duties, and weapons' firing could be heard in the *buon*. He asked what he should do, and I advised him to tell everybody. He did, and the major jumped on his shit until the man said I told him to do that. The major then shifted his anger to me. The rest of the night was free of problems and enemy firing. But in the morning, the elder from the *buon* where I'd heard the explosions brought ten dead to District and asked why District hadn't come to the aid of his *buon*.

☆
CHAPTER 12

June 1969

While I waited for transportation to Buon Dham, the district commander wouldn't look at me. The atmosphere was very uncomfortable, and I couldn't wait for my ride, so I started to walk down the road toward my *buon*. Bobleem picked me up before I got too far and told me that we had been assigned a new team leader because our captain had fallen sick. I found out later he had contracted hepatitis. Our team had received a first lieutenant.

Our new ell tee was a recent graduate from the adviser school in Di An and had been a basic training commander before being assigned to Vietnam. As soon as I met him, I didn't like him, nor did any of the other members of our team. When I walked into his hootch, he was sitting behind a makeshift desk. He wore spit-shined boots and a starched uniform. In the rear area, that was expected, but out in the bush, there was no place for it. Discipline was necessary, but not spit-shined boots. In addition, our ell tee decided we had all gone too native and put a curfew on our traveling around the *buons* and on people coming to our hootches. Because our captain had contracted hepatitis, we could no longer drink with the natives even if we brought the water. We were also restricted from participating in the sacrifices. I felt some of the rules would ruin the good rapport with the natives that had taken our team a long time to establish and that we needed to move among the people to find out what was going on in the *buon*. The ell tee disagreed with me. The only other person to say anything was Bobleem, who simply warned the ell tee that he should leave or he might die. Bobleem also mentioned to the ell tee the way the French had died at his *buon*. When the ell tee asked who would kill him, Bobleem said, "A tiger." I talked to Bobleem later, and he explained that he would turn himself into a tiger and eat the ell tee. When I told the ell tee, he freaked out and wanted to go to District the next day.

The ell tee was up at first light and wanting me to go with him to see the district commander. Bobleem wanted to go with us, but the ell tee would not agree. We got to District, and the ell tee was almost in tears as he told the district commander that Bobleem was going to kill him. The ell tee thought that the commander would fire Bobleem as our interpreter, but the ell tee forgot—or never understood—that Bobleem was born in Buon Dham; if anybody was to leave, it would have to be the ell tee. The commander said he wanted our whole team, including Bobleem, in his office the next day. The ell tee was quiet all the way back to our team room. Once there, the ell tee told us we would have to post a guard all night. We looked at one another in disgust, but the team sergeant made up a guard roster.

The night was long, and the ell tee never pulled a shift, so the rest of us had to pull two-hour stints. When morning came, we were off to see the wizard. The district commander again asked what had happened, and I repeated what had been said to me, and I told the commander that the ell tee was being unfair to Bobleem. The other team members agreed with me. The commander made a command decision and assigned the ell tee to a different team. When he said that, we team members had to suppress grins, but we looked meaningfully at each other. In our minds, we were celebrating. We returned to the *buon*, and while the ell tee packed his things, Bobleem went around the *buon* to spread the good word about the ell tee's leaving. Our weapons sergeant took the ell tee to District, and the rest of us had a party.

The rest of my time in Buon Dham, another six months, was spent trying to prevent disease and provide security for the *buon*. Before our team had come to Buon Dham, the people bathed in the local pond along with all the animals. I constructed a shower for the team and several other showers for the village. Before I left Buon Dham, the people boiled their drinking water and, for bathing, used the showers instead of the pond.

New people were arriving all the time, and District decided to send the new people to our *buon* because it was the safest and a model for other *buon*s. I was reassigned to Scherk's *buon* because his team's medic had rotated back to the States, and the District didn't want to send a new medic to a *buon* that was being harassed by the VC. I was ready for the change and thought it would be good just to be with my buddy.

I had learned how to speak the Mnong language while stationed at Buon Dham, but Buon Ma was a Rhade montagnard village, not Mnong, and the languages were different. The mission was still to win the confidence of the montagnards. We armed them and trained them in military tactics and helped them fortify Buon Ma. I gave the people medical assistance by treating their injuries and doing elementary dental work on them, mostly pulling decayed teeth. We were rewarded by being invited to attend and participate in ceremonial drinking and sacrifices. And we received numerous brass bracelets as symbols of acceptance and loyalty.

Buon Ma was located northwest of Ban Me Thuot, close to the Cambodian border. Consequently the *buon* received a lot of harassing fire from NVA as they passed the *buon* while marching in from Cambodia. Scherk's *buon* had a reaction force of about fifty armed men, but it was armed with World War II–era semiautomatic M-1 rifles, and the weapons were bigger than the people carrying them. Montagnards are a tough breed. They handled the weapons as best they could and made up for their shortcomings with a lot of heart. The rest of the *buon* was armed with crossbows and blowguns, the montagnards' traditional weapons for the hunt and defense.

My new team was short one NCO, so Scherk took on the responsibilities of that job. Our team leader, a Captain Wright, looked a bit like Robert Redford and was one of the smartest people I had ever met. He treated his NCOs with respect and let us do whatever we thought necessary to get our assignments done right. He thought of us as professionals and treated us as such. Lieutenant Redman was the opposite of the captain. Although we liked him, he couldn't do much, so the captain let him type reports based on information we gave him. Scherk and I handled all of the *buon* duties ourselves. The captain would help if we asked, but for the most part he just watched us perform.

My first night in the *buon*, someone outside our defenses fired off a burst of automatic fire. It could have been VC or some of the South Vietnamese troops who worked in our area on occasion. I spent numerous sleepless nights at Buon Ma, as did the rest of our team. Being on a team that had as much contact as the one at Buon Ma did, it was difficult to drink, so Scherk and I would occasionally smoke a joint or two. It was amazing how quickly we could come down from a marijuana high to handle a situation. Drunk, we wouldn't have been able to deal with almost any situation very well. I have to admit that occasionally we overindulged in *nampai*; sometimes we just had to forget about the war and think as civilians would in a war-torn country. The montagnard peoples had lived in that environment for thousands of years. If their instincts were bad, then my instincts wouldn't matter.

Scherk took patrols around the *buon* on occasion. During one of them, the patrol found signs of a tiger on the prowl. The people of the *buon* decided to stage a tiger hunt, because they didn't want a tiger setting up in their area, killing water buffalo or dining on children who might wander into the jungle. In addition, the tiger would have meant wealth for the man who shot it: The skin and teeth were worth a fortune. The bones could have been sold to the Chinese for a good sum. The Chinese used tiger bones in compounding traditional medicines.

Of course, to have a successful hunt there had to be a sacrifice. That night, out came *nampai* jugs too numerous to count or for me to remember. A pig was donated, and the party began. It didn't end even when most of us left the *buon* for the hunt; the women and people who didn't go on the hunt stayed up and finished off the food and drink.

In Buon Ma, the montagnards used elephants to haul logs and do heavy work. They also used them to hunt, putting bamboo carriers on their backs to carry hunters and supplies. Tigers could smell a man from miles away, but they apparently couldn't detect a man on the back of an elephant. The "driver" of the elephant sat behind the elephant's ears. He carried a three-foot bamboo stick with a hook on the end that was used to prod the elephant to make it obey his commands.

We loaded onto the back of the elephant and, using the handholds on the bamboo carriers, sat down cross-legged. I was too big to allow more than two people to fit on the back of the elephant I was on. Slowly swaying to and fro with each step of the elephant, off we went into the jungle. The guide on the hunt was the man who had found the tracks and sign of the tiger, and we were moving one behind the other, the guide on the lead elephant. Once we reached the tiger's last known position, the guide stepped down from his elephant and began to look for fresh sign. We hadn't gone more than a couple of klicks before we stopped, and the guide and a couple of other montagnards left to check things out, on elephant-back, while we stayed where we were. Our interpreter told us to be ready, because once the guide found the tiger they would make it move toward our location. We were to have the honor of first chance at the kill. We had been sitting on the back of the elephant for about an hour when the jungle came alive with automatic-weapons fire, the distinct sounds of AK-47s—and our people didn't have AKs. Then another sound startled me, the sound of a huge elephant running full speed in our direction. I watched as the guide and his elephant came racing through and passed our location, giving us only hand signals and yelling at the other montagnards to follow. It seems they had stumbled on a group of NVA infiltrating into Vietnam from Cambodia. It had never occurred to me how close we were to the Cambodian border. We followed quickly behind the guide to make a hasty retreat. I certainly didn't want to be captured while on a tiger hunt or to have someone killed. We didn't have a radio with us to call for help, so our only recourse was to get back to our *buon* and prepare for trouble. From there, we could call for support from District and the artillery that was available at another location.

I never realized how fast an elephant could run. It was difficult to hold on, and I was getting seasick as we rocked and bounced through the jungle. When we finally reached our *buon*, Scherk called District and told them we had spotted a large NVA force moving in our direction. At the same time, all of the men and women were called to arms and set up in a defensive posture. There wasn't any sleep that night, and every time something moved, a flare was sent up.

We never had any contact, so the next morning Scherk and I, along with thirty montagnards, went on patrol to see if we could find signs of the NVA. There was nothing. We probably scared them as much as they scared us. Needless to say, we didn't participate in any more tiger hunts. Of course, we still hunted for deer and monkey, but we made sure we brought along a radio and didn't go too far west.

A couple of weeks had passed when Scherk and I received word that an American and his interpreter had run over a land mine outside their *buon*. We didn't know at first who they were or which *buon* was involved, but after some research, we found out the dead man was Bobleem and the wounded man one of the advisers from Buon Dham. Scherk and I went to the funeral.

Buon Dham was about ninety minutes from where Scherk and I lived, and we had to promise our team leader that we would stop at District to pick up supplies and drop off our team leader's situation reports. Scherk and I laughed whenever we talked about all the paperwork District could create. We had reports on village strength, deaths, sickness, and anything else someone could think up to justify his existence. We stopped at District and did our chores, thinking that most of the advisers would be at or on their way to Bobleem's funeral. We got to Buon Dham, and five hundred people must have come to say farewell to Bobleem. The *nampai* jugs were two hundred in a line. To feed the people who attended the funeral, Bobleem's dogs had been sacrificed, along with a water buffalo. It was a custom to kill the dogs of the deceased. A priest or shaman beat the dogs to death, then threw their bodies onto a bonfire to burn off all the hair. Then they were butchered for the guests.

Bobleem's funeral lasted three days and nights. On the third day, Bobleem was carried to his grave by Scherk, myself, and four other montagnards who were related to Bobleem, followed by several hundred mourners all the way to the grave site until he was laid to rest.

Scherk and I stayed with the Americans who lived in the *buon*, but not one American from District or Province came to pay homage to a fallen comrade and leader of a Mnong tribe. Bobleem had served with the Americans since their arrival in Vietnam and supported the Americans until his death, but apparently none of those people at District or Province cared about the deaths of our allies. I have to admit, that when I first arrived in Vietnam, I didn't care either. However, as I lived with the people and began to mature, I realized we all were caught up in a political war where the little man suffered and the rich got richer. After I'd spent two years observing our presence in Vietnam, my feelings changed radically. I grew to understand the Vietnamese and montagnards and wanted to do whatever I could to protect them—from not only the VC, but from all the people who exploited and used them for their own gain. My experiences in Vietnam have made me a better and more sensitive person.

Scherk and I found out that Bobleem's widow should have received a death benefit from the Vietnamese government, but it never came. In fact, the Vietnamese government rarely paid any of the montagnard widows the benefits that they were due. So I went to the local authorities and asked what she had to do to receive the benefits that were due her. After several minutes of searching, the clerk produced a voucher that said she had been paid the money by the commander of the interpreters. I had the clerk make a copy of the paperwork and left with blood in my eyes. Clearly the man in charge of the interpreters had pocketed the money, a common Vietnamese practice when dealing with montagnards. Weapons in hand, Scherk and I went to have a face-to-face talk with the man, a captain in the Vietnamese army. Since his office was located near Province headquarters, we walked into the building and asked for him. Out came a small Vietnamese man wearing a tailored uniform. A cigarette hung from his mouth, and he looked like a gangster out of a bad movie. But he spoke perfect English and seemed more like a con artist than an officer.

Scherk asked if we could speak with him alone for a minute, and he agreed, probably thinking we had a shady deal for him. He led us into his office. I stood by the door as the captain sat behind the lone desk in the room. Scherk walked to the desk and hovered menacingly over the little man and asked him, in Vietnamese, what had happened to the money owed Bobleem's widow. Scherk showed him the copy of the voucher.

The cigarette fell out of the captain's mouth, and a look of fear suddenly overcame him. He was trying to think of an excuse, and his eyes were moving back and forth between me and Scherk, looking for help. Scherk told the Vietnamese he had one minute to tell us what happened to the money. The sum wasn't an enormous amount, but it was owed her, and we were there to see she got it.

Out of fear, the captain reached into his pocket and pulled out a roll of money a hundred times larger than the widow should have received. He gave it to Scherk and begged Scherk not to kill him.

Scherk peeled the proper amount from the roll and threw the rest on the floor; then he grabbed the Vietnamese and promised to kill him if he ever again stole money from a montagnard. Scherk also said that we were going to find out how many other people the captain had ripped off and report him to the authorities. We then left his office and returned to Buon Dham to present the money to the widow. Bobleem's widow was surprised and grateful for the money, and she asked us to stay and drink some *nampai*, but we had to get back to our *buon* before dark.

When we arrived, our team leader asked what mischief we'd been up to, because the District commander wanted to see us the next day. Of course, Scherk and I knew why he wanted to see us, and we'd kept the voucher copy for our defense. We knew that the way we had handled the problem was wrong and that something bad would probably happen to us for scaring the little son of a bitch. That night at our *buon*, Scherk and I got our stories together. We would tell the major that Bobleem's widow came to us about not receiving the money due her. All we went to do was to find out where the money had gone, and we hadn't threatened anybody. It was the Vietnamese captain's word against ours. Still, I felt that Scherk and I would end up getting the shaft.

The next morning, we put on our best uniforms and spit-shined boots and drove to District headquarters. On the way, we rehearsed our story. When we got to District we learned the major had left for a meeting at Province headquarters. The sergeant we spoke to didn't know when the major would be back. It would have been helpful if the major had radioed the *buon* to tell us he wouldn't be there. We didn't even know if he'd forgotten or wanted to make us wait for his return, but the NCO said that the major usually stayed the night at the Bungalow when he went to a meeting at Province headquarters. So Scherk and I returned to our *buon*, hoping that the major had already forgotten about us.

Our captain was on our side and said he would talk to the major, so Scherk and I repeated our story to him so that he could relate it to the major. We gave him the voucher and told him we had given the money to the widow. The captain said we shouldn't worry any more about the situation. We liked our captain and hoped we wouldn't get him in trouble.

The next day our captain was told to report to the major. Scherk and I thought the captain was going to get his ass chewed. As it turned out, Scherk and I were volunteered for an operation that was taking place in our area. Actually, Scherk was the only person volunteered, but I wasn't going to stay behind and answer the major's questions alone. Scherk was picked to assist on the operation because of his detailed knowledge of the terrain and the area. When the captain returned, he was accompanied by a Special Forces sergeant, the only American with a CIDG unit. CIDG stood for Civilian Irregular Defense Group, a montagnard unit that operated with Americans to raise the standard of living for and win the loyalty of the montagnards. Those montagnard soldiers were excellent fighters, brave men, and loyal to their advisers. When I served with SF, I had observed Mike Force, but never worked with any of the montagnard units. I had only heard stories of their bravery. Bobleem had served with a CIDG unit until he was wounded and lost his eye.

The Special Forces NCO briefed us on his intelligence reports. High-flying aircraft had picked up a large movement of NVA troops across the Cambodian border, and his montagnards wanted to go after them, but the montagnards were from a different area and didn't know the land as well as Scherk did. As the sergeant briefed Scherk, I sat and listened and kept my mouth shut. Scherk asked what kind of support the sergeant had and was told that he was under the control of the local Vietnamese artillery and air support. They also had to use Vietnamese medevacs, which was not wonderful because Vietnamese medevacs wouldn't fly at night, and if the unit being supported was montagnard, it was almost impossible to get the Vietnamese to fly out the wounded at all. But because of our presence with the CIDG, we would be able to call in American medevacs and use any other American support that was available. The mission was to take as long as necessary, which meant until contact was made.

Scherk and I packed for the duration. I carried a radio along with my other equipment. To support the mission, I would be responsible for calling in medevacs and anything else available in our province. The CIDGs were already camped outside our *buon* waiting for the order to move. We left early the next morning but only after drinking a couple of jugs of *nampai* with the Special Forces NCO. We called him Spike, and I don't remember his real name. He didn't wear a name tag, and I didn't want to be nosy and ask him for a life history. I could see that he had excellent rapport with his soldiers; it was clear to Scherk and me that the montagnards would die for the guy. Spike was tall, probably in his late thirties or early forties. He was skinny as a rail but could carry more than his share. He talked slowly and deliberately so that everyone understood what he had said. He was fluent in the language of his troops to the point of being able to joke with them. As we sat behind the *nampai* jugs, he talked constantly when he wasn't drinking, not to us but to his troops. Unfortunately, I didn't understand a word of that part of the conversation.

We walked into the countryside with a hundred or so troops in tow. The CIDGs moved quietly and fast, something I never saw the Vietnamese Rangers do. The sergeant had one element that was dressed in black PJs and walked point, that is, in front of our main body of troops. We were heading toward the area of our tiger hunt. I could tell those CIDGs had been together a long time because they moved cautiously but steadily. Every soldier was looking for something. When I had worked with the Vietnamese Rangers, the only man looking for the enemy was the point man; the rest of the troops followed like men on a chain gang. The CIDGs carried no noisy pots and pans or canteens or radios, and no one was smoking.

When we came to a trail, the column would stop while the black-clad montagnards checked out the area. We stayed off trails, paralleling them until we had to cross. Scherk knew which trails were old and which trails were new, and Spike chose to follow the new trails. We might move only fifteen meters and then stop again. The montagnards knew how to move and what to do when something went wrong.

The terrain around our *buon* and much of the surrounding area was the same—triple canopy—and it was very difficult to see the ground from the sky. It was also very difficult for us to see the sky. Our only advantage in that terrain was that someone on the ground could guide our air superiority on target. If the weather was bad enough to prevent that, then we had no advantage over the enemy. It would be a ground battle where the first side to spot the enemy and seize the advantage would win. Seeing the way the CIDGs moved, I knew we were tactically superior. I wished I had started with that type of unit, because if I had, I would have developed faster into a better infantryman. I knew I had already developed into a capable medic. At least, I wasn't afraid to try everything I had learned to save someone.

It took us most of the day to move eight or nine kilometers. The terrain was so thickly overgrown that it seemed to produce its own rain; something was always falling from the trees and bushes as we moved. The vines grabbed at our rucks and tripped some of us up. For the most part, the only one to fall was me. I caught every vine in the jungle on my ruck, even when the man in front of me slid through the vines without effort. I was afraid that I was making too much noise until Spike fell with a loud thud. I had become rusty since my Lurping days with the 101st. But Scherk was smooth and moved like a cat on the prowl.

As the sun went down, so did the visibility, and we had to stop for the night. Spike set out ambushes all around our perimeter; then we just lay back on our rucks until first light.

Out of shape and extremely tired, I fell asleep without effort. I had the radio, so every two hours I had to key the mike to let District know we were alive. Scherk checked to make sure I was doing the sitreps, but every time I had them done before he could say anything.

That was my quietest night in the jungle: I could hear people breathing, animals talking, leaves and drops of rain falling. The only things I didn't feel or hear were the leeches crawling on my face. On the last sitrep of the night, Scherk pulled three topped-off leeches from my face, and it bled for an hour. While we waited for the ambushes to return to our main body, we ate and went through the morning rituals. During that mission, I never saw anyone smoking, and that included Scherk, who was a nicotine addict. In the light of morning, Scherk laughed at my face, which was swollen and battered from the leeches. I really didn't care how I looked, but the spots itched worse than a mosquito bite.

As soon as the ambush parties linked up, we were on the move again—for about five minutes; then the point squad spotted movement. A large element must have been spotted, because Spike immediately sent out flank squads and set up our 60 mm mortar. I lay there thinking that I would really have to be careful before I fired my weapon. If the point squad came running back toward us while wearing VC garb, it would be difficult to tell if they were friendly or enemy. Fortunately, nothing happened, and we were on the move again. I was told later that if I saw a VC-clad soldier near my location, I was to engage that individual and kill him.

The rest of the day was without incident, and that night, I made sure to use more than enough repellent to keep the leeches away.

After three days out, we were running low on rations, so Spike called for a resupply mission. We stopped by a fast-moving, deep, clear stream. The water was over my head, but we could see to the bottom, and there were tons of fish. If I had been with the Vietnamese Rangers, they would have thrown a grenade into the stream and collected a lot of fish. Of course, the noise would have notified everyone within a ten-mile radius where we were. The montagnards carried bamboo fish traps on their rucks, so while we waited for resupply, we ate fish. I took advantage of the deep stream and dived in, boots and all. Voilá, a clean uniform and a drenched body; I was ready for the days to come. I didn't even know we had been resupplied until Scherk handed me a case of C rations. We buried all of our trash, and my ruck was as light as a feather until I put the case of Cs in it.

On our fifth day in the field, the point squad made contact by walking into the point of an NVA platoon. The NVA didn't fire; our guys cut loose and the enemy ran. Spike yelled at the troops and they dispersed into the jungle on line, moving at the run and yelling as they went. The point squad had killed six NVA and wounded three others. I treated the wounded NVA, and helicopters were called in to take them away. We didn't have any wounded. Along with the evacuation helicopters came gunships, and they were turned loose to rake the area in front of and behind us. There was no extraction for us, and we had to walk one and a half days to get back to the *buon*. That place had never looked so good, but the best thing about it was a shower.

Spike and his troops spent that night drinking *nampai* and eating everything in sight, while the local montagnards brought out their cymbals and gonged the night away. Scherk and I strolled away from the rest of the crowd and smoked a joint in private. We got back just in time to see Spike pass out. I was exhausted and was looking forward to a good night of sleep, so I drank only enough to satisfy the people who provided the *nampai*. Our captain left us alone until the next morning, when he wanted an after-action report. The paperwork was Scherk's; my job was to relax. After Scherk finished his report to the satisfaction of the captain, the captain told us we were to report to the major that morning, because the major wouldn't accept our account as the truth.

The major was standing in the front entranceway to his office as we pulled into the compound. We parked our jeep about three feet from him, got out, and saluted him in proper military fashion. He turned his back without returning the salute—a breach of military etiquette—so we realized the shit was going to hit the fan. We followed the major into his office, but he asked me to wait outside while he first spoke with Scherk. While I waited, I was trying to remember the story Scherk and I had made up. It wasn't hard because the story was mostly true. Only the threats we had made were eliminated from our account. Our only evidence was the voucher, and the captain had given that to the major.

Scherk came out of the major's office, and I was called in. I stood before the major's desk and reported formally. The major asked about what had happened, and I repeated our story. When I finished, the major remarked that I had learned my lines well, because it was the same story Scherk had told.

The major said it sounded rehearsed. I told him it wasn't hard to tell the same story when it was the truth.

The major then began to chew my ass about courtesy to an officer, saying that it didn't matter what that officer had done; it wasn't our responsibility to correct him. By the book, the major was probably right, but in my heart I wanted to tell him that he was full of shit. Instead I bit my tongue and kept my mouth closed; I was afraid of what he was going to do to us. After much ass-chewing, he called Scherk into the office and told us we were going to be separated and sent to different teams. I pleaded that I be the only one moved, because Scherk had such good relations with his *buon* and team. The major agreed. The major also said that he was going to investigate our story, and if anyone else said we were lying, we would be court-martialed. In the week before the major found a place for me to work, Scherk and I talked about what we were going to do for the rest of our time in Vietnam. We decided that when the tour was over, we would extend for a unit where we could work together. Scherk was a true professional soldier and knew his trade well. I would always want him on my side.

I was sent to a Rhade montagnard village outside Ban Me Thuot to work for MACV MAT 25 out of a compound much like the District headquarters. My team leader was a civilian named Robert Givens. The compound housed fifteen NCOs and ten officers. To this day, I don't know what their function was other than to create something to do. I never really talked to anyone except Mr. Givens, who was married to a montagnard teacher living in Ban Me Thuot. He visited her on the weekends.

I had forgotten about weekends off, but that team worked banker's hours. And once the team leader was gone, the compound turned into a party house. If there wasn't anything to do, then it was off to a minimall compound of well-constructed whorehouses enclosed by a cement wall. Guards at the gate admitted only American and Vietnamese officers.

And there, every Friday night, our black first sergeant had a party. He first asked the team members which ones wanted women; then he trucked them onto our compound. I have to admit that the women were exceptionally beautiful. The funny thing was that he collected all the money, and we didn't have to give the girls anything if we didn't want to. We all brought our own bottles of hard liquor and beer.

Although I never bought a woman from our first sergeant, I did participate in the steak, fries, and drinking marathons. Since I didn't know anyone, I was afraid to smoke grass in front of them. Those guys had powerful amplifiers and speakers that could handle 150 watts. After observing my first sergeant in action with all of his enterprises, I concluded that by the time he left Vietnam, he would be a millionaire.

Across from the whorehouse compound was an aviation unit, and those men had it made, too. Among other luxuries, they had a steam bath, and masseuses who gave real massages. I often sat in the steam bath for an hour or so, then had an hour-long massage. I hated to leave that place. I got so relaxed there that I sometimes fell asleep.

Once, as I was leaving the aviation unit's compound, I saw our first sergeant behind a two-and-a-half-ton truck filled with fifty-five-gallon gas drums that he was filling with gas from the aviation unit. Out of curiosity I followed him when he had finished. He drove to downtown Ban Me Thuot and off-loaded the fifty-five-gallon drums at a Vietnamese gas station. He disappeared inside, so I didn't see whether he received any money, but I would be willing to bet he received some kind of payment.

Some nights everybody played poker and always ended up borrowing money from the first sergeant. He would pull out a roll of bills that could choke a horse.

Come Monday, everything was back to normal; Mr. Givens would return, and it was business as usual. Of the whole group, Mr. Givens was the only man I could communicate with. He was sincere about his job and the montagnard people.

Mr. Givens hated the Vietnamese and their paperwork shuffle and didn't like the way the Vietnamese treated the montagnards. I never said anything to him about our first sergeant out of fear it would ruin the good thing those guys had. Besides, I felt like I was on probation because of what Scherk and I had done. I did tell Mr. Givens about the Vietnamese officer who had taken Bobleem's widow's money, and he confirmed that was common practice for Vietnamese officials. After I was on that team for about two months, because of the rotation of some of the team members, I became the NCO with the most in-country time—except for the first sergeant. I don't think he ever wanted to leave; he was getting too rich. I, on the other hand, wasn't getting rich, but I was meeting a lot of people and learning more about those people every day.

After observing my ambitious first sergeant, I decided to open a store in our compound. I provided supplies, and my montagnard girlfriend ran it. Our compound had about one hundred Vietnamese and montagnards for security, and they stayed in the compound except to shop for food and drink. The montagnards didn't have the luxury of a military club system, and they could not afford the prices in the local bars, so I opened a dry-goods store and a place for them to drink. The prices were cheap, and I made only enough money to cover expenses. The team leader didn't know that I was doing that, either. He didn't know about any of the extracurricular activities on the compound.

In the fall of 1969, Scherk called me by radio to let me know that he was ready to take his R & R and wanted me to go with him. I put in paperwork for Thailand, but Scherk and I planned on spending our time in Vietnam. When the orders finally came down, Scherk and I were on them. We met at the Bungalow and decided to spend our time at the beach in Nha Trang. We also decided to try to find a better job while we were on leave. Our tours were coming to an end, and we both wanted to stay in Vietnam.

When we finished the paperwork and were signed out of our units, we went to the supply sergeant who'd been using our jeep and recovered it. We had a couple of spare gas cans, enough to make it to Nha Trang.

The weather was perfect, sunshine and cool breeze. When the sun shines in the highlands, everything is green, and all of the flowers were in bloom. When we drove by an area that was full of magnolia trees, the scent filled the air. The countryside was really a panorama of beauty. Traffic across country was minimal, just the occasional bus packed with people on the inside and people hanging on the outside. The buses carried luggage on the roof, and people sat on that luggage just for the privilege of a ride. The only worry Scherk and I had was about going through the Korean lines. The Koreans could really be assholes, stopping Americans, questioning them, and searching their vehicles for no other reason than to mess with them. But we passed through the Korean lines without a problem. We never even saw one of them.

As we got closer to Nha Trang, we could tell because the houses got closer together and fruit stands appeared alongside the road. Our jeep had new MACV numbers painted on the bumpers so we could drive anywhere without the military stopping us. After all, we were American advisers.

We entered Nha Trang and went to the Nautique restaurant and hotel. We paid up front for the week just in case we ran out of money later. We could always go to a U.S. facility and eat in one of the many mess halls.

The Nautique sat across the street from the beach, and its rooms were individual bungalows arranged in a circle around a fountain. Each room had a small patio with a table and chairs, where we could eat breakfast or dinner and listen to the waves on the beach. The Nautique was like a compound in the middle of a jungle, and the aroma of wildflowers was always in the air, overshadowing any of the area's offensive odors. The restaurant had a screened-in patio that faced the beach, so flies and mosquitoes were at a minimum, and only the smell of insect spray was offensive.

As in any hotel and restaurant in Vietnam, women were available to drink with or sleep with, and I knew most of them from having lived in Nha Trang for six months. Most of the women had worked in the Nautique since the place had opened. The owner was a Frenchman who had owned the place since the French controlled the country. He was called Frenchy.

We parked our jeep in the rear of the compound and chained it to the building. Scherk said he was tired and was going to crash for a while. I was hungry and couldn't wait to eat some good seafood, so I left. But just as I got to the door of the restaurant, I realized I had forgotten my money. When I walked into our room, Scherk was snorting something. He looked at me as if I'd caught him doing something very wrong. On his bed were a bunch of small clear plastic vials filled with a white substance. It was heroin, refined opium. Why he'd been hiding it from me, I'll never understand. I'd done lots of drugs, but never pure heroin. To relieve his fear, I asked to try some. Heroin can be snorted, smoked, or injected intravenously with a syringe and needle. Scherk told me he hadn't been doing heroin long, but from the amount I saw on his bed, he was either selling it or he was hooked. I snorted some of the white powder, and it immediately made me lose my appetite. At that point, if I had eaten, I'm sure I would have vomited. I just didn't like it as much as I liked pot. After a joint, food tasted delicious, and I could drink all night. With pot, sex was more sensual.

I soon learned that Scherk didn't like to go out when he did heroin, so I hit the beach bars and, once in a while, took in a Chinese movie. At night I went to bars that had live music, but I was back at my hotel before the curfew for Americans; I didn't want to be picked up by the military police. Then, if

I wasn't tired, I would sit in the hotel bar until they threw me out. Scherk would be passed out by the time I got back to the room.

When Scherk and I had only one day left, we finally decided to research a job that we had been told about, a program or organization called Phoenix that was actively recruiting advisers for its mission. The term for Phoenix in Vietnamese is *Phung Hoang*, which is a bird of freedom. The mission of the Phoenix was to neutralize the Viet Cong infrastructure. In reality, it was a secret-police unit that sought to catch the Viet Cong who were living and working in South Vietnam. It targeted the leadership of the Viet Cong organization. Scherk and I went to the CORDS compound that housed the the headquarters of the organization and had an interview with the commander, a Colonel Millet. Before we left Nha Trang, we had letters of acceptance. Our trip back to Ban Me Thuot was fast; I couldn't wait to put in my transfer request.

We pulled into Ban Me Thuot and dropped the jeep off with our favorite supply sergeant. I returned to my *buon* and learned that my team leader was gone for the week; Scherk found out he was without a job. The province had pulled the advisers out of his *buon* and sent them all to other jobs. When the personnel clerk asked Scherk if *he* knew of an available job, Scherk pulled out his letter of acceptance from the Phoenix commander, then told the clerk he could be found at my *buon* when his orders came in. Unfortunately, the clerk told me I wouldn't be going anywhere because of the shortage of medics. Looking back on it, I think that some of our people knew of Scherk's problem with drugs and wanted to get rid of him. The only way I was going to be able to get to the Phoenix Program was to extend my tour in Vietnam, but to do that, I had to wait for my team leader to return to approve the paperwork.

Scherk and I went to my *buon* and waited for the return

of my team leader. That night Scherk and I joined the rest of my team in playing poker. I was smoking marijuana from packs that looked like store-bought cigarettes. A couple of the older guys complained that our cigarettes were moldy, but when they ran out of their own, they borrowed a couple from Scherk and me. Of course, they didn't realize they were smoking grass, and as time went on, they thought they were getting drunk on their beer. After about an hour, they developed the munchies and were having problems concentrating on the game. Then one guy dropped his cards on the floor and couldn't pick them up. Everybody started laughing and couldn't stop. The fun went on for about three hours before everyone gave up on the idea of poker and raided the kitchen for chow.

The next day I approached Scherk about his drug problem and told him he would have to stop before we arrived at our new assignment. We would be spending more time in the field, and not with Americans. We would have to set the example and be drug free. Scherk agreed with me and promised that he would quit, but he would have to get out of the *buon* environment to kick the habit.

My team leader returned from his vacation, and I told him about Scherk's problem with drugs and explained that the military didn't have any programs for drug users. The only thing the military did in those days was to give the individual jail time or throw him out of the service. I wanted to get back to a field unit and at the same time help Scherk kick his habit. My team leader said he admired my wanting to help Scherk but felt that was work for professionals. But, after about two hours of begging, the team leader endorsed my paperwork "approved."

Scherk had applied for leave en route to his new assignment, and I took my extension leave at the same time. We picked up our jeep for the last time and bade farewell to Ban Me Thuot. En route to our point of departure, we dropped the jeep off at the CORDS compound; I wasn't about to give the jeep away. Then we went to the air base and caught a flight to Saigon. We were to leave Vietnam from Saigon, and we had two days to wait until our flight left. I spent my time at the air force theater watching Stateside movies while Scherk disappeared downtown. It came time for our flight, and Scherk arrived at the last minute. I thought for sure he'd miss the flight.

The trip home was routine except that when we arrived in Tacoma, Scherk and I had to go through customs. Scherk was acting strange and had broken out in a sweat. When I asked if he felt all right, he said he was fine, but I knew when Scherk was lying, and that was one of those times. Something wasn't right. The closer Scherk got to the customs agent, the more he sweated, and the sicker he looked. Even the customs agent asked him if he was okay. The agent went through Scherk's things like a tornado. Nothing was left unturned. When he got to Scherk's shaving kit, he found the toothpaste had broken open and coated everything. The agent pointed that out to Scherk, then closed the kit. Scherk immediately recovered from whatever had bothered him.

We left customs and headed for the domestic-flight counter to find out about the next flight to Oakland. On the way, I asked Scherk what he was up to, but he wouldn't answer me. I was starting to have flashbacks about being put in jail for something I hadn't known about. When we got to the boarding area, I grabbed Scherk and said, "What the fuck is going on?" He said that he had smuggled a container of heroin in his shaving bag. I grew very angry and demanded to know what he was going to do with it. After all, he was supposed to be kicking the habit. He said he intended to sell it so we could live the good life while we were in the States! When we boarded the plane, I asked for a seat away from him. I just knew I would be the one who took the hit if he got caught. I wanted to sleep while in flight, but my anger overrode my ability to relax. Scherk knew I was pissed and didn't make an effort to approach me while I was on the aircraft, but as soon as we landed in Oakland, he told me he would get rid of the heroin. We went to where my Corvette was being stored, then on to Atascadero, where Scherk's parents lived. All the way to Atascadero, I didn't let up on how *I* was going to be clean when I returned to the bush.

We arrived at Atascadero early in the morning, and Scherk's stepsister opened the door. I can't remember her name, but it was something like Candi or Bunni. I do remember she was tall, slender, had big blue eyes that went great with her blond hair, and was very well built. She was just visiting her mother when we showed up. Scherk's stepsister wasn't married but lived with a rather wealthy man somewhere in L.A.

Without our knowing anyone, and with both of Scherk's parents working, there wasn't much to do or anyone to talk to. Scherk didn't know anyone except his stepsister, so we went to visit her at her mountainside home. It was beautiful, but for some reason, it didn't have any furniture. For a man who was supposed to be wealthy, her guy sure didn't have much other than the girl. When we arrived, Candi had a girlfriend visiting from New York, and she was also beautiful. We hit it off really well, but I had Scherk with me, so I couldn't do anything. The girl gave me her address and asked me to write to her once I got back to Vietnam. While we were talking, she gave us her views on the war in Nam, saying we shouldn't be there. At that point in my life, I felt we had a need to be there, so we argued for a while, then fell asleep on the empty living room floor.

When Scherk and I awoke the next morning, everybody was gone. So we left a note with our farewells, then went back to Scherk's home and said good-bye to his parents. While Scherk was talking to his parents, I found his heroin stash in a talcum powder container and dumped it down the toilet. The stuff was probably 98 percent pure, and I'm certain that any junkie who used it would have overdosed.

With the farewells said and my car packed, we hit the road, looking for adventure. But first we went to a local pawnshop and bought a couple of weapons to take with us. I got a .44 Magnum Ruger, while Scherk purchased a .357 Magnum. We both got western-style holsters. We also bought a couple of swords to use as machetes in the jungle. The store owner sharpened the swords to the point that we could shave with them. We had to wait three days to pick up the weapons, so we cruised down Highway 1 to see the ocean and stop in at Fort Ord to get paid. One of the benefits in those days before computerized, networked pay records was being able to stop at any military base and draw casual pay. I stopped at all military facilities and got paid whether I needed it or not, even though that meant that when I returned to Vietnam I would receive "no pay due" for a couple of months; I could live in Nam without money. After several days of sight-seeing, we swung back to pick up the guns. With swords in hand and guns on our hips, we hit the highway, traveling during daylight and finding a motel with a bar each night. We had plenty of money, and we lived like the rich and famous, eating and drinking whatever and whenever we felt like it. I had thought about stopping at Longmont, Colorado, to see Lana, but Scherk and I both wanted to see my parents, which I hadn't done since the annulment of my marriage to Monica, so we decided to forgo the stop.

Along the way, traveling through desert terrain, and it being secluded, we stopped often to fire our new weapons. We both got pretty good. Of course, with my weapon being a .44 Magnum, about all I had to do was point it at a target and I could hit it. But once we left the deserts behind, it became more difficult to find a place to fire the weapons.

We arrived in Culver, Indiana, in the morning, and everybody was already at work. Scherk and I went to find my mother first. From her office, we went to find my father. My mother knew where he was and called to let him know I was in town and looking for him. My father was counseling a cadet at the Culver Military Academy; he couldn't tear himself away from the military, and that was the closest thing to active duty he could find. At Culver he was able to share his experiences with the younger generation. All of the cadets loved him and my mother, and my parents often took in cadets for holiday meals when the cadets weren't able to make it home.

Scherk and I waited outside my dad's office until he was finished with the cadet. Through the window overlooking the school grounds, we watched the young cadets going through drill and ceremony. Scherk and I were both thinking about how *we* would be doing drill and ceremony once we returned from Nam. As if on cue, we looked at each other and declared, "No way are we staying in the military unless there is a war!" Well, that's the way I felt at the time, but as circumstances would have it, I did remain on active duty.

Finally, my father finished with the cadet and walked out of his office. With a big smile and a fatherly hug he welcomed me and Scherk home. He told me to give him a moment to clear his schedule and let people know where he would be. Of course, he told everyone we would be at the local VFW. The VFW was the only bar in town that opened early in the morning, and it was like a second home to my dad.

The VFW had changed dramatically since the last time I had visited the establishment, and it was a result of my father's influence. I had helped when the first stages of the remodeling had started but had never seen the completed project until that moment. It was truly a credit to the veterans who had worked on it. The bar was still located in the basement of the building. It was small, but held a pool table and could accommodate a small band. Without a word, the bartender handed my dad a beer and asked Scherk and me what we wanted. Let the drinking begin! We spent the rest of the afternoon drinking, playing pool, and telling war stories. It was one of the best times I had at home with my dad. My mother called the VFW after she got off work and told us to come home for dinner. By that time, the three of us were three sheets to the wind, and that we made it home without killing ourselves or someone else still amazes me. Dinner was ready when we walked in the door, and the smell of the house brought back many warm memories. Dinner was fabulous, but because of our drinking and being worn out, Scherk and I passed out after dinner.

Scherk and I slept in and didn't hear my parents leave for work the next morning. It was noon, and Scherk and I both needed a little hair of the dog. We hit the first bar we came to, Bob's Tavern, which overlooked Lake Maxinkuckee and had the best food in Culver, not to mention a pool table. There were only a couple of people in the bar, two of whom were local asshole brothers. When we walked in, everyone gave us ugly stares, as if we were creatures from another planet. We ignored the stares and ordered a beer each and a couple of burgers. While we waited for our food, Scherk and I played pool.

All the while, the two brothers continued to stare at us to the point of my asking the bigger of them what his problem was. He said he knew who I was, and he and his brother didn't like queers. It was a good thing I didn't have a pool cue in my hand, because I immediately saw red and wanted to kill this insect. Bob, the owner of the bar, knew me and was close at hand. He advised the brother not to bother us. Then Bob pulled me aside and told me that my former wife, Monica, had told people in town that she left me because I was gay. Just then Monica and her boyfriend walked in. Bob turned green; he wasn't having a good day. If looks could kill, Monica would have died that very moment. Her face turned ashen when she saw me. Her boyfriend wanted to leave, but Bob asked me and Scherk to leave because he didn't want any problems. I told him there'd be no problem, then turned to the ugly brother, looking him in the eye, and told him it was his lucky day—that he had been closer to death than he'd known, and that if he ever again mentioned thinking of me as a homosexual, I would personally rip his dick off, shove it in his mouth, and make him eat it. I turned to Scherk, who was watching my back, and told him it was time to go. On the way out, I stopped by Monica's table and told her not to be spreading rumors about me because of her inadequacies as a wife. Scherk and I walked out of the bar.

I really wanted to hit someone. But my parents lived in that town, and I didn't want any more problems, or to generate gossip for the small minds there. As we drove toward my house, I told Scherk it was time to leave before I did something stupid. It seemed to me that everybody in the States hated those of us who were serving in Nam. It was easy to say things about us when we weren't around to defend ourselves. I had a sister who lived in Chicago, and when we got to my parents' home, I left a note saying we were going to visit her. I just wanted out of that town and, for that matter, out of the country. Scherk and I stayed in Chicago just one night, leaving early the next morning for California. I couldn't wait to get back to Vietnam.

By then I definitely felt more comfortable in Nam than in the States. Even today I don't feel the same level of security and comfort I had there. That may sound crazy, but the only time I felt uneasy in Nam was while engaging the enemy and after a firefight. But stateside I live with the feeling of butterflies in my stomach every day. I worry about the tax people taking my house and how to support my family. It's a struggle to maintain sanity in our society, one that seems to have little sense of commitment to family or friendship. It seems everyone is out to get whatever he can without regard to anyone else or anyone else's welfare. For me, a good night's sleep makes everything better. Things do go away, especially in war in the lives of those guys who went to Vietnam at the request or orders of our government. We came back and are supposed to act the way we did before we left; it doesn't happen that way. I have friends in jail for murder because they couldn't deal with our society and the way they were treated after returning to the Land of the Free and the Home of the Brave.

Finally, after driving three days straight, Scherk and I arrived at Oakland Army Terminal. After getting manifested on a flight back to Nam, I put my Corvette in storage. We wouldn't be leaving until the following day, and we didn't want to stay at the army base, so we spent the night in a motel just outside the airport, where we had several beers and joints, then conducted a mock sword fight. After packing the next morning, I closed the curtains and found we had cut them to ribbons. We quickly pulled back the curtains and arranged them so no one could tell they had been killed. We made a fast exit to the airport, praying the sliced-up curtains wouldn't be noticed until we were well on our way back to Nam.

☆
CHAPTER 13

Phung Hoang (Phoenix Program)

In Western mythology, the phoenix is a bird with the wings of a bird (air), the tail of a fish (sea), and the legs/feet of a land animal (land). In Eastern mythology, the phoenix is a symbol of the empress, signifying peace, prosperity, happiness, and fertility (those were our goals) and is frequently depicted in Chinese restaurants and at weddings. It is a bird that rises up and out of the ashes of defeat and despair, slays all its enemies, and reigns for a thousand years.

The Isis (an Egyptian goddess) or ICEX (intelligence, coordination, and exploitation) Program was the test bed for the Phoenix Program. ICEX was officially created in July 1967, although basic structures had been in place for a year. It was placed under CORDS, and its trial was conducted in Saigon and Gia Dinh, a large metropolitan area. The concept of the Phoenix Program was modeled on the British success against Communist insurgents in Malaysia. The idea of the Phoenix and Isis programs was not to fight soldier against soldier in mass formations, but to utilize specific targeting to "neutralize"—that is, assassinate or imprison—members of the civilian infrastructure of the National Liberation Front. The Viet Cong infrastructure (VCI) were the leaders of the terrorist/revolutionary effort and, concurrently, also the leaders of the Communist party.

Article 10 of the constitution for the Republic of Vietnam made being a Communist and adhering to communism's ideology to overthrow the constitutional government through violence and terrorism a crime punishable by death.

Phoenix offices were set up from the national level down to district level. Their functions were to organize intelligence on the Viet Cong infrastructure. Through interrogation of civilians picked up by military units, captured enemy soldiers, and assets from intelligence units that had infiltrated the VCI, the Phoenix offices identified the people involved, including spies, terrorists, commo liasions, supply officers, political cadre, tax collectors, etc.

Persons to be neutralized were put on a "blacklist," according to specific leadership categories (defined in the "Green Book"). Persons placed on the blacklist had to be identified by three separate sources and from three separate agencies. Placing an individual on the blacklist at the province level had to be coordinated with the province (state) security committee, consisting of the province senior judge, the province chief of the National Police, and the province chief. The blacklist had to be coordinated with the CIA to avoid accidental neutralization of their resources. The blacklist contained six-digit UTM (map) coordinates for the province People's Revolutionary Party committees, listing the name and position of each member. Leaders were categorized as level A or B and were to be neutralized through three methods:

1. The *Chieu Hoi* program that gave the enemy incentive to come over to our side by rewards of money and property: buy them a farm, educate them in farm methods, pay them money, etc.—offer the hand of compassion, friendship, and protection. In turn, they told who, what, when, where, and how.

2. Arrest and trial by the province security committee (province judge; chief, Special Branch; province prosecutor).

Category A, if found guilty, a mandatory sentence of not less than two years on Poulo Condore (Island of the Condors), also known as Con Son Island. If they acted up, their terms could be extended.

Category B, sentence of one year, which could be extended if the prisoner did not reform.

3. Termination (execution or assassination). That was usually done by CIA-led Vietnamese organized into Provincial Reconnaissance Units (PRU). All KIA were photographed and thumbprinted, their documents and weapons recorded.

The director of Phoenix Program was William Colby, a CIA officer who worked in conjunction with a Vietnamese officer of the government's Special Branch. Colby would later become the little-loved director of the CIA.

The miltary commander of the Phoenix Program was legendary army officer Col. Lewis L. Millett, a recipient of the Medal of Honor during the Korean War. As a captain and the company commander of E Company, 27th Infantry Regiment, he led his company in a bayonet attack against a strongly held and fortified enemy hilltop position. Through brutal opposing fire, the attack soon turned into ferocious hand-to-hand combat. Though seriously wounded, he refused evacuation until the position was taken and secured.

Colonel Millett had also been responsible for establishing the Recondo School for the 101st Airborne Divison under the leadership of then Maj. Gen. William Westmoreland.

December 1969

It was a great relief to get back in country. Scherk and I were fortunate in acquiring transportation. As soon as we got off the civilian aircraft, we went to the MAC (military airlift command) terminal at Tan Son Nhut Air Base and were able to catch a flight to Nha Trang, where our jeep was being stored. We took a Lambretta (a vehicle that was part motorcycle and could squeeze in ten Vietnamese yet was barely large enough to accommodate two GIs) to the CORDS compound and did some in-processing. We reported to Colonel Millett, who we found to be very personable and genuinely concerned about anyone under his command. On spotting the French parachute jacket I was wearing, he was really taken with it and asked me numerous questions about it. I had received the jacket as a farewell gift from a montagnard friend who didn't want me to leave. In the spirit of friendship, and because I knew he liked and appreciated the jacket, I gave the jacket to Colonel Millett.

Scherk and I spent the night in Nha Trang, renewing old acquaintances. At first light we headed for God's country and the land of plenty. On our drive to our new home, the Central Highlands offered an unbelievably beautiful panorama, marred only by the sight of foreign armies and the destruction they brought with them.

Da Lat was located in the upper highlands in Tuyen Duc Province, directly west of Cam Ranh Bay and southwest of Nha Trang. Da Lat sat on top of a hill that looked more like a mountain from an aircraft making a landing. The only airstrip was Cam Le. It had the shortest runway in South Vietnam and sat on the highest tip of land in Da Lat. Many aircraft overshot the landing strip and crashed. Aircraft loaded too heavily couldn't get enough altitude to clear the end of the runway on takeoff and would crash. The landscape of Da Lat was home to large oak and pine trees and trees that I couldn't identify. These trees were foliated with green vegetation that enhanced the beauty of the area. There were also many rubber-tree and coffee plantations that added to the color of the area. The temperature actually got below fifty degrees during certain times of the year. The area had been a resort for the French during the period of French colonization. The countryside was filled with French-style villas. It was the only place that had real lettuce and vegetables that we had in the States. The city housed a university, a nuclear reactor, and the South Vietnam version of our West Point. It was truly a beautiful area, especially to live in. If there hadn't been a war, it would have been the biggest tourist attraction in South Vietnam. Great hunting as well, man and beast.

We arrived in the early afternoon and knew we had to report to the province headquarters but had no idea where it was. As we entered Da Lat, we stopped and gave a lift to an air force airman. In return for the ride, he showed us the way to province headquarters. Scherk and I were now assigned to MACV Advisory Team 26 (MAT 26), under the command of the military intelligence officer and Phoenix coordinator for Tuyen Duc Province, Maj. Erwin Minter. We reported to the province headquarters and were told that Major Minter was on operation with the 302d Reconnaissance Company. They said he would be gone for an undetermined time, which meant they would be gone until they made contact with the enemy. The only person who really knew what was happening at headquarters was Chu My, the pretty radio operator whose husband, an American staff sergeant named Jerry Beckett, was on the operation with Major Minter. Chu My filled Scherk and me in on the history of the American occupation and the problems that had gone on and were going on at that time in Da Lat. She spoke English better than I could; she spoke French as well as she spoke English. She was a very intelligent woman and with beauty to match. She was very happy to see us because it meant her husband wouldn't have to go on missions anymore. Everybody knew we were coming. Staff Sergeant Beckett was the operations sergeant for the province headquarters. Before I arrived in Tuyen Duc Province, S.Sgt. Jerry Beckett was the only NCO who would go to the field with the 302d, because the company made contact every time it went out. Staff Sergeant Beckett went because he knew that if there wasn't an American on the ground with the 302d, it would be very difficult to get artillery support, air strikes, and, most important, medevacs. On occasion, officers wanted to go to the field to earn their Combat Infantryman Badge; they weren't going out to support the mission, just to help their military careers and to be able to tell war stories. A captain who was stationed at the province headquarters told Captain Phong, the Vietnamese commander of the 302d, that before he left Nam he wanted to kill someone with a knife. Phong believed him and took him on a mission and gave him the opportunity to fulfill his fantasy; the guy chickened out, and Phong had to extract him from the field because he was scared. A week later, the guy transferred to some safe job in Saigon.

S.Sgt. Jerry Beckett had spent six years at District because he had met Chu My and married her. He wasn't going to leave her behind. When Scherk and I arrived, he was preparing to take her back to the United States. Jerry and his new wife had survived the Tet Offensive of 1968, when the Da Lat district had been overrun with Communist forces. He told me he had been sleeping in town with his wife when all hell had broken loose. His wife being an interpreter as well as a radio person for the district, they both went to the district headquarters to find out about the situation. Captain Phong and the 302d had been in charge of the security for the city. The Communists hadn't expected any problems in taking Da Lat but were surprised by Phong's company and their aggressiveness. It took several days, but Phong and the 302d took back the city, making the VC regret ever having tried to take it. With minimal losses suffered by the 302d, the VC suffered several hundred dead and wounded. Staff Sergeant Beckett did a lot during the siege of the 1968 Tet Offensive, providing air support, artillery, and medevacs for the wounded. The VC never would attack Da Lat again until the fall of Saigon, and even then Phong fought on, making Da Lat the last city in Vietnam to fall to the Communists.

Scherk and I had a couple of days before the company would return from its current mission, so we reported to the personnel clerk at province headquarters, who in turn sent us to a first sergeant located at a secure American compound on the other side of town. We were afraid to tell anybody we had our own jeep out of fear they would confiscate it, so we told the clerk we would find our own way to the American compound. After driving all over the area, we did find the compound, but any VC who had wanted to kill a few Americans would have had no problem. Da Lat was organized into nine city quarters, eight of which were "red," VC controlled, and one "green," government controlled.

The compound was guarded by military police who carried pistols, and the compound area was surrounded by a brick wall with trees and bushes all around. It would have been an easy place to crawl up to the wall and toss a couple of grenades over and do some terrific damage.

The first sergeant was sitting behind his desk reading when we found him, and he stood to greet us as we walked in. The company clerk at the Phoenix compound had told him of our coming, so he was expecting us. He asked us for our orders and, to his dismay, realized that we didn't belong to him. His whole demeanor changed from that of a nice guy to that of an asshole. He was expecting new NCOs to help him with his daily struggles, and he'd thought we were them. He'd read our orders assigning us to the Phoenix Program. He told us he didn't have room at that time for us to live, but that something would be available in a couple of weeks. In other words, he didn't want anything to do with us. He left it up to us to find our own living quarters, which was fine with us. We already knew where we were going. He mentioned that there was an air force detachment that might be able to put us up. We thanked him and couldn't wait to get out of his office, but the first sergeant insisted we have a tour of his compound, showing us his twenty-four-hour NCO club, mess hall, and the security around his facility. After an hour, we were able to get away and go to a hotel we had spotted on the way to the first sergeant's compound. We spent the next two days checking out the neighborhood and meeting the local people. We stayed away from the American compound but checked with province headquarters to find out when the 302d Company would return from the field.

At the beginning of our third day in Da Lat, we received word the company was home and the military intelligence officer wanted to see us. His office was located behind and next to the province headquarters. When we arrived, Major Minter was in his small office, behind a desk that was overflowing with paperwork. He welcomed us and told us to have a seat until he finished the after-action report. Major Minter was a tall, thin, balding man but was in great shape. Finally he threw down his pen and asked if Scherk and I were hungry. We replied, "Yes, sir!" We got into his jeep but were afraid to tell him about our own transportation, and he drove us to a local restaurant that wasn't usually frequented by common American soldiers. The place became our favorite place to eat. It was the best food I had ever eaten in Vietnam. All through the meal we told Minter about our experiences and our desire to get to the field as soon as possible. He explained that he already knew of our experience and said we didn't have to prove a thing to him; we would have to prove how good we were to the commander of the 302d, Captain Phong.

We told him about meeting with the first sergeant, but he explained that we wouldn't be living at the American compound because we would never know when we would be going on a mission. He would make sure we got quarters allowance and separate rations, which meant a lot more money per month. Scherk and I knew we had found a home! We finished eating, and Minter asked where we were staying, and we told him of the hotel. He asked how much we were paying for our rooms. When we told him, he said that after we met Captain Phong the price would go down. Minter said he was going back to his quarters to rest and that the next day he would give us a rundown on our mission and what he expected from us. He offered to take us to our hotel, but by then we felt comfortable enough with him to tell him of our jeep at the province headquarters. He said that was good because he wouldn't have to get us a vehicle! He dropped us off at our jeep and told us to see him in the morning. Scherk and I went back to our hotel to celebrate our newfound fortune. We both passed out early and couldn't wait for whatever the next day would bring.

We were up at dawn, ready to meet our famous Vietnamese commander. Captain Phong was in conversation with Major Minter when we arrived at the office. Major Minter introduced us to Captain Phong. The company commander of the 302d Reconnaissance Company was Capt. Le Xuan Phong, a well-proportioned man physically, but a giant as a tactician, soldier, and leader of men. "Xuan" means "Spring Wind." Phong is the bravest man I have ever met. He was what the word *hero* was invented for. The first thing that caught my attention was his eyes. They looked very intelligent and searched my face for information. He saw my Special Forces patch and told me he, too, used to be Special Forces. We bonded that very moment, and Phong became not only my commander but would eventually become my brother-in-law and one of my best friends, even to this day. Captain Phong held a formation of his troops and introduced us to all of them. The 302d Reconnaissance Company *(Trung Sat Dai Doi)*, about three hundred strong, was manned half by montagnards and half by Vietnamese, all of whom were born and raised in the Da Lat area. His three hundred soldiers had been with Phong for many years and were loyal only to him—loyal not because he was feared but because he was loved. Phong was one of the few Vietnamese officers who took care of his soldiers and their families. He made sure the soldiers were paid on time, and if a soldier needed extra cash, he gave it to him. If a soldier was killed in the line of duty, Phong made sure his immediate family was taken care of.

The TOE of the 302d *Trung Sat Dai Doi* (Company) was as follows: the commanding officer was rated as a captain, the executive officer a first lieutenant; first sergeant, master sergeant (E-8); five platoon leaders, second lieutenants; five platoon sergeants, sergeants first class (E-7); eight squad leaders, sergeants (E-5). The company was broken down into five platoons with four twelve-man squads per platoon. Four of the platoons were rifle platoons with two M-60s and one 60 mm mortar per platoon. The riflemen were authorized for M-16s, M-1 carbines, M-14s, BARs, LAWs, and M-79s. But most of Phong's soldiers carried Communist weapons to confuse the enemy. Phong carried a CAR-15. The fifth platoon was a small element and was essentially the headquarters element of the company. There was one medic per platoon. The authorized strength of the company was 245 men. Phong actually had more soldiers than he was authorized, but higher command never said anything about it.

Minter told me that I would be going on a mission the next day with the AK squad and to prepare for a two-week stay in the field. The point squad for the company was called the AK squad because all of its members carried AK-47s and dressed in the uniforms of the enemy. Scherk would monitor the radio while I was in the field. Scherk wasn't happy with that decision. After all, I was a medic and he was the infantry soldier. But he never said anything to Minter, only to me when we returned to our room. Phong must have seen something in Scherk's eyes that made him leery of taking him; maybe it was the drugs. As it happened, Scherk was never to go alone with Phong's unit; an American would always accompany him.

The night went fast, and I went to Major Minter's office for my operation order. Phong was with Minter and several other Vietnamese officers. I watched as Phong planned the mission as other people gave him information. The process took about two hours. After the briefing, Phong turned to me and asked if I was ready. I told him yes, and he said this was just a recon mission with the AK squad and that we were not to make contact. He said he had chosen me because of my experience with recon units. He then showed me where we were going and told me to make sure I coordinated with the medevac people. He added that he had already coordinated with the air force and artillery. He then wished me luck and told me I would see the enemy within the next twenty-four hours. Boy, was he right.

With a reaction company in the rear if we got into trouble, we left the comfort and safety of Da Lat.

☆
CHAPTER 14

Upon returning to the rear, I had to undergo debriefing, writing up for the major everything I had seen and heard on the mission. While everyone else was taking a much-needed shower, I had to tell my boss about being pissed on. At first he didn't believe me, but after talking to Phong's soldiers, he had a good laugh at my expense. Scherk was waiting for me with a beer in hand. Of course, he had to take a few shots at me about my golden shower. As I was completing my report, Phong walked into the office. After he conferred with Major Minter, he turned his attention to me. Phong has a way of making you listen to every word he said (still does). It's not just respect; it's his eyes, which probe into your very soul. His eyes are full of knowledge and wisdom of life and death. Phong has the ability to look at you and make you feel that he can read your mind. Which he can! With a slight grin, he asked me how I liked working in Da Lat. I told him I liked it and left it at that. Not really knowing Phong yet, I didn't want to show too much interest or act conceited, the way most of the American advisers seemed to. Phong turned and left the building, and Major Minter gave me a brief history about Phong and our methods of operation.

Phong was born in 1940 in Da Lat, while the French still controlled Indochina. After the French surrendered to the Germans, the Japanese took control of the area. Before the war, Phong's father was a big-game hunter and guided for

Europeans and other foreign dignitaries. Phong would follow in his father's footsteps and also become a big-game hunter and a guide much in demand. Phong's father employed a montagnard whose skills as a hunter, woodsman, and tracker were unsurpassed. Under the tutelage of this montagnard, Phong was taught the lessons of the jungle, the hunter, and the hunted. His father and his stepfather had specialized in hunting the tiger. While other boys were playing, Phong roamed the jungles and the countryside, learning every inch of the terrain and every sign left there by animal or human.

When Phong became of age to hunt, which was at the very young age of seven or eight years old, his father instructed him on the weapon he would hunt with: an M-1 Garand, a very heavy weapon for such a small kid. After learning and firing the weapon to his father's satisfaction, Phong was to be tested for his courage. His father had a pit dug, eight by eight by eight feet deep, the bottom of the pit lined with fire-hardened bamboo punji stakes, and the entire pit covered with bamboo and palm leaves. In the center of the tiger trap was placed a slaughtered goat. This was the lure for a tiger and Phong's first big-game kill. Tigers feast at night and have an extremely sensitive sense of smell and excellent night vision. Phong had to wait in hiding for the tiger to appear and kill the tiger with one shot. That would be the only chance he would get. The tiger could come from any direction, and if the tiger smelled Phong, he would be the tiger's meal. Phong's father knew what he was doing and, explaining to Phong, placed him in a bough of a tree, camouflaging carefully Phong's smell and small body. The most important part of this lesson was the art of patience, both physical and mental. Phong sat in the darkness of the night, listening to the sounds of the jungle sing around him. Suddenly the sounds were replaced by a deadly silence. Phong had been trained, and cleared his mind of the most powerful enemy: fear. Phong could feel more than see the tiger as it approached the bait. He quietly positioned himself to make the kill. He had to be sure his shot was accurate and perfectly timed so the tiger would fall into the pit as he shot it. A wounded tiger in the darkness of the jungle meant danger for everyone. A shot rang out, and the tiger fell into the pit, dead before it hit the bottom. Phong's father had been close by and reached the pit before Phong could jump out of the tree. Phong's father and montagnard teacher started singing the praises of Phong: "Phong the killer of tigers."

As dawn gave light to the pit, helpers were carefully lowered into the pit, and a sling was tied around the beast. The tiger was then pulled out of the pit. Because he had killed the tiger, Phong cut the tiger's heart out and ate it, thereby acquiring the "soul of the tiger." It was a rite of passage, and a skill that Phong later in his life would use against his enemies.

Phong's father fought with the French resistance against the Japanese, but after the war, the French tried to regain power, and the country was split once again between the north and south, the Communists and the Democrats. Phong's father was a leader of the Democrats and was executed in front of his family and soldiers as an example to others who supported foreign powers. He was beheaded with Phong watching. Phong was only ten, but from that point he hated Communists, even to this day. Phong's mother never let Phong forget who killed his father. She remarried a year later, to a man half French, half Vietnamese. He was also a big-game hunter, and he continued to train Phong in the ways of the land and the kill. Phong's mother tutored Phong in language and math to give him everything he needed to become more educated. Phong finished high school and had learned French, English, and Vietnamese. He went on to a college-level school that specialized in math. But to his mind, the greatest skills he had learned were the ways of the jungle and the hunt. He wanted to use those skills to find and kill Communists or any other enemy. The government required that all young men of age had to serve their country. The French were gone, and the North and South were at odds with each other. Phong's hatred for the Communists had been nurtured by his mother. Phong made a vow to avenge his father's death, even if it meant his own demise. He enlisted in the South Vietnamese army and attended an officers school that was similar to Officers Candidate School (OCS) in the U.S. Army. The Americans were aiding the south with Special Forces advisers, and Phong wanted to learn from the best, so he joined a Special Forces unit. The unit he joined fought in Tuyen Duc Province, and Phong's knowledge of the terrain that he and his stepfather had hunted for many years was of crucial importance to the advisers. Even while Phong was assigned to his Special Forces unit, word got around of his hunting skills and his knowledge of the terrain. On several occasions he was asked to take dignitaries on a hunt. The people would always get the kill but didn't want to keep the meat, so Phong would make extra money by selling the meat to local restaurants. Because of his bravery, hunting skills, and knowledge of the terrain, Phong was eventually promoted to lieutenant and given a reconnaissance platoon that would be instrumental in locating and killing the enemy.

Phong received the American Silver Star (the highest award the United States will present a non-American) for saving the life of an American adviser and several other high-ranking Vietnamese. He had led a six-man recon team into a base camp that had been overrun and occupied by the NVA in the Ben Het area. With the Silver Star, he was also promoted to the rank of captain and given command of the 302d *Trung Sat* and assigned to the Phoenix Program.

Phong was a big-game hunter and knew not only the terrain but the people who lived there. Only the people who were corrupt feared Phong. Over the years, Phong became known as the Gray Tiger, a cunning but deadly opponent—a name given to him by the enemy. Major Minter stated he had worked with several Vietnamese officers and quite frankly was never impressed by their professionalism or honesty. He was sure there were many great Vietnamese soldiers who had proven themselves on the battlefield and will never be heard of. But Phong was born to be a leader and a great soldier. There are several books written by Vietnamese authors who were witnesses to his actions from the sidelines. Most advisers who worked with Vietnamese considered themselves superior to their counterpart until they met Phong. Other Vietnamese officers wouldn't guarantee the safety of their adviser, but Phong would. He would tell us the size, type, and strength of our enemy before we would engage them. The Gray Tiger would give us a time and location of contact just from looking at the surrounding terrain. He was a remarkable hunter. But the best thing was that he knew how to kill the enemy and did it with the fierceness of the tiger he was named after.

Major Minter explained to me that the performance plan our district worked under for the Phoenix Program called for the neutralization of ten VCI per month. In the time I spent in the Tuyen Duc Province, we exceeded our quota by close to 300 percent. Early in the conflict, Tuyen Duc Province was VC controlled in eight of nine city quarters. By the late sixties and early seventies, the entire province was considered Amber/Green, red being controlled by VC, amber being partially VC controlled, and green being clear of VC control.

Neutralization of identified targets was conducted in the jungle regions through pattern analysis. Sources of information would report VCI leaving base areas and trails on a regular basis and being led by montagnards to collect taxes in villages, propagandize the people, and punish people who cooperated with the United States.

A typical mission scenario for a targeted individual, Major Minter explained, was that Phong would set up an ambush based upon specific targeting, reading of trails, stealthiness, and pattern analysis of the enemy movements through that area; the same principles that were employed so well in hunting the tiger. Concealed in triple-canopy jungle, with the colors of the flora and foliage in greens, golds, and reds, the company would observe a not-too-secret VC trail. Phong would anticipate the "target" at a specific time and place. Our company would set out claymore mines on the trail the VC would be traveling and detonate the mines when the target was identified by an informant. Usually the leader of the VC would be in the middle of the column, and after an intense eruption of mines exploding and small-arms firing, we would move slowly through the kill zone, searching bodies and looking for documents and identity cards. I would be issued a small Petri camera, and it was my responsibility to take pictures of the bodies. Documentation was crucial, Major Minter pointed out; then we would strip the bodies and leave them for the tigers to feast on. The Gray Tiger had already had his feast and was ready to move on to the next meal.

With the background information Major Minter had given me, I had a greater respect for Phong. I couldn't wait to learn as much as I could from this warrior. What I did learn would help me survive the numerous conflicts with the enemy I would encounter with Phong and his company. I would go on to serve three years with Phong and his soldiers.

One week later, we received information that several high-ranking VCI targets were operating northwest of Da Lat with NVA troops. After receiving the intelligence summaries, Phong worked out an operations order to intercept and neutralize the blacklisted targets. I would be going out on the mission not only as the Phoenix representative but as the company medic.

It was barely dawn, and the sun's golden light generated hot, humid vapor over the upper canopy of the jungle, little of

which penetrated to the cool, dark jungle floor where Phong
and his black suits waited. The monkeys playing in the upper
branches were our security. Suddenly they commenced to
chatter the alert!

Phong watched as the first NVA troopers slowly appeared
on the trail. He also observed that the cautious troops were
carrying brand-new weapons. He smiled and said, "Welcome
to South Vietnam; I like that new AK!" As the NVA troop approached, our scouts reported that NVA were flanking the
trail. Phong estimated that contact was imminent; the element
of surprise appeared to be in danger; the monkeys in the overhead canopy alarmed the neighborhood with more frantic
chattering. Phong gave the signal that immediately ignited
five claymore mines, creating earsplitting hellfire, propelling
thousands of ball bearings, ripping, tearing, smashing skulls,
lifting bodies into the air, and then smashing them into the
ground, completely devastating the point squad of the young
men of the advance element of *Nong Troung 1* (Work Site
One), otherwise known as the 1st North Vietnamese Army Division. Yes, the NVA also had their cherries! Phong's black-
suited AK squad poured AK-47 firepower into the ambush kill
zone, their unique cackle causing confusion among the young
NVA soldiers. The American-made CAR-15s, M-16s, and
M-60s opened up on full auto, popping skulls and ripping
off limbs, followed by the thud of handheld 60 mike-mikes
(small portable mortars), a second of graceful silence, and
then the devastating roar of broken hot steel pelting the
ground-hugging butts of young red-starred, sun hat–helmeted
khaki suits receiving their first baptism of hellfire. Maybe
there would be Crosses of Gallantry for our heroes. B-40s
blasted off, screaming and thundering unmercifully back and
forth around and through the witless targets.

Phong smiled. "It too good!" Then he slunk into a tiger
crouch. "Flankers!" He assumed full alert, his left hand pulling the pin off a willy pete (white phosphorous grenade) and

flinging it far forward over the heads of his men, the WP curling as gracefully as a football and landing on target in the kill zone, signaling "peel the banana," as well as creating shock, pain, and death with everlasting hot phosphorous and beautiful white smoke to conceal the withdrawal of the good guys. The NVA commander signaled "caution," then "withdrawal," assuming properly that his FNGs might encounter a dug-in regimental-size force, drawing them into a kill zone even Geronimo would envy!

It was my first introduction to the combat workings of the 302d. Starting at the very top with Phong, any command worked its way down through the platoon leaders (officers), platoon sergeants, squad and fire-team leaders, to the privates. I was amazed and impressed at the efficiency and expediency with which an order was acted upon. And it all started with Phong. He led from the front and by example. He was one intricate living, breathing, ass-kicking, death-dealing machine.

About this time, I met my favorite person in the district, Chi Ly, Phong's wife. Phong had met Ly while she was attending school to become a Catholic nun. It was love at first sight, and they have been together since, through more hardships and trials than any couple should have to endure. Of exceptional beauty, she personified to me the perfect female in wisdom, compassion, nurturing, and the loving heart of a mother. She was raising a family in the middle of that crazy war. She was also combat hardened and not a stranger to weaponry and its use. On several occasions, she drove Phong's jeep through enemy-held territory to bring us much-needed ammo and supplies. She was also very accomplished in cooking Vietnamese food. On returning to the district after a mission, I looked forward to one of her home-cooked meals. She also took care of Phong's soldiers' families while they were in the field. If a family needed money, food, or anything Ly could provide, she would handle it. If one of the soldiers was killed, she would personally take charge and see that the grieving family was properly taken care of. Chi Ly is a small woman in stature but a giant in heart and soul.

Early one morning, I was called to the district headquarters to prepare for a mission. As I approached the headquarters building, I saw Phong watching his NCOs prepare his soldiers for another exercise in death. I wandered up to him and was greeted by his big tiger grin. He asked me, "Are you ready to kill VC today?" In a kidding manner, he told me to be prepared to call for air support if he requested it. I found out later he wasn't kidding. Unknown to me at the time, we would engage a local VC force in the Duc Trong District. After much planning and preparing, Phong, his soldiers, and I loaded onto trucks that would take us to the staging area to begin our hunt.

After getting off the trucks, we walked for hours, going up and down steep hills and through thick foliage, with wait-a-minute vines making progress that much harder. At a hand signal from Phong, we came to a stop. I was grateful because of the rapid pace the little guys were setting. I was *ready* for a rest stop. I was used to walking with Americans, and we moved a lot slower.

Phong was studying his map when one of the AK squad members returned from a point recon and started conversing with him, pointing in the direction we were moving. The AK squad had located an enemy base camp that seemed deserted. Phong, myself, and one other man went forward to recon the base camp. After checking it out very carefully, we knew it was well used. Phong said they would be back.

Phong had an incredibly perceptive mind when it came to finding and utilizing terrain to tactically engage an enemy; he knew how the enemy would react to a given situation. I recognized later the brilliance of the trap he set for the enemy. It was the basic hammer-and-anvil tactic. He set up three ambushes, in three different areas around the base camp where the terrain naturally funneled movement, stocking each

ambush site with fifteen to eighteen men, who set out a gen-
erous amount of claymores. The rest of the company he
moved to where we formed a sizable front against the enemy
base camp, keying on several large trails leading from the
camp. We also set up a large number of claymores. The ambush sites were directly opposite our location, and 150 to 200
meters from the base camp. Either location could be the
hammer or the anvil. He set trail watchers on all the trails
leading into the base camp for early warning for all the
elements.

After the people were in place, Phong looked at me and said
we would have contact in one hour. Well, Phong was wrong; it
was thirty minutes before the exploding of claymore mines,
the popping and cracking of AK, and M-16 small-arms fire
turned into a roar. Everybody in our position was fully alert,
waiting for the enemy to appear before us. Right where Phong
said the enemy would be coming from, a large body of VC
carrying everything from AKs to B-40s came scurrying down
the trail, only to be met with the deadly explosion of claymores, followed by a huge volume of our small-weapons fire,
taking their feet out from underneath them as parts were being
blown from their bodies. The smell of gunpowder and blood
mixed to give the air the odor of death.

Excitement written over his face, Phong shouted for me to
call for air support because we had attacked a larger unit than
he had estimated. I quickly radioed back to province headquarters, relating what Phong had told me and saying that we
needed support. At the time, an American artillery unit in the
area was supposed to support us, but it was busy supporting
someone else. The only thing available was the Vietnamese air
force, flying old prop-driven, straight-wing, World War II–
vintage A-1 Skyraiders. We'd picked a bad time because the
American air force was already engaged in heavy combat support somewhere else. I told them we'd take whatever support
we could get.

Phong quickly had us on the move because the enemy had regrouped and was on the offensive, wanting to make us pay for the damage we had caused. Trying to fix us in place, they started using mortars. Fortunately, we hadn't taken any casualties. It was my job to provide support for Phong, but it was also my job to search enemy bodies for documentation and to take pictures of the slain foes. Phong looked irritated with me because I was taking too long checking out the enemy dead, but I had already called in the coordinates for the air strike and was waiting for a reply. I needed to gather information for Major Minter. Later, after processing the recovered documents off the dead VC, it was determined that the enemy unit we had engaged was the VC Main Force Company 816, plus several advisers from the North.

I heard the aircraft before I got a response from District on an ETA (estimated time of arrival) on the aircraft. Through a radio relay, Phong was able to talk to the aircraft and direct them where he wanted their ordnance dropped. The pilots and their aircraft were very good. I had never been that close to air support, and it was frightening how much devastation the aircraft could provide. I thought the smell and smoke from our firefight were bad, but the aircraft's bombs made me feel as if I were in hell. Not only was there a lot of fire, smoke, and smell, but the ground shook and the air heated up from the bombs and napalm they were dropping. It seemed like the A-1s were flying just one foot over our heads as they made their approach, but they actually were one hundred feet above the ground. Those prop-driven aircraft could linger over the target area longer and could bomb with much more precision than jets. I had used jet aircraft for support before, but because of their fuel consumption, they couldn't stay around for very long. From that day forward, I tried to get those Skyraiders for support on all our missions.

After breaking contact and using the Skyraiders for cover, we made it back to the staging area. Our trucks were waiting for us, and they sure looked good, because I was exhausted and ready to wash off the smell of blood and napalm.

After we all had much-needed showers, some of the AK squad members asked me to accompany them to the local brothel, Madame Thai's. It was a haven for the 302d Company, because most brothels had been established for GIs and didn't want Vietnamese to patronize their establishments.

That day, I met the famous Ba Thai for the first time. She was in charge of about a hundred beautiful prostitutes and seemed to like me right away because I could speak more of the language than the GIs' usual "Do you want to fuck?" Ba Thai was about forty years old but looked twenty. She had long black hair with a body that could be described only as a perfect ten. She had larger breasts than most Oriental women and displayed them with pride. After our first encounter, I would spend many nights acting like a breast-fed baby. The best part of the experience was that I didn't have to pay. I was a member of the 302d *Trung Sat*, and that was pay enough for her. Occasionally, I would do Ba Thai favors by getting her cigarettes or liquor, but for the most part, she took care of me.

After my night at Ba Thai's, it was time to return to District. It was early morning, and no other American was around. Having the place to myself, I processed all the information that we'd captured and was able to begin a file that would become a reference for future use. Before I had taken my shower and gone into town, I had given the film to Major Minter, along with all of the papers I had found on the bodies. He had added them to the files he had prepared since his arrival at District. Major Minter was a meticulous record keeper and frequently knew more about the enemy than the enemy knew about themselves. By the time I came in, he'd already had the film developed, and the pictures were put on a board like the wanted posters in a post office. We had killed some important people, and he was proud of it. When it came to neutralization of the Viet Cong infrastructure, Major Minter was the brains behind the plans. From the information we had obtained, we could figure out who was supplying the enemy locally, or at least which hamlet or village. Based on that information, we would set up surveillance of the village roads and observe any strange meeting or occurrences. The information we got from that would determine where our next ambush would be.

When I look back now, it was Big Brother watching, using standard gestapo tactics. I regret having participated in some of those tactics. For instance, on one occasion we had ambushed a road leading out of a village that had been suspect for a long time. We made contact, killing four Viet Cong. We took the bodies and displayed them in the middle of the village for all to see what happened when people were sympathetic to the Communists. Some of these dead enemy had relatives in that village. When I watch old movies about Germany during Hitler's reign, I hate myself for doing some of the same things he did. But at the time, I thought I was doing the right thing.

I would spend many days and nights in the field with the 302d *Trung Sat* and, for the most part, loved every minute. I had become an accepted family member of the company and was treated as an equal. Off duty, we would party together, love together, and, when we lost a comrade, we would weep together. I had gone so native that I would shun fellow Americans because they didn't understand my reationship with the people. I didn't like the way many Americans treated the Vietnamese, as if they were a second-class people in their own land. Most of the locals were more cultured and sophisticated than most of the GIs serving in Da Lat.

During an invitation to one of Chi Ly's great meals, I was introduced to Ly's sister Francoise, a student home on school break. She was beautiful, intelligent, and very sexy. It was love at first sight, but I didn't know how to approach her and get to know her better. And I felt guilty because of my association with the famous Ba Thai. Not to mention she was seventeen years old, and I was close to thirty. Also, she was the sister-in-law of Phong. When she was there during family meals, I would catch her looking at me and winking. Then one night while I was sleeping over at Phong's, I was startled awake by a naked body climbing into my bed. It was Francoise! I was used to being the aggressor, but now I was the prey. We made love all night until I passed out from exhaustion with a smile on my face. I had finally met the woman I wanted to be with. From then on, whenever Francoise was in town, I would spend my time with her. I didn't stop going to Ba Thai's, because that was where the AK squad and I hung out after a mission, but I stopped whoring around.

Going on all the missions with the 302d for over a year, I had developed a great rapport with the soldiers, and especially the AK squad. Scherk would go to the field occasionally, but for the most part that job was left to me. Scherk was having problems with his use of drugs—not in the field but in the rear. One incident that comes to mind concerns the time we were picking up some laundry from a local shop when we were stopped by MPs because the area was off-limits to Americans. One particular MP didn't like us because we never listened to anything the MPs said. And he thought we considered ourselves outside their control. In truth, we didn't give a shit. That day they were out to make an example of Scherk and me. After we left the laundry, the MPs pulled their weapons and shouted at us to put our hands on our heads, then proceeded with a full-body search. Unknown to me, Scherk had a vial of heroin on him, and the dickhead MP found it. The MP acted like he had busted the biggest drug dealer in the world. They called for backup, and in about two minutes, Scherk was handcuffed and on his way to the provost marshal's office. Scherk started yelling that the MP had planted the vial on him. Later he had to take a drug test, and the results went against Scherk. I knew Scherk was still doing drugs because once in a while I would do it with him. For the most part, I had quit because Phong hated it. But the members of the AK squad *all* did heroin and opium, and I always liked going to the opium den with the boys. I suppose that if I had lived my whole life in a war, I would have chosen a similar way to escape the ugliness of watching friends die in combat. Hell, just the pressure I felt at the thought of getting myself killed was enough reason to smoke. Scherk was given an Article 15, fined some money, and put on house arrest for one month. That didn't bother Scherk, because we went back into the field for three weeks.

The three-week trip was more a hunt for tiger, or whatever other big animal Phong could find to hunt, in the Don Duong area, which was located in the highlands of Vietnam. Before we could hunt for wild game, the area would have to be secured, so Phong sent out several ambush teams to the area. Major Minter was on that trip and insisted that he carry a radio. For an old man, he could carry his own, not to mention that he was fearless at the onset of a firefight. Scherk had found himself a new weapon, a sawed-off M-14.

The ambushes were set in place around us in a 360-degree perimeter. They were there for about ten minutes when one of the ambush teams engaged an enemy force. Almost at the same time, two other ambush teams started firing. Phong called on the radio to the teams, and they reported back that they were in heavy contact with a far superior force. Major Minter immediately called for artillery support. Phong and the reaction force of a hundred men went to the area of the heaviest contact.

Three of Phong's men had been wounded, and Phong asked me to help them. The small-arms fire was so heavy that I had to crawl to the wounded to administer help. The first soldier I came to was dead. The next soldier was wounded in the leg, and he was putting a tourniquet on his upper thigh. The wound was a gaping hole, but it was clean. I slapped his hands away from the tourniquet and loosened it to see how much blood flow he had. It wasn't bleeding at all, so I took off the tourniquet and applied a pressure dressing. I then grabbed the guy by the shirt collar and, low-crawling, dragged him back to where I could get up, then carried him to the rear of the action. I dropped him off at the company CP and went back to the action. By that time, we were starting to receive heavy RPG and B-40 fire. It seemed like hours before we started to get artillery support, but when it came, it poured, and it was welcome. With a hundred men behind him, Phong led a charge that Custer would have been proud of. Every one of us was screaming at the top of his lungs, and we must have scared the shit out of those VC, because they took off running. Soon after the artillery stopped, gunships arrived and started hosing the area with their miniguns.

The whole fight must have taken two hours, but it seemed like twenty-four. I was hoarse from yelling obscenities at the enemy and exhausted from carrying wounded people to the safety of our command post. We had run into a base camp manned by two companies of NVA regulars, and we had kicked ass. They must have thought we were crazy. We killed thirty-five and captured two B-40s and twelve brand-new, Chinese-made AK-47s with fiberglass stocks. I carried one of them to the field for the rest of my tour with Phong.

Phong walked into the NVA base camp cussing up a storm because he had received a wound to the groin. It hadn't hit anything vital, just left a bullet burn on his inner thigh close to his testicles. Phong wanted to pursue the enemy because they had almost shot his balls off, but Major Minter talked him out of it. We had three dead to take care of. I took pictures of the enemy bodies, and Scherk went through the bodies looking for documents. From documents Scherk found, that one action netted several Viet Cong names and exposed several local officials of the South Vietnamese government who were sympathizers to the Communist party.

After returning to the rear area for some rest and recreation in the town of Don Duong, the AK squad and I hit the local bars in a small village called Song Pha. After consuming vast quantities of *Bier* 33 and gorging myself on tons of Vietnamese food, I returned to where we were staying, a house that belonged to Phong's sister Chi Can. To my surprise, Chi Ly and Francoise were there. Unfortunately, on seeing me intoxicated, Francoise made it clear that she didn't want anything to do with me. Phong laughed and left me to pass out from exhaustion and intoxication. Scherk had found the local opium den and, along with a couple of the AK squad members, stayed there until the next day.

We returned to the NVA base camp where we had made contact. Phong was sore from his wound and didn't want to walk any farther, so he decided to set up camp in the enemy complex. He put out listening posts all around so that we wouldn't have any surprises. With several small hootches framed with bamboo and covered with elephant grass, the base camp resembled a tiny village. Long tables in the middle of the camp had been used for eating and meetings. Phong's cook set up his kitchen close to the long bamboo table, and we were served our meals there.

Later in the day, Phong's three-quarter-ton truck arrived with his hunting rifles and ammo. As soon as it was dark, Phong told me to get in the truck with some of his soldiers because we were going hunting. Phong drove the vehicle while one of his soldiers took a handheld spotlight to shine it across the wood line looking for the telltale glow reflected from an animal's eyes. I didn't know that Phong had already scouted the area we were hunting in and had found evidence of a large animal in the area.

We drove around for about an hour when suddenly the soldier with the spotlight told Phong to stop. Phong jumped in the back and grabbed his M-14 hunting rifle while the soldier shined the spotlight on the startled animal. Phong saw it and fired, dropping whatever it was with one shot. Quickly we off-loaded the truck and went to the spot where the animal had dropped. Phong had shot a huge animal called a gaur, with a head as large as an elephant's. I had never seen an animal like it before and hadn't even known it existed. Shaped like a water buffalo but very massive, it had horns that didn't seem to fit its large head. Phong said the animals had been known to attack and kill people. He took some of the meat and distributed it among his soldiers and sold the rest to a local restaurant. We had steaks that night. They were tough and did not have quite the same flavor as stateside beef, but they were good, for those with good teeth.

Our last week at Don Duong before we were to move back to Da Lat, a montagnard whom Phong had grown up with told him that his stepfather had been shot by the Communists while hunting. Phong came and asked me to help patch up his stepfather. The man had been shot in the lower leg, and the bullet had almost severed the leg. Because of the seriousness of the wound, there wasn't much I could do. It wasn't bleeding badly, and the old montagnard must have given Phong's stepdad some opium, because he was feeling no pain. I applied a pressure dressing and a splint and told Phong we had to get his dad to a hospital as soon as possible. The closest one was in Phan Rang, and we would have to drive over good and bad roads.

Early the next morning, we left Song Pha and headed for Phan Rang. By then whatever Phong's dad had been taking had worn off, and he was in terrible pain. He would never scream when we hit the bumps in the road, but I could tell that he wanted to. After a couple of hours we arrived at the hospital, and when the doctors saw the wound they immediately took him into surgery. We stayed there until they were finished and his father awoke from the general anesthesia. The surgery took about three hours, and the doctors said he was lucky to keep his leg. Phong was angry about his dad's being shot and wanted to hunt down the people who did it. The old montag-nard said he would show Phong where it had happened. We left Phong's dad at the hospital and went to prepare for another mission: a mission of revenge.

After we returned to Song Pha, Phong gave his troops a warning order to prepare for a mission in the area in which his stepfather had been shot. We walked into the area of operation because there wasn't any transportation available. After pa-trolling for about ten kilometers, we stopped for a chow break. I was leaning back on my rucksack when Phong started yelling into the handset of his radio. Phong then turned to me and said, "VC! VC!" The VC had found our frequency and were talking to Phong. Phong told the VC commander that he would meet him anywhere, just Phong and his men and the VC, and fight it out between them. The VC said he would, ex-cept that he felt Phong would cheat and call in an air strike. Phong tried to convince the VC to meet him but to no avail.

The VC knew where we were, but we couldn't locate them. Our troops had found numerous well-used trails, but we couldn't find the enemy and make contact. Disappointed, Phong decided to return to base camp. Finally, a cold beer and decent food.

While we were sitting around a table at Phong's sister's house, Phong was talking about not being able to get trucks for transportation to and from the missions. He said we were last on the priority list for vehicles. I told Phong I could go to the air force base in Cam Ranh Bay and see if I could find someone to give us a truck. With his permission, I took Phong's jeep and four of the AK squad. We arrived in the early afternoon at the bridge and gate that led into the air force base. I was afraid the security guards wouldn't let us on the base be-cause we looked like mercenaries. But as we approached the gate, the air force policeman on duty asked me for my ID card, then asked each man in the AK squad for his Vietnamese ID.

It was really too easy. Knowing that it would be a good

place to establish a contact, I went to the closest transportation company's enlisted club and took the boys in for a drink. It wasn't long before a couple of off-duty soldiers approached us to find out if we were mercenaries. I told them we worked for the CIA and we were out looking for a truck to transport my troops. One of the GIs said he could get anything I wanted, so I gave the soldier a French parachute jacket and a captured VC weapon. The GI told me to meet him early in the morning by the base wash point. A convoy would be leaving at that time, and we were to fall into the line of trucks leaving the air base.

We drank a few more beers, then went to Cam Ranh Bay town to wait for morning.

We arrived at the front gate of the air base as the sun was coming up. After the routine check of ID cards, we drove to the wash point to wait for the convoy to arrive. We didn't have to wait long. With each vehicle having to stop at the front gate for a paper check before exiting the air base, the vehicles started stacking up. The guy who had promised to give us a truck came skidding to a stop in a ten-ton truck, jumped out of the behemoth, ran over to our jeep, and shouted, "There it is!" He then took off running and jumped into another truck, leaving the ten-ton truck sitting in the middle of the road. Of course, no one in the AK squad knew how to drive that type of truck, so I jumped into the cab and read the gear diagram plate situated on the covering of the gearbox. I found first gear, and we were moving, not very fast, but we were able to keep up with the other trucks in line.

The next obstacle was getting through the front gate. As we got closer to the gate, I noticed that by that time the guards were just waving the trucks through. I was praying they would do the same for me, and they did. Once we drove over the bridge, the convoy headed in one direction, and we headed in the opposite. At first, we couldn't go very fast because I couldn't figure out how to shift the truck into the higher gears. Finally, after much trial and error and with a lot of grinding of gears, we were on the move. I was returning to Phong with a ten-ton truck that didn't have a trailer in which to haul anything. What the hell was Phong going to do with the vehicle?

When we got back to Song Pha, one of the local advisers was visiting with Phong. When he saw the truck, he asked me where I got it. I told him it belonged to the company. The vehicle didn't have any markings on it, American or otherwise. The adviser was a young lieutenant who was trying to make a name for himself by catching an NCO stealing. He asked where I had just come from, and I told him that I had just come off a mission and for security reasons I couldn't tell him anything else. He wasn't satisfied with that answer and left to make some calls. Meanwhile, Phong was looking at the truck, and then he looked at me with an expression showing that he thought I was crazy. "What am I going to do with that?" he asked. I explained to him that I had no choice but to take the truck because if I hadn't, we would have been caught by the military police. Phong yelled for one of his soldiers who knew how to drive the truck, and within seconds, it disappeared. An hour or so later, the ell tee returned and asked me where the truck was. I told him the vehicle had been taken back to the motor pool where we had gotten it. He told me some CID (Criminal Investigation Division) personnel were on their way to our location and they would have some questions for me. The ell tee had a smug look on his face, which I wanted to wipe off. But by then, Major Minter had arrived on the scene and told the ell tee to fuck off. With the lieutenant protesting, Phong and our company packed up and went back to Don Duong, leaving the ell tee standing there looking dumbfounded.

We had actually gone to Phong's stepdad's home in Don Duong to avoid the American advisers back in the rear area and also to set up a base camp to hunt for meat. While Phong, myself, and a few other people were sitting around poking at a campfire, the soldier who had taken the truck returned and handed Phong what seemed like a million dollars in Vietnamese piasters. Phong handed me the money and said he had sold the truck to a logger, who had buried the truck until things got cold. I told him I didn't want the money, but he insisted I take it. I asked him if it was okay with him if I gave it to his soldiers, and he said yes. So we held a company formation, and I went down the ranks giving everybody a payday. If anyone in that company hadn't liked me before, they sure loved me that day. We didn't get much hunting done that day, and Phong decided to return to Da Lat. So we again packed up and headed back to the warmth and hot food of Ly. Ly and Francoise had departed when we left Song Pha and were waiting for us in Da Lat.

The day after our return to Da Lat, I was summoned to the commander's office to talk to a couple of CID agents about a truck the ell tee claimed I had stolen. The CID hadn't received any reports of missing vehicles, and talking to me was just a formality. I told the agents the ell tee was seeing things and was trying to get me into trouble because he was jealous of me. That was the last I heard about the truck—except from Major Minter, who knew the whole story. But my talents would come in handy one more time.

Major Minter was summoned to Saigon to a meeting and wanted Scherk and me to accompany him. We drove our issued Japanese jeep to the meeting. Since we had to spend the night at a local hotel, our jeep would have to sit in the street all night. Scherk and I took a heavy chain and locked the jeep to a lightpost that was under our window so that we could keep an eye on it while we were in the hotel. Even so, when we got up the next morning, the jeep was gone. Major Minter had visions of paying for the jeep out of his own pocket, so Scherk and I told him we would have a jeep for him when he returned from his meeting.

Scherk went to the airport, and I went to the local PX (post exchange) on a hunt for a jeep. It didn't take me long to acquire a vehicle, because an air force airman in a hurry left his jeep running. By the time he returned, I was already out the gate of the compound. I went to the hotel and waited for Scherk to return. About thirty minutes later Scherk also arrived with a vehicle. So all we had to do was wait for Major Minter. His meeting lasted about two hours, and when he returned to the hotel in a taxi, he saw us sitting in our *new* jeeps, personal gear loaded, and ready to return to Da Lat. We didn't want to hang around very long because there had to be air force police out looking for the jeeps.

Our new jeeps weren't Japanese jeeps but brand-new American-mades and much better vehicles, and Major Minter was afraid someone would question our having those jeeps instead of the one we'd been issued. At some point the colonel did mention something to the major, but the major never mentioned anything to Scherk or me during the time we served together. I never stole another jeep for the rest of my time in country.

Since my time at Da Lat was getting short, I asked Francoise to marry me, because I didn't want to leave Vietnam without her. We were married in a Vietnamese ceremony and applied to the U.S. government for permission for her to return with me. As fate would have it, about that time my job at the district was eliminated, and I had to return to the States. Major Minter would stay longer, but Scherk and I had to go. I received orders to A Company, 75th Infantry (Ranger) at Fort Hood, Texas. I promised Francoise I would be back and to keep the faith. It wasn't easy to leave her, but I knew Major Minter would do whatever he could to push our paperwork through and get her on the way to me.

I arrived at the Waco, Texas, airport and took the shuttle bus to Fort Hood. I was in-processed through personnel, then sent to my company, a newly formed unit consisting only of Ranger School–qualified soldiers. At my interview with the first sergeant, he told me I would be going to Ranger School within weeks. Before I left, I was put through a pretraining course that included land navigation, squad tactics, rappelling, knot tying, and patrolling techniques. In other words, everything I'd had in Special Forces training and a repeat of everything I went through in Nam. But I kept my mouth shut and did everything I was told to do.

After pretraining, I was sent to Fort Benning, Georgia, to Ranger School. I might as well have been a private all over again. But the hardest part of Ranger School was the lack of sleep and the one meal a day. The training was good but nothing I hadn't endured during my first four years in Vietnam. At Benning we had classes in warning and operation orders, land navigation, and numerous other subjects, including physical conditioning like rifle PT, and the Bear Pit (a version of King of the Mountain or Last Man Standing). After Benning, we were shipped off to Dahlonega, Georgia, for mountain training and more long days and nights without sleep and food. We were graded on a merit/demerit system by the instructors, and by our peers. So if people didn't like someone, he was gone. The RIs (Ranger instructors) were all Vietnam vets, but they didn't care who we were or what we had done in the war; we were just Ranger candidates. We patrolled the hills of Georgia, rappelled down Mount Yona, and played at being team leader and assistant team leader. After two weeks, we were sent back to Benning for a day of rest before continuing on to Florida to survive the swamps and mosquitoes of the jungle we played in. We stood waist-high in swampy water while RIs instructed us. Believe it or not, it does get cold in Florida. After two weeks, we returned to Benning to graduate. Victory Pond never looked so good, and that is where we graduated.

I hadn't been back at Fort Hood for more than a day when we were being sent to the desert for more training. As it turned out, a desert phase had been added to Ranger training. During the time I was in the States, I spent more time in the field than I did when I was in Nam. I wrote to Francoise and Minter as much as I could, and I put in transfer papers (1049) to go back to Nam. My dad had a friend in personnel, my paperwork went through, and soon I was on my way back to Vietnam.

I arrived in Vietnam thirty days early so I could have some time with Francoise and all my friends in Da Lat. For the first three weeks, being there was like being home. I was being assigned as an adviser to the Ranger Training Center in Duc My, a little town outside Nha Trang, so a week before I was to report to my new assignment, I drove down with several members of the AK squad to check it out. That area also housed the National Training Center and Cambodian Training Center. The rank structure at my new assignment was a full colonel (O-6) as commander, a lieutenant colonel (O-5) as executive officer, a lieutenant colonel in charge of the Ranger Training School, two majors, two captains, and one lieutenant, followed by one E-8 first sergeant, an E-7 supply sergeant, an E-6 cook, and last but not least, one E-6 medic (me). Needless to say, I was low man on the totem pole.

The compound I was to live in had a swimming pool, an officers club, and tennis courts. On arriving, I went to the compound to meet the man I was to replace, an overweight E-7 who had never seen a day in combat. He never even shook the hand I extended, jumping on my shit like I was some private-e-nothing.

An arrogant man, he first didn't like the idea of my riding around in a jeep loaded with Vietnamese dressed up like VC. Before I could even introduce myself to him, he told me I couldn't bring my friends onto the compound and that I needed a haircut and a good polishing of my boots. I asked him when his last day was, and he told me it was the day before I was to report. I then turned to him and told him to go fuck

himself and that if I saw him in Nha Trang, I would kick his
big, sorry, fat ass. He couldn't believe I had said that to him
and told me he was reporting me to the colonel for being dis-
respectful. Wishing I had gotten a different assignment, I
turned and left with my friends. I had one week to enjoy my
friends, and especially my wife.

The village of Duc My was small, but I found the only hotel
that I could put Francoise in. By then I had been back in
country for a month, and Francoise told me she was pregnant.
I was ecstatic but scared about there not being adequate
medical facilities in the area for her.

When I arrived to report for my new duty assignment, the
officers and soldiers were having an award ceremony for a
lieutenant who was receiving an Army Commendation Medal
for services rendered. I had on starched fatigues, spit-shined
boots, and a fresh haircut. After the ceremony, I met the first
sergeant, who showed me around the compound and my aid
station. He was a great guy but way overweight. I told him
about my run-in with the man I replaced, and he said not to
worry about it.

My next step was to meet the colonel. The only name I remember for the compound was Gilligan's Island; Gilligan was
the name of the colonel. I reported to him by first knocking on
his door, then waiting for his response, "Enter." I felt like I was
back in basic training. The colonel was behind his desk, his
executive officer standing to his right. The XO was a nervous
man who jumped every time the colonel said something. It
was almost as if a big sign floated over his head saying ASS
KISSER.

I stood at attention and reported to the commander with a
snappy salute. He returned the salute in a half-assed manner
and told me that he heard I had visited the compound earlier
and that I had been insubordinate to one of his NCOs. I looked
at the first sergeant, and he gave me an "I didn't know" look.
That asshole medic had gone to the colonel and never told the

first sergeant anything. I denied everything. He then told me that Vietnamese were not allowed on the compound, and that we were not to fraternize with our counterparts. Everything I had learned about establishing a strong, mutually respectful relationship between the Vietnamese and us was going out the window with that commander. In the morning, I was to go to work at the training camps and then straight back to the compound with no stopping in between. While listening to him, I was trying to figure out what I would tell Francoise about the man and our situation. I felt that it was not a good time to tell him I was married to a Vietnamese. I left his office with the feeling that I was in trouble and had better try to find a new home.

Several interpreters were assigned to the unit, and I immediately made friends with all of them. The interpreters would be my link with Francoise until I could figure how to get out of my situation. I would give the interpreters messages for Francoise. The first message was that I wanted her to return to Da Lat until I could set things right. Then I went to work, hoping the colonel would come to see my value as a soldier instead of thinking of me as a dirtball.

My first job was to inventory the aid station and clean it up. It was obvious to me that my predecessor hadn't done his job as a medic. The aid station had only the bare essentials, such as aspirin and bandages. There were no IV setups or any type of real medication. I did find a stethoscope and a blood-pressure cup. After the cleaning and inventory, I sat down and made a list of items to requisition. I then screened the medical records of all the men in the unit that I was responsible for. With such a small organization, that didn't take long.

I then decided to go to the training centers and see how I was to help the soldiers who were going through training. I had my own jeep, so off I went to check out the different training sites. My first stop was the Ranger training area, where I found one of the advisers working with his Vietnamese counterpart. The adviser was one of our majors, and he looked surprised to see me. It seems the fat medic before me had never left the compound. I was learning a whole new concept of being an adviser. From what that major said, the medic before me had been more of a gofer for the colonel than anything else. Everybody on the compound had been afraid to seek medical attention from the fat guy because he hadn't known what the hell he was doing.

Later that evening, the Ranger adviser, an American lieutenant colonel, came to me with a sore throat and swollen lymph nodes. Not having my own lab, I couldn't do a throat culture, so I treated him as if he had strep throat. The lieutenant colonel told me he had no allergies so I gave him a shot of penicillin and some throat lozenges. The very next day, he said he felt a lot better. The following afternoon, I was talking to the first sergeant about my situation when I noticed how red his face was. I asked if I could take his blood pressure, and he agreed. His blood pressure was dangerously high, high enough to kill him. I told him I was sending him to the closest military medical facility that same day. He protested, but the medic rules. Later the first sergeant was medevacked to the States. I hated to see him leave because he was my only ally and my only way out of the organization.

I had been at Duc My for two weeks and still hadn't been able to see Francoise. She would write me letters and give them to my interpreter friend. She refused to return to Da Lat and wanted to see me. Our compound was guarded by Vietnamese soldiers, so I went to them and told them I needed to sneak into town to see my wife, and they covered for me by not telling anyone. I continued to do that for the next month. Then our organization lost another NCO, the cook, and the colonel thought that the cook's responsibilities should be mine. After all, officers have to eat, and NCOs were there to prepare it for them—so the colonel thought. Actually, we had Vietnamese cooks, and the mess sergeant just prepared the menu and ordered and picked up supplies. My new position would allow me to visit with my wife when I went into Nha Trang for supplies. What I didn't know was that the executive officer followed me everywhere I went.

On my return to our compound after picking up supplies for the first time, the colonel was waiting for me. He told the XO to inventory the foodstuffs, that I had brought back. Somehow one can of peaches was missing, and the colonel accused me of selling it on the black market. I defended myself, but those two really believed I was crooked. The only reason they didn't punish me was because the colonel had received the citation for my Bronze Star for valor. When the colonel called me into his office and handed me the medal, he stated that he, too, could have gotten a Bronze Star if he had just added that he also had helped a wounded soldier.

No ceremony, not even a congratulations. Of course, if I had been part of their clique, I would have been presented the medal in formation for all to see. I noticed the XO had a smile on his face as I walked out of the colonel's office. That night I went into town to be with my wife and didn't realize the XO was watching the gate through binoculars and saw me leave.

Again I was called into the colonel's office, that time to be reprimanded in writing for leaving the compound without permission. I had had enough, so I told the colonel why I was going into town. I told him I was married to a Vietnamese and she was pregnant. I also told him I wanted a transfer out of his organization. Both the XO and the colonel looked at each other and smiled, then the colonel turned to me and said, "Request denied," telling me I was dismissed.

I went back to my quarters and didn't know what to do. Franscoise sent me a letter saying I needed documents signed by my commander in order for the paperwork to be processed to allow her to go to the States. The interpreter handed me the paperwork, and I went to the commander, asking him to please sign the documents. He refused on the grounds that he didn't believe GIs should marry indigenous personnel. I told him I was already married and this paperwork was just a formality. He looked at me with contempt and said, "There is no such thing as Vietnamese wives, just Vietnamese whores." He then told me I was restricted to the compound and not allowed to leave for any reason. I turned and left his office with a *lot* of anger building in me.

I found the interpreter and told him to tell my wife that the colonel had refused to sign the papers. Later that night, a soldier came to me and informed me that my wife had suffered a miscarriage of the baby and was bleeding internally. I had to go to her because the only medical attention she would receive was what I provided. I left the compound with the XO watching me. By the time I arrived, Francoise had stopped bleeding. I told her we would make arrangements for her to return to Da Lat, and I would follow in a couple of weeks.

I returned to the compound, and everybody was up as I entered. The colonel was standing by the gate and ordered me to go to the bunker and stay there until further orders. The bunker housed our principal radios and was to be used in case we were attacked. It was usually manned by the interpreters for radio watch. I was now assigned to permanent radio watch. I spent two weeks in the bunker, leaving only for bodily functions or to take a shower. I would have the interpreters smuggle me beer or whiskey, but alcohol served only to heighten my depression. As my luck would have it, the XO walked into the bunker as I was finishing a can of beer. He told me I was relieved and to report to my quarters for house arrest. All of my pent-up emotions came to a head. In a cold killing rage, I went back to my hootch and grabbed a grenade, walked back to the bunker the XO was in, pulled the pin on the grenade, threw it into the bunker, closed the bunker door, and started back to my hootch. As I was walking back, I heard the explosion of the grenade. Everybody came running with weapons in hand, helmets and flak jackets on, thinking the compound was under attack. It was, but not by the VC.

The supply sergeant ran over to me to tell me that the XO had been wounded and needed my help. I knew I was in trouble right then because I hadn't gotten the job done. I looked at the sergeant and said, "Fuck him!" I followed the sergeant to the bunker, and the XO was dragging his ass on the ground the way a dog does when it has worms. When I had pitched the grenade in, it had rolled underneath the desk and came to rest directly under his oak chair. When the grenade blew, it sent slivers of wood up his ass and shredded his lower legs. With deep satisfaction, I saw that the grenade had really done some damage to him, though regrettably not enough to snuff him.

When he spotted me, he got hysterical, screaming that I had just tried to kill him. Suddenly everyone's weapons were pointed at me. I was escorted to a room, and a guard was placed on the door.

It wasn't long before a helicopter flew in, and I was taken to Nha Trang and put into the local jail. Some CID agents interviewed me, asking me why I tried to kill the executive officer. I was really tired of the bullshit, and I told them he was an asshole who deserved to die. I spent one night in the Nha Trang jail; the next day I was taken to Long Binh Jail (LBJ) to await my Article 32 investigation. An Article 32 is like a pretrial hearing where all the facts are presented to determine if a general court-martial is called for.

Well, mine was, and while waiting for the investigation to be finished, I was visited by a brigadier general who asked me why I had committed the crime. I told him the whole story, and he told me the army would take care of its own. Shortly after his visit, Francoise was allowed to visit me. The general had signed her paperwork, and she was going to be able to go to the States.

At that point, I was worried about how long I would be in

jail and what I would do after I got out—if I got out. After one month in Long Binh Jail, I went to trial for attempted murder. I pleaded guilty with extenuating circumstances. I had some of the officers and NCOs testify on my behalf. They all said that I had been treated with prejudice by both the executive officer and the colonel, and I hadn't been allowed to visit my wife or have her come onto the compound.

After all the evidence and arguments were presented, the panel of six men (three NCOs and three officers) retired to decide my fate. It took them only an hour or so to come to a decision: I was sentenced to thirty years at hard labor, with twenty-nine years suspended, reduced to the grade of private, and fined $10,000. The saving grace was that I wasn't given a dishonorable discharge and thrown out of the army.

I was taken back to my jail cell to await transportation to the States. I was allowed one more visit with my wife, who said she already had tickets to the States and that my parents would take care of her until my time was up.

The worst part about leaving Vietnam was going in handcuffs and leg chains and walking through the airport with guards. I was going home, but not with honor. I had disgraced my profession, my family, and, most of all, my integrity. I really wanted to die. I had to focus on making amends for my mistakes.

I arrived at Leavenworth, Kansas, Disciplinary Barracks (DB). I was stripped, searched, and showered, then given a prisoner's uniform to wear. I was in-processed and told the rules: seven steps up or seven steps down. It was a format toward a goal of rehabilitation. I had a choice of soldiering my way out of the situation, or I could get out with no redemption for my sins. I choose to go up. After three months in the DB, I was allowed to go to the United States Retraining Brigade (USARB) in Fort Riley, Kansas. That was a compound that housed soldiers who had made mistakes and were given the opportunity to make amends. If they straightened out, they could stay in the army.

I was made a platoon sergeant of forty-five ex-cons who just wanted out of the army. The program was like basic training: a lot of work details with marching and discipline, but also classes on anger management. The officer in charge was a social worker who evaluated our performance. I made sure every soldier did his job and didn't create problems. Occasionally I had to take a soldier into the latrine to show him the error of his ways by kicking his ass, but I was determined to earn my way out of my situation, stay in the army, and regain the respect of my family and fellow soldiers. The program was nine weeks long, followed by either a discharge or reclassification to a different job skill. As I already had three job skills, I decided to stay as a medic.

During my time at USARB, Francoise and my parents came to visit, and Francoise and I were married American style in the jail church. My best man was my active-duty platoon sergeant, and all of the members of my platoon attended. I was the only prisoner ever to be allowed to leave the compound to spend the honeymoon night with my wife. I returned early the next day to continue my training to its completion. After nine weeks, I was put back on active duty and assigned to Irwin Army Hospital at Fort Riley, Kansas. It took me six months to recapture the grade of E-6. During that time, Francoise became pregnant with our first child, Alan III.

EPILOGUE

In April 1975, a year later, Vietnam fell to the Communists, and Phong went into hiding with several hundred other soldiers who hated the North Vietnamese. They all thought the Americans would be coming back and wanted to be ready when they arrived. Francoise had been in contact with her mother and sister, but they couldn't say a lot about Phong. Six months after the fall of Saigon, Phong told his soldiers to go home, because he realized the Americans wouldn't ever be coming back. Because the Communists were looking for him in Da Lat, he went to Saigon to turn himself in under a different name. If they had discovered who he was, they would have killed him. The Communists sent him to an area around Hanoi where the prisoners had to build their own prisons. I didn't hear anything from Phong and thought I would never see him again. I continued in my determination to redeem myself for all the trouble I had caused.

After regaining my rank, the next step was to ensure my ability to stay in the army and retire. In order to reenlist, I had to apply for a waiver from the Department of Defense. That was granted, and I was authorized to reenlist for six more years. I stayed in Kansas for five years and was then transferred to Germany, where I worked in a clinic for three years. While in Germany, we had two more children, a daughter, Shannon, and a son, Erich. I was wrestling for the army, and the kids would go with me to watch when I wrestled in tournaments. I was then transfered to Fort Benning, Georgia, where I worked as a Pathfinder instructor and became a member of the Silver Wings (the parachute demonstration team). I also played football for the Fort Benning Doughboys. Those were good times because I was back with the Airborne, and life in the army was good. My job and the extra activities I participated in left Francoise alone (her choice) most of the time. Francoise and I had started to drift apart. I was promoted to E-7 and received orders to 10th Special Forces Group in Germany. The kids wanted to go, but Francoise didn't, so I took the kids, and Francoise stayed at Fort Benning.

My new assignment in Germany was with ARSOFE (Army Special Operations Forces, Europe). I worked at a training facility called Platoon Confidence Training, the only Ranger-style unit in Europe. Our headquarters was located in Flint Kaserne, Bad Tolz, Germany. We trained in Sachsencam, Germany, about three miles from headquarters. We would take infantry-platoon-size elements and train them in team, squad, and platoon tactics. It was a grueling two-week course of rifle PT, land navigation, and road marches. It ended with a field exercise on which the platoons were graded. When I arrived, I was the senior medic, but I was moved into a first sergeant position when I made E-8. That was a surprise because I made the promotion list in the secondary zone shortly after I arrived in country. But before I could be promoted, I had to attend the First Sergeant Academy in Munich, Germany, an eight-week course. After graduation I became first sergeant, ARSOFE.

My company consisted mostly of senior NCOs and officers, and my job was all administrative and extremely boring. The only diversion from the boredom was that I led the USAEUR (United States Army Europe) army parachute demonstration team. There I met M.Sgt. R. L. Donahue (Ret.), who was selling parachutes. I purchased fifteen of them for my team, and R.L. spent many hours teaching me how to put those canopies together and how to pack the main chutes and the reserves as well. Reserve parachutes could be packed only by qualified riggers, so whenever I packed a reserve, it was under his supervision. When I met him, R.L. was an *old* soldier, about sixty-two years old, who had been a paratrooper when I was still in diapers. R.L. taught me how to run the team and how to carry out demonstrations. Whenever he was in the area, he would show up for all the demonstration jumps we had.

We traveled all over Europe doing jumps into the opening of festivals, rodeos, and any other event that was highly visible to the public. One of the biggest was the Allied annual celebration of the three big nations (America, England, France). We jumped onto Juli Strasse in front of the victory column. The other big event was the jump into the Berlin Olympic Stadium for the European Police Show. That jump was supposed to be a day jump, but the opening ceremonies took so long, we couldn't exit the helicopter until after dark. As it became dark, the wind picked up, and we really should have canceled, but we were all professionals and decided to go on with the show. We exited over East Berlin and had to fly looking over our shoulders because the wind was so strong. Any wrong calculations and we would have landed in the parking lot. I was the first person out of the helicopter, followed by my mentor, retired Master Sergeant Donahue, then the rest of the team. I experimented by turning my canopy with the wind to see how fast I was moving and discovered it was *way* too fast. I turned back into the wind and prayed I would make the stadium. When I could see the edge of the stadium under me, I turned into the wind. Fortunately it was perfect timing, and I landed in the middle of the field to the roar of 150,000 people. Every time one of my troops landed, the stadium erupted with a roar. That was the most technically difficult jump I ever made. And I had it on video. At least I used to have it—but my youngest son taped over it with an MTV program.

One day I received a letter from Panama City addressed to

my home in Georgia. It had been forwarded to me in Germany and was about a month old. It was from Phong, who had escaped from Vietnam with his family and had been picked up by a German-registered freighter, the *Cap Ademore*. He was to arrive in Hamburg two days after I had received his letter. It had been twelve years since I had last seen Phong and his family. I was shocked at the good fortune and decided to surprise him at the place they would dock.

It was a four- or five-hour drive to Hamburg from Bad Tolz. On arriving in Hamburg, I went into the immigration office and talked to the man in charge, convincing him I would be responsible for Phong and his family. I arranged it so that Phong could get off the boat and come with me to Bad Tolz. It would be only a couple of hours before the boat docked, but it seemed like years. Suddenly, there he was on the highest part of the ship, directing other Vietnamese around him. I found out later that the ship's crew put Phong in charge of all the boat people they had picked up. Next I saw Ly and their daughter, Ngan. I yelled at the top of my lungs, "Phong! Phong! Ly! Ly!" Finally Ly saw me and instantly started crying. Pointing to where I was, she grabbed Phong, and he, too, began to shout and cry. Phong grabbed one of the ship's crew members and pointed me out in the crowd. It took a while, but finally they were allowed to leave the ship. Phong reached me first, crying and talking at the same time, saying, "My friend, Cornett, you save me and my family. I stay with you!" I told him yes, he would be staying with me. I had a Van-a-gon bus and loaded what meager belongings they owned into the back of the van. It was time to take them home.

Before I had left Bad Tolz, I had talked to my commander about what I was going to do, and he agreed with me. As long as I was in Germany, Phong and his family could stay with me and my children. The trip back to Bad Tolz was quiet because everyone was emotionally drained. Most of the conversation revolved quietly around the loss of one of Phong's sons. When

Phong escaped from Vietnam, he and his family did it in small launches that were to meet a "bigger" boat (twenty-five feet long) and then sail to freedom. Phong's son's boat never arrived at the bigger boat. Phong and Ly wanted to go back and find him, but the other refugees wouldn't let them. From accounts told to them, the police had arrived shooting, and they feared their son was dead. Every time Ly talked about her son, her eyes welled up with tears. Phong believed his son was dead.

We arrived at Bad Tolz late at night. I showed Phong, Ngan, and Ly where they could sleep. But Phong wanted to talk. Our conversation ended up on the subject of how we could get him to the United States. I had no idea just then, but I told him I would never leave him or his family again. The military community of Bad Tolz was great; they gave donations of money, food, and clothing. Most of all, they welcomed Phong and his family with open arms. America might have forgotten those people, but the military community hadn't.

Jerry Beckett was now a sergeant major and worked in Heidelberg, Germany. I called him and told him I had Phong with me. Jerry made it in record time to visit. It had been a long time since Jerry and Phong had seen each other. Once we were all together, Jerry said we had to make a plan to get Phong to the United States. We would write to the U.S. ambassador to Germany and anyone else who could help us start Phong's paperwork shuffle.

I called Major Minter in the States. By that time, he was working for NASA out of Maryland. He also wrote to senators, congressmen, and other politicians to solicit help in obtaining what we needed to get Phong where he wanted to be. After a year of paperwork and telephone calls, we were denied on all fronts. But I had made a promise to Phong that I would get him to the States, and I was going to keep that promise.

Once a month, we flew military teams from Fort Devens, Massachusetts, to Bad Tolz. After they'd completed their mission training, they had to rotate back to the United States. With my career on the line, I put Phong in a uniform and told him not to speak to anyone. Both of us boarded one of the military flights back to the States. My only worry was that the pilots, the team leader of the rotating team, or immigration would notice something when we got to the States. But we didn't have any problems. I left Phong with Minter and flew back to Germany.

It would be another year before Phong could get Ly back to the United States. She stayed with me until I had to return to the United States. After my departure, Ly was given housing by some of the military families who had befriended her. Phong and his family are all now living in California and doing very well. I have since retired and at least once a year visit Phong and Ly. She is still the best cook.

Phong had spent ten years in a POW camp, enduring horrendous pain and suffering, both mental and physical, all of which will be detailed in his coming book, *The Gray Tiger*.

☆
GLOSSARY

AA Antiaircraft.

acid pad Helicopter landing pad.

aerial recon Reconning a specific area by helicopter prior to the insertion of a recon patrol.

AFB Air force base.

air burst Explosive device that detonates above ground.

air strike Surface attack by fixed-wing fighter-bomber aircraft.

AIT In the U.S. Army, Advanced Individual Training that follows Basic Combat Training.

AK A Soviet-bloc assault rifle, 7.62 mm, also known as the Kalashnikov AK-47.

AO Area of operations, specified location established for planned military operations.

ao dai Traditional Vietnamese female dress, split up the sides and worn over pants.

ARA Aerial rocket artillery.

ARC Light A B-52 air strike.

arty Artillery.

arty fan An area of operations that can be covered by existing artillery support.

ARVN Army of the Republic of (South) Vietnam.

A-team Special Forces operational detachment that normally consists of a single twelve-man team composed of eleven enlisted men and one officer.

ATL Assistant team leader.

A Troop or **Alpha Troop** Letter designation for one of the aerorifle companies of an air cavalry squadron.

bac si Vietnamese for doctor.

baseball Baseball-shaped hand grenade with a five-meter kill range.

BC Base camp.

BCT In the U.S. Army, Basic Combat Training every trainee must complete upon entering service.

BDA Bomb damage assessment.

beat feet Running from danger.

beaucoup or **boo koo** French for "many."

beehive Artillery round filled with hundreds of small metal darts designed to be used against massed infantry.

berm Built-up earthen wall used for defensive purposes.

Bird Dog A small fixed-wing observation plane.

black box Sensor device that detects body heat or movement. They were buried along routes used by the enemy to record their activity in the area.

black PJs A type of local garb of Vietnamese farmers, also worn extensively by Viet Cong guerrillas.

blasting cap A small device inserted into an explosive substance that can be triggered to cause the detonation of the main charge.

blood trail Spoor sign left by the passage or removal of enemy wounded or dead.

Blues Another name for the aerorifle platoons or troops of an air cavalry squadron.

body bag A thick, black plastic bag used to transport American and allied dead to Graves Registration points.

break contact Disengaging from battle with an enemy unit.

bring smoke Placing intensive fire upon the enemy. Killing the enemy with a vengeance.

B Troop or **Bravo Troop**   Letter designation for one of the aerorifle companies of an air cavalry squadron.

bush   The jungle.

buy the farm   To die.

C-4   A very stable, pliable plastique explosive.

C & C   Command and control.

CA   Combat assault.

cammies   Jungle-patterned clothing worn by U.S. troops in the field.

cammo stick   Two-colored camouflage applicator.

Capt.   Abbeviation for the rank of captain.

CAR-15   Carbine version of the M-16 rifle.

Cav   Cavalry.

CCN   Command and Control (North), MACV-SOG.

Charlie, Charles, Chuck   GI slang for VC/NVA.

cherry   New arrival in country.

Chicom   Chinese Communist.

chieu hoi   Government program that encouraged enemy soldiers to come over to the South Vietnam side.

Chinook   CH-47 helicopter used for transporting equipment and troops.

chopper   GI slang for helicopter.

chopper pad   Helicopter landing pad.

CIDG   Civilian Irregular Defense Group. South Vietnamese or montagnard civilians trained and armed to defend themselves against enemy attack.

clacker   Firing device used to manually detonate a claymore mine.

CO   Commanding officer.

Cobra   AH-1G attack helicopter.

cockadau   GI slang for the Vietnamese word meaning "kill."

Col.   Abbreviation for the rank of colonel.

cold   An area of operations or a recon zone is "cold" if it is unoccupied by the enemy.

commo Communication by radio or field telephone.

commo check A radio/telephone operator requesting confirmation of his transmission.

compromise Discovered by the enemy.

contact Engaged by the enemy.

CP Command post.

Cs Combat field rations for American troops.

CS Riot gas.

daisy chain Wiring a number of claymore mines together with det cord to achieve a simultaneous detonation.

debrief The gleaning of information and intelligence after a military operation.

DEROS The date of return from an overseas tour of duty.

det cord Timed burn fuse used to detonate an explosive charge.

diddy boppin' Moving foolishly, without caution.

didi Vietnamese for to run or move quickly.

DMZ Demilitarized zone.

doc A medic or doctor.

double canopy Jungle or forest with two layers of overhead vegetation.

doughnut dollies Red Cross hostesses.

drag The last man on a long-range reconnaissance patrol.

dung lai Vietnamese for "don't move."

Dust Off Medical evacuation by helicopter.

DZ Drop zone for airborne parachute operation.

E-1 or E-2 Military pay grades of private.

E-3 Military pay grade of private first class.

E-4 Military pay grade of specialist fourth class or corporal.

E-5 Military pay grade of specialist fifth class or sergeant.

E-6 Military pay grade of specialist sixth class or staff sergeant.

E-7 Military pay grade of sergeant first class or platoon sergeant.

E-8 Military pay grade of master sergeant or first sergeant.

E-9 Military pay grade of sergeant major.

E & E Escape and evasion, on the run to evade pursuit and capture.

ER Enlisted reserve.

ETS Estimated termination of service.

exfil Extraction from a mission or operation.

extension leave A thirty-day furlough given at the end of a full tour of duty after which the recipient must return for an extended tour of duty.

FAC Forward air controller. Air force spotter plane that co-ordinated air strikes and artillery for ground units.

fast mover Jet fighter-bomber.

field Anywhere outside "friendly" control.

finger A secondary ridge running out from a primary ridge-line, hill, or mountain.

firebase Forward artillery position usually located on a prominent terrain feature used to support ground units during operations.

firefight A battle with an enemy force.

fire mission A request for artillery support.

fix The specific coordinates pertaining to a unit's position or to a target.

flare ship Aircraft used to drop illumination flares in support of ground troops in contact at night.

flash panel A fluorescent orange or yellow cloth used to mark a unit's position for supporting or inbound aircraft.

FNG "Fucking new guy." Slang term for a recent arrival in Vietnam.

FO Forward observer. A specially trained soldier, usually an officer, attached to an infantry unit for the purpose of co-ordinating close artillery support.

fougasse or **phou gas** A jellied gasoline explosive that is buried in a fifty-five-gallon drum along defensive perimeters and, when command detonated, sends out a wall of highly flammable fuel similar to napalm.

freak or **freq** Slang term meaning a radio frequency.

G-2 Division or larger intelligence section.

G-3 Division or larger operations section.

ghost or **ghost time** Taking time off, free time, goofing off.

gook Derogatory slang for VC/NVA.

grazing fire Keeping the trajectory of bullets between normal knee to waist height.

grease Slang term meaning "to kill."

Green Beret A member of the U.S. Army Special Forces.

ground pounder Infantryman.

grunt Infantryman.

gunship An armed attack helicopter.

H & I Harassment and interdiction. Artillery fire upon certain areas of suspected enemy travel or rally points, designed to prevent uncontested use.

HE High explosive.

heavy team In a long-range patrol unit, two five- or six-man teams operating together.

helipad A hardened helicopter landing pad.

Ho Chi Minh trail An extensive road and trail network running from North Vietnam down through Laos and Cambodia into South Vietnam that enabled the North Vietnamese to supply equipment and personnel to their units in South Vietnam.

hootch Slang for barracks or living quarters.

horn Radio or telephone handset.

hot A landing zone or drop zone under enemy fire.

HQ Headquarters.

Huey The Bell UH helicopter series.

hug   To close with the enemy in order to prevent his use of supporting fire.

hump   Patrolling or moving during a combat operation.

I Corps   The northernmost of the four separate military zones in South Vietnam. The other divisions were II, III, and IV Corps.

immersion foot   A skin condition of the feet caused by prolonged exposure to moisture that results in cracking, bleeding, and sloughing of skin.

incoming   Receiving enemy indirect fire.

Indian country   Territory under enemy control.

indigenous   Native peoples.

infil   Insertion of a recon team or military unit into a recon zone or area of operation.

intel   Information on the enemy gathered by human, electronic, or other means.

jungle penetrator   A metal cylinder lowered by cable from a helicopter, used to extract personnel from inaccessible terrain.

KIA   Killed in action.

Killer team   A small Lurp/Ranger team with the mission of seeking out and destroying the enemy.

LAW   Light antitank weapon.

lay dog   Slang meaning "to go to cover and remain motionless while listening for the enemy." This is SOP for a recon team immediately after being inserted or infilled.

LBJ   Long Binh Jail. The in-country military stockade for U.S. Army personnel convicted of violations of the U.S. Code of Military Justice.

LDR   Leader.

lifer   Slang for career soldier.

LMG   Light machine gun.

LOH or **Loach**   OH-6A light observation helicopter.

LP   Listening post. An outpost established beyond the perimeter wire, manned by one or more personnel with the mission of detecting approaching enemy forces before they can launch an assault.

LRP   Long-range patrol.

LRRP   Long-range reconnaissance patrol.

Lt.   Lieutenant.

Lt. Col.   Lieutenant colonel.

LZ   Landing zone. A cleared area large enough to accommodate the landing of one or more helicopters.

M-14   The standard-issue 7.62 mm semiautomatic/automatic rifle used by U.S. military personnel prior to the M-16.

M-16   The standard-issue 5.56 mm semiautomatic/automatic rifle that became the mainstay of U.S. ground forces in 1967.

M-60   A light, 7.62 mm machine gun that has been the primary infantry automatic weapon of U.S. forces.

M-79   An individually operated, single-shot 40 mm grenade launcher.

MAAG   Military Assistance Advisory Group. The senior U.S. military headquarters during the early American involvement in Vietnam.

MACV   Military Assistance Command Vietnam. The senior U.S. military headquarters after full American involvement in the war.

MACV Recondo School   A three-week school conducted at Nha Trang, South Vietnam, by cadre from the 5th Special Forces Group to train U.S. and allied reconnaissance personnel in the art of conducting long-range patrols.

MACV-SOG   Studies and Observations Group under command of MACV that ran long-range reconnaissance and other classified missions over the borders of South Vietnam into NVA sanctuaries in Laos and Cambodia.

mag Short for magazine.

Main Force Full-time Viet Cong military units, as opposed to local, part-time guerrilla units.

Maj. Major.

Marine Force Recon U.S. Marine Corps divisional long-range reconnaissance units similar in formation and function to U.S. Army LRP/Ranger companies.

McGuire rig A single rope with loops at the end that could be dropped from a helicopter to extract friendly personnel from inaccessible terrain.

medevac or **Dust Off** Medical evacuation by helicopter.

MG Machine gun.

MIA Missing in action.

Mike Force Special Forces mobile strike force used to reinforce or support other Special Forces units or camps under attack.

montagnard The tribal hill people of Vietnam.

MOS Military occupation skill.

MP Military police.

MPC Military payment certificates. Paper money issued U.S. military personnel serving overseas in lieu of local or U.S. currency.

NCO Noncommissioned officer.

NDP Night defensive position.

net Radio network.

NG National Guard.

no sweat With little effort or with no trouble.

number one The best or highest possible.

number ten The worst or lowest possible.

Nungs Vietnamese troops of Chinese extraction hired by U.S. Special Forces to serve as personal bodyguards and to man special strike units and recon teams. Arguably the finest indigenous forces in Vietnam.

nuoc mam Strong, evil-smelling fish sauce used to add flavor to the standard Vietnamese food staple—rice.

NVA North Vietnamese Army.

OP Observation post. An outpost established on a prominent terrain feature for the purpose of visually observing enemy activity.

op Operation.

op order Operations order. A plan for a mission or operation to be conducted against enemy forces, covering all facets of such mission or operation.

overflight An aerial reconnaissance of an intended recon zone or area of operation prior to the mission or operation for the purpose of selected access and egress points, routes of travel, likely enemy concentrations, water, and prominent terrain features.

P-38 Standard manual can opener that comes with government issued C rations.

pen flare A small, spring-loaded, cartridge-fed signal flare device that fired a variety of small, colored flares to signal one's position.

peter pilot Military slang for the assistant or copilot on a helicopter.

PFC Private first class.

Pink team An aviation combat patrol package comprising a LOH scout helicopter and a Charlie model Huey gunship or an AH-1G Cobra. The LOH would fly low to draw enemy fire and mark its location for an immediate strike from the gunship circling high overhead.

pith helmet A light tropical helmet worn by some NVA units.

point The point man or lead soldier in a patrol.

POW Prisoner of War.

PRC-10 or **prick ten** Standard-issue platoon/company radio used early in the Vietnam War.

PRC-25 or **prick twenty-five** Standard-issue platoon/company radio that replaced the PRC-10.

PRC-74 Heavier, longer-range radio capable of voice or code communication.

Project Delta Special Forces special unit tasked to conduct long-range patrols in Southeast Asia.

Project Gamma Special Forces special unit tasked to conduct long-range patrols in Southest Asia.

Project Sigma Special Forces special unit tasked to conduct long-range patrols in Southeast Asia.

PRU Provincial reconnaissance units. Mercenary soldiers who performed special military tasks throughout South Vietnam. Known for their effective participation in the Phoenix Program, in which they used prisoner snatches and assassinations to destroy the VC infrastructure.

Ps or **piasters** South Vietnamese monetary system. During the height of the Vietnam War, 100P was equal to about $0.85US.

PSP Perforated steel panels used to build airstrips, landing pads, bridge surfaces, and a number of other functions.

P training Preparatory training. A one-week course required for each new U.S. Army soldier arriving in South Vietnam, designed to acclimatize new arrivals to weather conditions and give them a basic introduction to the enemy and his tactics.

Puff the Magic Dragon AC-47 or AC-119 aircraft armed with computer-controlled miniguns that rendered massive support to fixed friendly camps and infantry units under enemy attack.

pulled Extracted or exfilled.

punji stakes Sharpened bamboo stakes, embedded in the ground at an angle designed to penetrate into the foot or leg of anyone walking into one. Often poisoned with human excrement to cause infection.

Purple Heart A U.S. medal awarded for receiving a wound in combat.

PX Post exchange.

radio relay A communications team located in a position to relay radio traffic between two points.

R & R Rest and recreation. A short furlough given U.S. forces while serving in a combat zone.

Rangers Designation for U.S. long-range reconnaissance patrollers after January 31, 1969.

rappel Descent from a stationary platform or a hovering helicopter by sliding down a harness-secured rope.

reaction force Special units designated to relieve a small unit in heavy contact.

rear security The last man on a long-range reconnaissance patrol.

redleg Military slang for artillery.

REMF Rear-echelon motherfucker. Military slang for rear-echelon personnel.

rock 'n' roll Slang for firing one's weapon on full automatic.

round eye Slang for a non-Asian female.

RPD/RPK Soviet-bloc light machine gun.

RPG Soviet-bloc front-loaded, antitank rocket launcher, used effectively against U.S. bunkers, armor, and infantry during the Vietnam War.

RT Recon team.

RTO Radiotelephone operator.

ruck Rucksack or backpack.

Ruff-Puff or **RF** South Vietnamese regional and popular forces recruited to provide security in hamlets, villages, and within districts throughout South Vietnam. A militia-type force that was usually ineffective.

saddle up   Preparing to move out on patrol.

same-same   The same as.

sapper   VC/NVA soldiers trained to penetrate enemy defense perimeters and to destroy fighting positions, fuel and ammo dumps, and command and communication centers with demolition charges, usually prior to a ground assault by infantry.

satchel charge   Explosive charge usually carried in a canvas bag across the chest and activated by a pull cord. The weapon of the sapper.

Screaming Chickens or **Puking Buzzards**   Slang for members of the 101st Airborne Division.

SEALs   Small U.S. Navy special-operations units trained in reconnaissance, ambush, prisoner snatch, and counter-guerrilla techniques.

search and destroy   Offensive military operation designed to seek out and eradicate the enemy.

SERTS   Screaming Eagle Replacement Training School. Rear-area indoctrination course that introduced newly arrived 101st Airborne Division replacements to the rigors of combat in Vietnam.

SF   U.S. Special Forces or Green Berets.

SFC   Sergeant first class (E-7).

Sgt.   Sergeant.

shake 'n' bake   A graduate of a stateside noncommissioned or commissioned officer's course.

short rounds   Artillery rounds that impact short of their target.

short timer   Anyone with less than thirty days left in his combat tour.

single canopy   Jungle or forest with a single layer of trees.

sitrep   Situation report. A radio or telephone transmission, usually to a unit's tactical operations center, to provide information on that unit's current status.

Six Designated call sign for a commander, such as "Alpha-Six."

SKS Communist-bloc semiautomatic rifle.

sky To run or flee because of enemy contact.

slack Slang for the second man in a patrol formation. The point man's backup.

slick Slang for a lightly armed Huey helicopter primarily used to transport troops.

smoke A canister-shaped grenade that dispenses smoke, used to conceal a unit from the enemy or to mark a unit's location for aircraft. The smoke comes in a variety of colors.

Snake Cobra helicopter gunship.

snatch To capture a prisoner.

Sneaky Pete A member of an elite military unit who operates behind enemy lines.

snoop and poop A slang term meaning "to gather intelligence in enemy territory and get out again without being detected."

socked in Unable to be resupplied or extracted due to inclement weather.

SOI Signal Operating Instructions. The classified codebook that contains radio frequencies and call signs.

Sp4. or **Spec Four** Specialist fourth class (E-4).

Spectre An AC-130 aircraft gunship armed with miniguns, Vulcans, and sometimes a 105 mm howitzer, with the mission of providing close ground support for friendly troops.

spider hole A camouflaged one-man fighting position frequently used by the VC/NVA.

Spooky AC-47 or AC-119 aircraft armed with Gatling guns and capable of flying support over friendly positions for extended periods. Besides serving as an aerial weapons platform, Spooky was capable of dropping illumination flares.

spotter round   An artillery smoke or white phosphorous round that was fired to mark a position.

S.Sgt.   Staff sergeant (E-6).

staging area   An area in the rear where last-minute preparations for an impending operation or mission are conducted.

stand-down   A period of rest after completion of a mission or operation in the field.

star cluster   An aerial signal device that produces three individual flares. Comes in red, green, or white.

starlight scope   A night-vision device that utilizes any outside light source for illumination.

Stars and Stripes   U.S. military newspaper.

stay behind   A technique involving a small unit dropping out of or remaining behind when its larger parent unit moves out on an operation. A method of inserting a recon team.

strobe light   A small device employing a highly visible, bright flashing light used to identify one's position at night. Normally used only in emergency situations.

TA   Target area. Another designation for AO or area of operations.

TAC air   Tactical air support.

tail gunner   Rear security or the last man in a patrol.

TAOR   Tactical area of responsibility. Another designation for a unit's area of operations.

TDY   Temporary duty.

tee tee or *ti ti*   Very small.

ten forty-nine or **1049**   Military Form 1049, used to request a transfer to another unit.

thumper or **thump gun**   Slang terms for the M-79 grenade launcher.

Tiger Force   The battalion reconnaissance platoon of the 1/327, 101st Airborne Division.

tigers or **tiger fatigues**   Camouflage pattern of black and green stripes usually worn by reconnaissance teams or elite units.

time pencil   A delayed-fuse detonating device attached to an explosive charge or a claymore antipersonnel mine.

TL   Team leader.

TM   Team.

TOC   Tactical operations center or command center of a military unit.

toe popper   Small pressure-detonated antipersonnel mine intended to maim, not kill.

Top   Slang term for a first sergeant, meaning "top" NCO.

tracker   Soldiers specializing in trailing or tracking the enemy.

Tri-Border   The area in Indochina where Laos, Cambodia, and South Vietnam come together.

triple canopy   Jungle or forest that has three distinct layers of trees.

troop   Slang term for a soldier, or a unit in a cavalry squadron equal to an infantry company in size.

tunnel rat   A small-statured U.S. soldier who is sent into underground enemy tunnel complexes armed with only a flashlight, a knife, and a pistol.

URC-10   A pocket-sized, short-range emergency radio.

VC   Viet Cong. South Vietnamese Communist guerrillas.

Viet Minh   Short for Viet Nam Doc Lap Dong Minh, or League for the Independence of Vietnam. Organized by Communist sympathizers who fought against the Japanese and later the French.

VNSF   South Vietnamese Special Forces.

warning order   The notification, prior to an op order, given to a recon team to begin preparation for a mission.

waste   To kill the enemy by any means available.

White Mice   Derogatory slang term for South Vietnamese Army MPs.

WIA   Wounded in action.

World   Slang term for the United States of America or "home."

WP or **willy pete**   White phosphorous grenade.

XF   Exfil. Extraction from the field, usually by helicopter.

xin loi or **sin loi**   Vietnamese for "sorry" or "too bad."

XO   Executive officer.

Xray team   A communication team established at a site between a remote recon patrol and its TOC. Its function is to assist in relaying messages between the two stations.

Yards   Short for montagnards.

zap   To kill or wound.

The bloody history of the 101st LRP/Rangers
by one of its own.

SIX SILENT MEN
Book One
by Reynel Martinez

In 1965, the 1st Brigade of the 101st Airborne Division was detached from the division and assigned to Vietnam. Reynel Martinez provides a personal account of the first faltering steps of the brigade's provisional LRRP unit as the men learn how to battle the VC and NVA while surviving the more pernicious orders of their own, occasionally thoughtless, high-level commanders. SIX SILENT MEN: Book One provides an often bloody but always honorable chronicle of courage under fire.

The compelling chronicle continues in

SIX SILENT MEN
Book Two
By Kenn Miller

After working on their own in Vietnam for more than two years, the 1st Brigade LRRPs were ordered to join forces with the division once again in the summer of 1967. It was a bitter pill to swallow for this formidable band of soldiers, but swallow it they did as they went on to become one of the most highly decorated companies in the history of the 101st.

Published by The Ballantine Publishing Group.
Available in your local bookstore.

FORTUNE FAVORS THE BOLD
A British LRRP with the 101st

by James W. Walker

Born in England to a British father and a Canadian mother, James Walker was raised at the British Sailors Orphan Home following the divorce of his parents. After he joined the British army as a teen, his mother, who was by then living in the States, bought his way out of the military and brought him to America—where he volunteered for the army, then went Airborne. In 1965, as an Airborne trooper in the 82d Airborne Division, he took part in the invasion of Santo Domingo.

But in 1967, in Vietnam, James Walker became "Limey," the only British citizen in the 101st LRRPs. He and the other LRRPS were given every sort of assignment: long-range recons, surprise raids on villages, trail watching, even herding stray cattle with helicopters. Back in camp, however, they did nothing to diminish their reputations as hell-raisers—especially Walker, whose outlandish behavior eventually made him possibly the only healthy enlisted man ever denied the "privilege" of an extension of his tour in Nam.

Published by The Ballantine Publishing Group.
Available in bookstores everywhere.